Risking together

PUBLIC AND SOCIAL POLICY SERIES

Marian Baird and Gaby Ramia, Series Editors

The Public and Social Policy series publishes books that pose challenging questions about policy from national, comparative and international perspectives. The series explores policy design, implementation and evaluation; the politics of policy making; and analyses of particular areas of public and social policy.

Australian social attitudes IV: the age of insecurity
Ed. Shaun Wilson and Markus Hadler

Globalisation, the state and regional Australia
Amanda Walsh

Markets, rights and power in Australian social policy
Ed. Gabrielle Meagher and Susan Goodwin

Risking together: how finance is dominating everyday life in Australia
Dick Bryan and Mike Rafferty

Wind turbine syndrome: a communicated disease
Simon Chapman and Fiona Crichton

Risking together

How finance is dominating everyday life in Australia

Dick Bryan and Mike Rafferty

SYDNEY UNIVERSITY PRESS

A catalogue record for this book is available from the National Library of Australia.

NATIONAL
LIBRARY
OF AUSTRALIA

ISBN 9781743325728 paperback
ISBN 9781743325711 ebook
ISBN 9781743320228 Kindle

Cover image by Joe Frost, *Denistone*, 2016, acrylic on polyester,152.5x198 cm, photograph by Michel Brouet.
Cover design by Miguel Yamin.

Contents

List of figures

List of tables

List of abbreviations

ABN	Australian Business Number
ABS	Australian Bureau of Statistics
ABSs	Asset-backed securities
ACCC	Australian Competition and Consumer Commission
ACTU	Australian Council of Trade Unions
ADI	Authorised Deposit-taking Institutions
AER	Australian Energy Regulator
AICD	Australian Institute of Company Directors
ALP	Australian Labor Party
APRA	Australian Prudential Regulation Authority
ASIC	Australian Securities and Investments Commission
CME	Chicago Mercantile Exchange
CPI	Consumer price index
CV	Coefficient of variation
DB	Defined benefit
DFA	Digital Finance Analytics

FINSIA   Financial Services Institute of Australasia

GDP   Gross Domestic Product

GFC   Global Financial Crisis

HES   Household Expenditure Survey

HILDA   Household Income and Labour Dynamics in Australia

HPI   Henderson Poverty Index

LMI   Labour market intermediaries

LP   Labour productivity

MBSs   Mortgage-backed securities

NFL   National Football League

P&I   Principal-and-interest

PAYG   Pay as you go

PMG   Postmaster General

RBA   Reserve Bank of Australia

RMBSs   Residential mortgage-backed securities

TAFE   Technical and Further Education institutes

TLM   Transitional labour market

USFD   US Financial Diaries

Preface

This book takes ideas we have been developing about finance, risk, class and theories of value and links them to empirical research on Australian society. We want to be able to make abstract theory concrete, and use empirical detail to inform innovation in theory. Writing it was in part motivated by our engagement with trade unions, activist and civil society groups, through which it became apparent to us that there is need for a more detailed exposition of what has been happening in the Australian economy and society more broadly, especially associated with the rise to prominence of issues of finance. So we started writing this book because we wanted to work out how, and communicate about, the impact of an era of rapid financial change as it is experienced on the streets, in homes and in jobs. This book follows up our 1999 book, *The global economy in Australia* and, in important respects, it is the next phase of that earlier research.

Writing it has been a bigger project than might appear, for we have also been using the Australian data to help think through some thorny theoretical issues, coming to the realisation that some conventional theoretical categories are being superseded by historical change. The theoretical issues do not appear in this book. Indeed we are pleased that it has been written without any 'deep' theoretical exposition: anything that looks even a bit theoretical has been partitioned off to two appendices. For those not interested in theory, the book can be read without engaging the appendices. We have sought to make the book readable to a wide audience in the hope it will stimulate debate.

As well as avoiding explicit theory, we also wanted to avoid some politically populist issues, especially 'bank bashing'. There is an alarming amount of evidence with which to hit banks over the head, and their opportunist, deceptive and illegal practices keep providing more and more instances. But the issues we focus on are not about the impact of some bad apples: our objective is to depict a society dominated by an ideology of financial calculation that would be there even if financial institutions operated with complete honesty and prudence. This book ends with a challenge to those who want real social and economic change to pursue it via a close understanding of how finance works; not one built on a moral critique of bankers.

Some of those to whom we issue the challenge will not like it – it requires political organisations, and especially trade unions, who want to pursue more collective communal social and economic goals, to think differently and for them to move on from the terrain that they have occupied for the last century. Amongst those who share our call to move on politically, there may well be disappointment that we do not engage issues of the environment, or Indigenous communities, or the regions, or refugees in as much detail as they would no doubt like. Our relative neglect of these issues is not that we think they are unimportant; it is that we have analysed the areas where we feel we have expertise. Others have and will continue to pursue important social and economic issues not adequately addressed in this book. We hope the framing of finance we develop here will assist them in their projects.

In preparing this book we have had extensive assistance. We have benefitted greatly from the research assistance of Tanya Carney, Nigel Douglas and graphic design of Nadine Goss. Tanya prepared Appendix 2 and helped enormously to make the evidence we present current by the updating of data as the book was being finally prepared for publication. The Australian Research Council provided the funding that enabled us to undertake this research. The staff of Sydney University Press also warrants particular mention. They took on the publication of this book with energy and enthusiasm and have made what can be a difficult process remarkably straightforward.

There are many people with whom we have discussed the content of the research in this book. With some we have ongoing disagreements, but all have influenced our thinking: Scott MacWilliam, Chris Jefferis, Randy Martin, Bob Meister, Robert Wosnitzer, Akseli Virtanen and associates at the Economic Space Agency, Sue Himmelweit, Simon Mohun, Andrew Wells, Janet Burstall, Phil Toner, Nick Coates, Peter Fairbrother, Bruno Tinel, and participants in the Australian Working Group on Financialisation, especially Lisa Adkins, Fiona Allon, Melinda Cooper and Martijn Konings, where some ideas in this book were 'road tested'.

Our families have been incredibly supportive throughout, including during some very difficult and sad times.

Introduction

Something is changing in wealthy societies such as Australia, to create a sense that economic security and its affordability are becoming beyond reach. Life is now full of financial costs, risks and uncertainties.

Whether the issue is paying the rent or mortgage, ballooning health care and utility bills, childcare, after-school fees and university fees, or managing superannuation and buying into a retirement village, we are increasingly exposed to risks and costs that are getting more complex and harder to manage. To access life's necessities, we are required to sign financial contracts, which embed exposure to risks, but at the same time our sources of income to pay for those costs are also getting more uncertain and volatile. We are told we just have to manage those risks and it's the way life now is.

Ordinary people have always carried financial risks, but the change we address in this book has been occurring at an escalating rate since the 1980s. We are living through a historic social experiment aimed at reinventing households' capacities to take on more and more risk in labour markets, as borrowers, as consumers and, indeed, as inputs into new financial products. The book examines this social experiment so as to reveal its dimensions, to challenge its normalisation, and to think about what is needed to resist its impact. It doesn't have to be this way.

A significant change in the last 30 years, more stark as each year passes, is that financial stress is now not just about being poor. It has always been unacceptably hard for the poorest people in society – by definition they are in permanent financial stress. Securing even a basic subsistence is now getting riskier and tougher for many more people. This is especially the case in big cities. Anglicare (2017) reports that in the Sydney and Illawarra region:

> The lack of private rentals affordable for single people and families struggling on either benefits or the minimum wage is a serious concern. The end result is people spending more than 50% of their low income on rent so they struggle to pay bills, afford electricity or even access enough food. Many are at risk of homelessness and hunger.

The poorest people don't buy houses, yet, in 2017, with interest rates at historic lows, almost a quarter of households with a mortgage reported being in some degree of financial stress. Digital Financial Analytics' mortgage stress modelling estimates that 21.8 percent of households report they have to cut back on normal expenditure and increase their use of credit cards. This estimate is based on a survey of 52,000 households (North 2017). Others, often younger but not 'poor', but with a lack of stable income, are locked out of owner occupation by the price of residential real estate.

A growing number of people feel that a decent, secure lifestyle is rapidly slipping out of reach: that they are only one misstep or unlucky event from being unable to pay the household's bills. People feel this vulnerability individually, and indeed it is framed in wider discussion as their personal problem, to be privately managed or endured. It is readily talked of by conservative critics as being caused by greed (borrowing too much), laziness, ignorance, or poor judgement. They tell us that the remedy lies in greater self-reliance, personal responsibility and moral resilience, more modest aspirations, as well as respect for legal and contractual obligations. At home it is felt as anxiety, failure and shame.

This book will show that, along with rising inequality, there are widespread changes in people's experiences of finance and of social risk that are generating this sense of vulnerability and insecurity. This book develops the argument that it is issues of the social production and distribution of risk, even more than the social distribution of income, that define the challenges of the current era. Our analysis will show that the growing vulnerabilities of ordinary people are systematic, not accidental, and collective rather than just individual experiences. When large numbers of people experience the same 'private' matter at the same time, it should be assumed that the drivers are social in foundation and momentum.

In the United States we have seen the election of Donald Trump be widely attributed to this phenomenon of people feeling economically disenfranchised and financially precarious. The same has been said of the 'Brexit' vote in Britain and the anticipated rise of right-wing nationalist, populist governments in Europe. These are generally depicted as the products of protest voters, expressing anger at governments that have done nothing to address their increasingly precarious lives. But voter anger won't deliver the desired outcomes. It is already apparent that Trump and Brexit will not improve the lot of ordinary people: in fact they will probably make things worse. In these places, the anger about a lack of security in work and income, and a lack of affordability of, or even access, to basic consumption, housing, health care and education, is likely to rise.

So how might communities creatively and effectively push back against these changes? We think the answer is not about protest votes for populist, maverick national leaders. Nor, indeed, is it simply about advocating thoughtful policies to make our society more caring and equal. Of course that would be a good outcome, but it is devoid of strategy. Policy is about framing what you believe to be 'right' as credible legislation. Getting such a policy taken up is a different matter. Strategy is how you change cultures and debates so as to make the right policy look not only possible but also desirable. For a strategic agenda there is a need to rethink ways of getting policy traction: ways that are designed around challenging what is new and different in an increasingly risky and precarious society.

So our further goal in this book is to build the case for strategic interventions in the name of securing decent living standards, including what we call 'household unionism'. We know existing trade unions, despite a proud tradition of winning many important conditions and rights, are struggling to maintain their relevance and strength. One reason is that, increasingly, people's relations with

3

'capital' (employers, corporations) and the state (governments and regulators) are occurring in financial dealings beyond the world of paid work, and hence beyond the focus of traditional trade unions. Household unionism is the term we use for organisations that engage, and in certain ways represent, ordinary people in these emerging dimensions of their daily budgetary and financial encounters with capital and with the state. These organisations may be our current trade unions taking a decisive turn to mobilise around how ordinary people are exploited in the increasing trading of life-course risks, or some alternative, yet to emerge, form of unionism.

Household unions cannot magically eradicate social and economic risks, just as trade unions can't eradicate poor working conditions and insecure employment. But they may be able to challenge the systematic nature of risks being shifted onto ordinary people. And even if taking on more risk is the unavoidable direction of change in the current era, we need organisations through which people face risk with a collective strength, not individual vulnerability. In the terms of our dear friend, the late Randy Martin, we are all being asked to take on more and more life-course risks. If we must take on this risk, we need to find ways to 'risk together'. This book is an explanation of why we need to risk together, in the hope that we can build ways to do it, and ways to avert the need to do it.

Asking the right questions

This book doesn't take a standard approach to social and economic analysis, and we want to be upfront about how it differs. In current debate there are three popular issues of economic focus. (Of course the environment and refugees lead a long list of other issues of importance. These will not feature centrally in our analysis, for reasons of emphasis, although both are indeed in important ways issues of risk and vulnerability.)

The first issue is growing inequality. Incomes in Australia are polarising over time and the share of national income and wealth going to working people is declining while those at the very top are accelerating away from the rest (Cowgill 2013; Leigh 2013; Bankwest Curtin Economics Centre 2014).

Growing inequality is indeed a critical issue, and it is now receiving long overdue attention. However, inequality is at best only part of the story. The reality is that a considerable proportion of the population, reaching well into middle-income levels, is experiencing or vulnerable to financial stress; not just those at the bottom of the income distribution. Janet Yellen (2014), now Chairperson of the US Federal Reserve Board (the US central bank), has noted: 'According to the Board's recent *Survey of Household Economics and Decision making*, an unexpected expense of just $400 would prompt the majority of households to borrow money, sell something, or simply not pay at all'. Moreover, the lot of the majority of ordinary people would not change dramatically if the post-tax incomes of the top 10 percent of income earners were dramatically cut. Our society may then be statistically fairer, but it won't feel socially much different. The critical, underlying issues are, we believe, not so much to do with income inequality per se but with what Morduch and Schneider (2017: Chapter 1) call the 'hidden inequality': how financial volatility and risk potentially and actually impact differently on people of different incomes, wealth and life circumstances.

The second issue in popular focus is the rise of what is being called 'neo-liberalism', generally meaning that governments are selling off public assets and introducing markets into more and more facets of both economy and society. Clearly this term 'neo-liberalism' captures some broad trends in society, and we will use this term occasionally. But it has also become a bit of a catch-all term to describe any government policies we don't like. Critiques of 'neo-liberalism' do not, we believe, tell us enough about the ways in which a systematic process of risk shifting is becoming central in social and economic change.

The third issue in popular debate is growing levels of government and household debt. By certain measures, both are higher than at any previous time. Certainly, issues of debt broadly engage our issue of finance and risk. Our concern is that a focus on debt in isolation gets too alarmist, pitched as predictions of spectacular crashes, and feeding a populist anti-bank politics. We also believe this framing misses many of the more critical issues of financial innovation and management.

After all, Australian state debt is third lowest of all the Organisation for Economic Co-operation and Development (OECD). The OECD is made up of the 20 most industrialised countries of the world. As a percentage of GDP, Australia ranks third lowest for general government spending, fourth lowest for general government revenue and eleventh lowest for general government debt (OECD 2016). While Australian households do indeed carry a lot of debt by global standards, they also hold a lot of assets, in housing and superannuation. The level of debt per se doesn't capture the issue. It is the risks associated with that debt and with other things that make debt repayable: it is that interest rates for borrowing are uncertain, as are the values of assets bought by debt – be it a house, shares or an education – and the working and retirement income from which the repayments are made is more volatile. Put simply, we need to move beyond headline predictions of bursting debt bubbles to a more nuanced appreciation of financial and social change.

In aggregate, we are concerned that these three popular issues tend to generate policy advocacy that turns out to be quite conservative: a desire to take us back to a previous era where there was less inequality, more state involvement in the economy and less debt. But history doesn't go backwards.

How, then, might we go forward? How might we reframe the concerns underlying the three popular issues, to look at the evolving financial risks of ordinary people, in a way that seeks not to reinstate the past but to challenge and perhaps even harness existing economic trends, unappealing as they are? To do that we will need to go inside the world of finance, to see how it thinks and calculates and how it systematically creates markets for risk imposed on people in their work and in their families. Only by getting inside the mindset of finance can we work out how we might challenge its rule.

Loading up household financial stress

The *1998–99 Household Expenditure Survey* conducted by the Australian Bureau of Statistics (ABS) was the first official survey to ask people whether they felt under financial stress: it asked whether financial constraints meant people had to forego buying or doing things they would once have considered part of normal life. Over 40 percent of people reported that they had had to cut back on something.

This was the first official measure of financial stress in Australia. It suggested that the benefits of a period of long-term economic growth were not leading to better, more stable living standards.

No one really named the change at the time, but the banks and other financial institutions already understood its significance. At around the same time as the ABS started surveying financial stress, banks and credit rating agencies were starting to do the same thing, because they understood that household financial stress, leading to failures to meet contractual payments, could impact directly on bank profitability. The financial institutions wanted to find out what sorts of people in what sorts of circumstances might default on their loans. What the surveys all showed, broadly, was that households were facing growing volatility in both their income and expenditure patterns and that the levels of financial stress kept, and still keep, rising (e.g. Illion 2014).[1]

A 2015 survey by the Wesley Mission (2015) estimated that 44 percent of households are under financial stress. A survey by Digital Financial Analytics (North 2016), using 2015 data, indicates that based on then-current interest rates, about 13 percent of households with an owner occupied loan and 27 percent with investment properties would be in financial discomfort if rates were to rise at all, and that more than one-third of households said they would be in difficulty if rates rose by 3 percent.

Broadly, the causes of stress were and remain pretty basic. The key ones are: loss of income and especially unemployment, ill-health or personal mishap, and relationship breakdown. The evidence shows that the three are often closely connected.

The late 1990s, when that first ABS survey was conducted, was a period of rapid economic reform as global competitiveness placed pressures on local industry. In Australia it was the time of the first Howard government. It was reforming rapidly, including in the areas of employment and health: both areas where shifting of risks was occurring

---

1   Illion (formerly known as Dun and Bradstreet) is a global company producing data for corporations. For a more detailed study, at the frontier of household data capacity, see Farrell and Greig (2015).

and causing financial stress in households. Labour market reforms in the name of 'flexibility' were making employment less secure and incomes less predictable. Health and welfare reforms were stripping back access to public health, requiring private insurance, and restricting access to a welfare safety net. What's more, these sorts of reforms have continued under governments of all persuasion – albeit at different paces.

Little wonder that there is growing financial stress. Corporations and governments alike have been implementing policies to get people to work harder and longer, in less secure jobs, with less social and personal financial reserves and in a more volatile economic and financial environment. People are quite simply facing greater risk and uncertainty across their life course.

Jump forward a decade to the 2007–8 Global Financial Crisis (GFC). There were massive household defaults in the United States, associated with so-called subprime lending, and in Europe too. In Australia, the previous decade's increases in labour market insecurity, cuts in state-funded health and welfare, as well as mounting contracted household financial obligations, might also have led to a mortgage crisis. At the time, some were predicting disaster. But in Australia there were comparatively few defaults: a very small increase. In Australia in the early 2000s no more than 10 percent of loans were 'subprime' (Bailey et al. 2004: 50–51).

Why did Australia fare so well, comparatively, in the midst of the GFC?

At the time of the crisis, Ken Henry was Secretary of the Australian Treasury and hence principal government adviser on economic policy responses to the crisis. Henry later reported that senior Treasury and Reserve Bank officials had already planned for such an economic shock (they had, as he later recounted, been 'war gaming' such scenarios for some time), and they had developed a simple strategic set of spending and interest rate proposals for government as a response. Henry summarised the strategy as: 'Go hard, go early and go to households'.[2] As a result, when the GFC hit Australia, the government applied a rapid fiscal stimulus in the form of cash payments to households, home insulation programs, school hall building, a revamped first home buyers grant etc., along with a rapid reduction of interest rates and

---

2   Ken Henry 2012, interview transcript, ABC Television, *7.30 Report*, 15 May.

government guarantees for banks and bank deposits. Many people complained that the spending was profligate. But it was a fast injection of spending into the economy and it was at least in part because of this spending strategy that Australia had a comparatively gentler ride through the GFC.

The contrasting negative US experience of subprime loans being foreclosed on a large scale causing massive destruction of wealth and social pain, and the generally positive Australian Treasury policy of demand stimulus, reveals a rarely uttered dictum: households – the wellbeing of ordinary people – are the key to economic *and* financial stability.

So a dilemma is immediately apparent. We see that ordinary people, and their capacity to work, spend, save and pay their bills, are the key to economic and financial stability, yet they are taking on more and more financial stress because of the combined effects of more volatile incomes and expenditures, more risks and constrained spending capacity. In short, households are expected to be a critical source of stability and indeed profitability, but at the same time they are more financially precarious!

Is it a crash waiting to happen, as it did in the USA in 2007–8, or are there new social and economic agendas being played out in ways not yet clearly apparent?

Later chapters will demonstrate that the absorption of financial and economic risk and uncertainty by households – whether in their role as workers, consumers, citizens, borrowers and investors – is the critical social and economic story of the last three decades. Yet the dilemma is, by and large, simply ignored in mainstream policy debates.

'Financialisation'

This shift of risk and uncertainty onto workers and households can, we believe, be understood as a process of 'financialisation'. This term is not just about banks, superannuation and hedge funds, though it includes them. It is also about the incorporation of financial ways of thinking and acting into corporate and government decision-making, into work relations, into media commentary on economic and social issues, and into our homes and home life too. Financialisation sees each of us being treated as if we were a business, where we are expected to perceive of ourselves, our families and our communities as transactions on balance sheets of assets and liabilities, and as business-like profit and loss accounts. We are asked, and indeed required, to manage a growing range of financial risks and costs that now come our way, as if we were a small business.

The incorporation of financial ways of thinking and acting – often without us knowing it – is seeing more and more facets of life being measured and 'performance' evaluated, with an increasing number of them being converted into prices. Things once accessed without direct pricing (often at token cost) – be it schooling, health care and roads – are now being explicitly priced. In workplaces, more and more parts of the job (and wage) are being measured, priced and performance evaluated; in schools, funding attaches to student test scores. We are being asked to consider multi-year service contacts with lots of fine print for everything from mobile phones, car insurance, energy, health insurance, education, and the list keeps growing. People increasingly believe that to supplement their volatile incomes they should rent out rooms in their homes on Airbnb or use their car to drive for Uber, or earn additional income on Airtasker. We even see people, unable to afford to purchase a home to live in, buying investment properties, while paying rent. Everything, it seems, even private life, is to be seen as a financial opportunity, and imperative.

These sorts of changes and the financial stresses that attach to them are presented as normal; indeed economically and even morally right. The Howard government, for example, could load up the preconditions of household financial stress and extol the cultural virtues of home and family values all at the same time! The trading and shifting of many life-course risks to ordinary households is a massive social experiment, but it is becoming the new normal.

The term 'shifting risk' is pretty alien to most people's conversations. Indeed it can often lead people to tune out, content with the moral certainty that finance and risk is all about speculation, that it is 'bad' and it should simply be avoided or condemned. Perhaps those judgements are in some sense 'true', but this book will show that individual ethical judgements and responses will not be enough to turn back the tide of financialisation. We simply can't avoid the consequences of risk shifting on our own, so we therefore need to understand it: to split finance and risk trading open; to reveal its social agendas in order that they might be effectively challenged.

Outline

In building the analysis, we start with a chapter that introduces the ideas of financialisation, risk and uncertainty (Chapter 1) and another which outlines the ways in which financial markets have developed products to trade risk (Chapter 2). The proposition we are building towards is that ordinary people – the significant majority of the population – in their roles as workers, citizens, savers and householders, cannot avoid being players in the market for risk. But, critically, they are systematically disadvantaged in these risk markets. Indeed the markets are structured so as to systematically transfer risks to those who can least afford to carry them.

In Chapter 3 we take the framework of risk shifting to the domain of employment, both because more precarious employment is a critical expression of risk shifting, and because we want to drive home the argument that risk shifting in the workplace can be seen as just one dimension, albeit the most widely discussed one, of a wider process of systematic risk shifting.

In Chapter 4 we explore the other dimensions of risk beyond employment and show that people are not just workers for wages but are also becoming risk-absorbing financial subjects in a wider context, in relation to debt and credit (especially for mortgages), savings for old age (superannuation) and in consumption (contracts for utilities, insurance). We show that individual and household financial contracts – be they for mortgages, credit cards, student fees and loans, insurance, mobile phones, internet services, gas and electricity, or retirement homes; indeed any contractual or compulsory financial extraction – are being reconfigured as inputs into financial products called securities, and sold into global financial markets as financial assets. This process of 'securitisation' changes dramatically the household's relations with finance, for even the mundane processes of insuring the car, paying the mobile phone and electricity bills and the mortgage open up new financial processes of risk shifting. It is a frontier of global financial innovation.

Accordingly, in Chapters 5 and 6 we change the focus to the household itself, and the way household contracts involve risks to be managed. In Chapter 5 we build the argument that, in a financialised world, households are being asked to manage their finances as if they were a personal hedge fund, balancing assets and liabilities and all the time having to gamble on which risks to take, and which to insure against. Yet households are not hedge funds: they are organised around norms of social stability, not constantly buying and selling assets in search of financial gain. They want a place to live and basic goods and services like utilities, a car and an education. These are not voluntary expenditures to be undertaken or not according to predictions of future price movements: they are the stuff of subsistence. We show that in valuing stability and norms in a financialised world, households become systematic targets for risk shifting.

In Chapter 6 we look at how governments and financial markets actively monitor (and increasingly manage) household risks so as to measure and minimise the risk of default on their contracts. We see growing levels of detailed surveillance of people's daily lives, beyond their knowing and their capacity to refuse. Put simply, we no longer have the choice of whether to play in financial markets: we are involved by virtue of being workers, consumers and citizens. The effect is that people become further and further drawn into compliance with financial ways of thinking even though this compliance is systematically deleterious.

In Chapter 7 we reframe this confronting and even oppressive story of risk shifting, so as to explore a politics of challenge and transformation beyond conventional resistance in the workplace. We do not come up with simple answers, as if there were a single, logical antidote to the processes of financialisation we have identified. Instead, we try to think how to turn the momentum of finance against itself, so that those who are systematically disadvantaged might imagine and build an alternative politics.

Finally, we include in Chapter 8 a version of our analysis trimmed down to its core propositions. It is not a direct summary of chapters – it takes a different path through the issues. It presents the takeaway ideas that we hope people will discuss, debate, critique and, most importantly, engage with and extend.

1
Financial ways of thinking and the risks they reveal

Everyone is worried about house prices. Young adults are worried that house prices are rising too quickly for them to ever own a house. House owners are worried that there may be a house price bubble and that it may (or, depending on where you live, has already) burst, sending prices crashing. Old people are worried their housing asset growth may see them lose access to welfare services. Renters are worried that higher mortgage repayments flow through to demands for higher rents. Governments are worried that investors with tax concessions are driving homeowners out of the market. Investors are worried they will lose the tax advantages they count on. Regulators are worried about high levels of borrowing. Banks are worried that people may default on their loans.

The strange thing is that the more house prices rise, the more everyone worries that they will lose in the housing market. How can it be that everyone is worried? It's all about exposure to financial risk and, as the stakes get higher, so does the risk exposure.

Over the past 30 years finance has become a bigger and bigger part of daily life. Martin (2002) refers to the 'financialisation of daily life', and he's not referring just to housing but to all the different sorts of financial contracts we sign which lock us into payments, but without knowledge of what the financial future holds. We sign contracts for long-term loans, but don't know long-term interest rates, house prices or our future income; we pay into superannuation but have no knowledge about the future value of the assets our superannuation funds purchase. We buy insurance without a capacity to comprehend the fine print and we sign contracts with utilities companies (gas, water, electricity) with no specification of the future prices we will have to pay. We sign up for childcare and university tuition, and after it starts the fees keep rising. We go into retirement homes, and face all sorts of contingent financial fees that make it impossible to know the real cost of occupancy.

At the same time, the fears of sickness and unemployment, and the resulting loss of income, impact on everyone. Many people are only one or two pieces of misfortune away from being financially washed up. Anxiety about financial insolvency is real and it's occurring in one of the wealthiest societies in human history.

In a nutshell, the more we are forced to get into financial contracts in order to access life's necessities, the more our lives become exposed to financially volatility: subject to changes that are often outside our control.

Conversely, despite these burdens of volatility, many people have had great financial success over these same 30 years. Ten or more years ago, borrowing to purchase a house may have severely stretched the household budget, but it has seen many people who did borrow now having a level of wealth they could not have imagined at the time of purchase – so long, that is, as house prices in their suburb or town don't crash!

Whether people have ridden financial volatility to gain or loss, the experience of risk and uncertainty in financial matters haunts us all. If we are to understand what's going on in the world of finance as more than fortune and misfortune, we need to go beyond the question of winners and losers and look at the fragility and volatility that lie embedded within finance. This takes us to a consideration of financial ways of thinking, and how those ways increasingly frame our lives.

A financial way of thinking

What is new here is not just that finance has become important to ordinary people; it has always been important. It's that there are changes in finance that make so many parts of daily life come into financial calculation. Companies, governments and financial institutions are all innovating policies and products that require that we be financial 'players'. Finance is, quite simply, the new game in town and we are players even if we don't yet know it.

The new game is seen in the complex calculations that must be performed when we sign an employment contract, a mobile phone or insurance contract and even enter 'dream team' competitions in a favourite football code. What we will show as our argument unfolds is that these sorts of contracts – whether critical, like employment, or for fun, like dream team competitions – are working their way into our lives as something 'normal' and even mundane.

So let us turn, briefly, to the employment contract, the phone contract, the health insurance and the dream team to build toward that argument. These issues are considered in detail in later chapters, so here we just get the flavour of the new financialised game.

Employment used to be based on the (contested) principle of 'a fair day's pay for a fair day's work' and a wage was fixed around the need to provide families with a basic standard of living (a living wage). This connection between work and subsistence is increasingly being broken, as more and more people are offered work of uncertain hours and uncertain numbers of days a year. Work is also being casualised and jobs shifting from being wage work to self-employed/subcontracted.

So what is 'financial' about that? It is that more and more employment contracts are designed to ensure companies only have to pay workers when they are needed, and people get paid only for exactly what they do rather than what is needed in terms of living standards or reward for effort. In some circumstances it is cheaper to use casual labour; in others, it's more profitable to turn workers into self-employed subcontractors. In both cases, the risks of work availability and other costs are transferred to the worker, with no regard for the ramifications on overall worker income. If the customers do not turn up at the restaurant, the casual worker is told to go home. If it rains on the building site and work can't be performed, the subcontractor gets no income.

Hence for many people and the households they live in, and especially younger and poorer ones, their income from work is increasingly volatile. Precise data are not collected in Australia, but they are in the US, and while employment conditions in the USA are different, and generally more precarious than in Australia, it is important to note what the US data show. US Financial Diaries tracks the finances of 235 low- and moderate-income households for a full year to collect highly detailed data on how families manage their finances on a day-to-day basis. Here is what they report about income volatility:

> The households faced substantial swings in income from month to month. On average, they experienced 2.5 months when income fell more than 25 percent below average, and 2.6 months when income was more than 25 percent above average. The volatility is summarized by an average coefficient of variation (CV) of monthly income (within year, averaged across households) of 39 percent. The CV is greatest (55 percent) for households below the poverty line, but the CV remained relatively high (34 percent) and steady for households with income from 100 percent of the poverty line up to 300 percent. Thus, in the non-poor sample, greater income did not imply notably greater income stability. (Hannagan and Morduch 2015)

Volatile income then challenges the capacity to meet basic needs on a regular basis. As many of these needs are now obtained by contracted financial obligations – the rent, electricity, car loan, health insurance – this also has direct implications for meeting financial contract obligations.

What is the advice to workers in this position? For the influential US financial institution JP Morgan Chase (2016), the answer is clear:

> Americans experience tremendous income volatility, and that volatility is on the rise. Income volatility matters because it is hard to manage. The typical household faces a shortfall in the financial buffer necessary to weather this volatility. Moreover, the decline in real wages since 2009 for all income groups except the top 5th percentile means that life is harder to afford in general, but even more so when earnings dip below average. Rapidly growing online platforms, such as Uber and Airbnb, have created a new marketplace for work by unbundling a job into discrete tasks and directly connecting individual sellers with consumers. These flexible, highly accessible opportunities to work have the potential to help people buffer against income and expense shocks.

So the advice on how to handle employment volatility is to accept the change and respond by turning your home and your car into a small business. Can there be a clearer statement about employment and daily life being financialised?

But JP Morgan Chase ends with a caution:

> The 'Online Platform Economy' [personal services like Uber and Airbnb] offers fewer worker protections than traditional work arrangements, however, which has led some to claim that the Online Platform Economy represents a fundamental shift in the nature of work.

This is the deep impact of financialisation: that traditional notions of 'work' and 'employment' are changing, and the risks of change are being borne by individual workers. We will pursue these issues in Chapter 3.

Telephones did not use to have complex contracts. The Postmaster General's (PMG) Department installed a single phone in the front hall of your home. The charges for its use were legislated by parliament. There were no pre-paid phones, 12- or 24-month contracts, contracts bundles with mobile phones and loss or damage insurance. Now, there are massively complex contracts with fine print terms and conditions and detailed price structures, with high cost penalties if you talk outside the standard times, places, or standard durations. To be sure, phones are way better and more versatile now than that earlier era, but along with the technological change has come a conscious agenda to transfer financial risks in service provision to the household. The consumer financial regulator Australian Securities and Investments Commission's (ASIC's) 'Smart Money' website (2015) gives the following warning about mobile phone contracts:

> Play it safe and work out your budget before you shop. Add up what you earn, subtract what you spend on rent, food, bills, petrol, fares and any other regular expenses. The money left over can be spent on things you want, including your mobile. Know your limits so you don't end up in debt. If you don't pay your mobile bills on time you could end up with a poor credit rating and even have problems getting a loan in the future.

To get the calculation right means thinking of yourself as a small business, doing computations about likely usage, costings and your likely future income and expenses. ASIC advises, for example:

> To get the right contract and choose the best capped plan for you, work out:
>
> - Do you really need the maximum memory capacity, Bluetooth, infrared and extra accessories (hands-free, car kit, adaptors)?
> - How much data do you need to download per month? ...
> - How many calls you would make in a month
> - How long your calls usually last
> - What time you usually make calls (e.g. before and after school hours).[1]

This is all about monitoring yourself as a financial subject.

Moreover, as we will see in later chapters, the financialisation of phone contracts extends beyond the pricing of service provision. Those contractual payments we make on our phones are themselves being 'onsold' into global financial markets, either directly by the telco being listed on global stock markets, or indirectly, as components of asset backed securities. These securities involve peoples' monthly payments being bundled together and sold as a future income stream. Investment banks will pay a lump sum now to get ownership of those future payments.[2] Ensuring the value of these securities is one of the reasons that mobile phone companies assemble extensive data about you, to determine whether to offer you a phone contract, and, if you miss a payment, to work out whether to cancel your contract or offer you the chance to make it up. Even in this mundane phone contract you are the subject of many different types of risk calculation and financial market exposure in ways that are not easy to see. To elaborate more will get us ahead of ourselves (see Chapter 4), but it is a signal that finance has a reach into parts of our daily lives most people have no awareness of.

---

1 ASIC 'Buying a mobile'. www.moneysmart.gov.au/life-events-and-you/life-events/buying-a-mobile
2 See Appendix 1 for a more detailed explanation and Chapter 4 for a discussion of securitisation.

Health insurance used to be for the rich (or very risk averse): for everyone else, there was the public health system. Now there are tax penalties for those who do not have private health insurance and the public system is run on a shoestring, offering a service that certainly gives an incentive to be privately insured for all who can afford it. But health insurance, like mobile phones, now comes with hugely complex contracts of base payments and 'extras'. An Australian Competition and Consumer Commission (ACCC) report 'Information and informed decision-making in private health insurance' (2015)[3] reached three primary conclusions about health insurance contracts:

- First, there are ... complexities in private health insurance policies, which reduce consumers' ability to compare policies and make informed choices about their future medical needs.
- Second ... there are increasing policy limitations and exclusions leading to an increased risk of unexpected out-of-pocket expenses and general dissatisfaction with the system.
- Third, [there are] examples where representations by insurers to consumers ... may be at risk of breaching consumer laws.

Here, as with mobile phones, you are asked to calculate your own risks about what coverage you want, at what price, and what health risks you are prepared to pay for, and to situate these calculations in complex, and sometimes misleading, contractual choices. It's a risk-based, financial way of thinking about health. And these insurance payments too are developing a new financial life as inputs into asset-backed securities. Michael Gannon, President of the Australian Medical Association, is highly critical of health insurance policies:

Some policies are designed to do no more than avoid the tax penalty if you don't have health insurance. Others offer nothing more than treatment in a public hospital, which is the same as being uninsured. These are junk policies. They should be banned. (Gannon 2017)

---

3   The ACCC 2013–14 report 'addresses issues specific to the reporting period, it also gives broader consideration to the enduring impact of these issues on consumers' (ACCC 2015: 1).

Following a football team once meant going along to a suburban ground and, on the side, perhaps entering the workplace annual tipping comp and possibly a wager at the pub. Now it means paying to watch games on pay TV (so more contracts) and more elaborate betting, often adding multiple contingencies into a single bet. There are now bets where you back your preferred team for a win, but you can 'cash out' of a bet during the game at the odds prevailing at the moment you cash out, or where you get your money back if your team loses but the crowd is above a certain level, or a certain player scores. In financial terms, you are invited to go long on the team, and short on the crowd, etc. That is a complex bet on which to calculate the odds!

Television coverage of a game has also included betting company advertising, reporting to viewers the real-time odds offered by bookmakers. In 2013, a high-profile bookmaker was incorporated into the Channel 9 television rugby league commentary team, to add a 'financial perspective' to the game, by converting commentator analysis into bet prices. It was soon abandoned as a case of bad taste for family viewing. In 2017 restrictions were introduced to preclude betting advertisements during many categories of sports broadcasts.

Moreover, new dimensions of sports betting have arisen with the internet and the compilation of more elaborate sports data. The industry of 'fantasy sports' has emerged, permitting fans to play games of player and team (i.e. asset) management, strategically trading player profiles in an online market, according to price and form metrics from each game, to build a 'dream team' which you hope will deliver better game-day data than other people's dream teams. In the USA there are over 30 million traders and the industry is worth over $US3 billion dollars. *The Wall Street Journal* followed one trader in the US National Football League named Cory Albertson:

> Using tactics more familiar to a hedge-fund manager than to your average sports enthusiast, Albertson is earning thousands of dollars almost every day. One NFL Sunday, he took home more than $100,000. 'It is like securities trading,' Albertson explains, 'and athletes are the commodities.' ... On this night, Albertson is making projections for how each player will perform in the evening's professional basketball games – 12 games, involving a total of almost

300 players. It is painstaking, almost menial work. As fuel for his calculations, Albertson imports statistics from the Web into a complex algorithm he built over a period of months, and then tweaks the numbers to reflect injury updates, matchups and other factors. (Reagan 2014)

It is not just individuals who engage in this betting. Australian hedge fund The Priomha Group specialises in sports betting. According to the company website:

The Priomha Group was formed in 2010 with a vision to pioneer the development of an uncorrelated [meaning they don't move with other market indicators like the stock market], alternative asset class. Founded by a group of senior business and gaming executives, they had identified the opportunity to secure superior returns through the application of mainstream portfolio and investment management techniques to the nascent industry of sports and event investment.

Through extensive research, due diligence, fundamental analysis and the use of technology, the Group has been able to develop a rigorous system grounded in statistical data, much the same way as has been achieved in more traditional financial markets, to produce superior returns.[4]

Generally society doesn't think about things like health, phones and sport as 'finance', for they are just about daily life. But the changes we have seen recently are bringing financial ways of thinking into daily life: we start to think of calculating about the pricing of risks (bets) as an integral part of life. But further, as we will see in later chapters, this is not just about bringing financial calculation into the home; it is also about bringing the home directly into global financial markets.

---

4   The Priomha Group, http://priomha.com/about/.

A financial way of calculating

A financial way of thinking leads to a financial way of calculating. What do we mean by financial calculation? We mean not just managing mortgages, credit cards and telephone banking, although these are certainly expressions of it, but something far deeper and more pervasive. It is that financial calculation is about making clear, quantified risk–return choices. Some choices may be trivial – like fantasy sports competitions – but others prove critical and (retrospectively) can be disastrous, with choices about superannuation a leading case here. It is one thing to have dud players in your fantasy sports team, but dud assets in your superannuation portfolio can do long-term damage to your fund balance and may mean a loss of living standards later on, in old age. So the deeper dimension of financial calculation in everyday life, which is not generally discussed, is that when things become financial they become competitive, risky and uncertain. There are going to be losers as well as winners, and in a world of risk and uncertainty it is often hard to know in advance what the conditions for success or failure will turn out to be, especially for non-specialists like households.

In popular language, and presented in financial advertising, it is framed as opening up more individual choice: you can choose your mobile phone provider and contract details that best suit your particular needs. It is the same for your health and car insurance, or for that matter your bank. Superannuation funds offer literally hundreds of choices in how and in what to invest. And trading in fantasy sports keeps your mind sharp, and facilitates more sophisticated workplace conversations than simply 'Who will win next week?'

Surely choice is good: it expresses the capacity of individuals to follow their own judgements. It is that, but it also has two standard problems that go with it. First, increasingly we cannot choose to not choose. Playing fantasy sports may not be compulsory, but superannuation is, health insurance virtually is, and your health costs in general are an unavoidable issue. Going to university or other tertiary training like vocational education and training is deemed vital to career success, but it invokes fees, which must be repaid. To not purchase a health insurance contract means taxation penalties and being forced to rely on an increasingly under-funded public health system. Not going for a dental check-up may save money in the short run, but risks serious problems down the track. Having a mobile phone or driving a car is virtually essential, at least for many lifestyles. If you wish to work in many occupations or industries, you are required to take out an ABN and work as a labour-only subcontractor, so purchasing workers' compensation, income protection and public liability insurance then become necessary as well.[5]

The effect is that to be a part of society we are required to make continual financial choices, and to manage a growing range of social risks through various financial contracts. But on many things the fine print (the risk allocation) is so complex that we simply finish up taking a punt on this or that selection: 'My friend/parent/workmate is happy with Vodafone, or with NIB insurance, or with First Colonial superannuation fund's balanced fund'.

The second problem related to the culture of choice is that with choice there can be complex and inadequately informed decisions, and, worse, it may be difficult if not impossible to know which is right and which is wrong until it is too late. It may take months or even years to show up positively, or negatively.

A financial way of calculating, at least as we will refer to it in this book, is increasingly requiring a sophistication in calculation: if you base it on what your friends buy, or on 'taste', or on influential advertising, and then rest on the idea that we can all make mistakes, it means you are not playing by the new, albeit unstated, rules of the game. Increasingly, we are being expected to have read the fine print, and be canny about contracts. Critically, we are being made liable for all the contractual commitments we make. Being responsible financial decision makers and reliable payers on our contractual commitments is becoming a moral imperative, similar to (indeed, perhaps replacing) 'hard work' and 'thrift'.

Social protection against harmful contracts is concurrently narrowing. The government says it wants to cut red tape in financial regulation, to facilitate choice and market forces. The corollary is that

---

5   See Chapter 3 for a consideration of the risks of subcontracting, and the argument that it has increased as a form of work so as to shift risks to workers.

ordinary people get less protection: we are just expected to be 'financially literate'. The Australian Securities and Investments Commission (ASIC) is the part of the state that regulates financial industry products and services, and its resources are being cut, not increased. Greg Medcraft was its Chairman until 2017. When asked at a 2014 Australian Institute of Company Directors (AICD) event about the regulator's resource cuts, Medcraft replied:

> We will look to hold gatekeepers to account within the resources that we have, but individuals taking responsibility for themselves remains a core part of our system … That would be my warning to everybody: take responsibility for yourself. (Millan 2014).

Financial calculation for all of us is becoming a demanding and precise process. It involves measurement, and where (most) things cannot be measured precisely there are probabilities attached to the estimates.

But, you might be saying, 'I don't think about things that way'! Indeed you may not, but the organisation that is selling you the mobile phone, or the insurance, or, for that matter, the employment contract certainly is. The contracts they present to you are not about guesses or designed by marketing departments simply looking to sell an appealing product designed just for you: they are about precise actuarial calculations, with people in back rooms using big datasets, building 'algorithms' (formulae and models) to calculate how punters like you will act. The contracts you sign with banks, service providers and with employers are the living logic of risk, and so, even if you are not aware of it, you are involved in the pricing and trading of risk. In fact you are almost certainly exposed to more financial risk than you imagine!

A consequence of each of us being objects of risk calculation is that we each have a risk report card (or cards) which identifies how financially reliable we are. In Australia one such risk report card is called a credit record.[6] According to Illion, one of Australia's two main credit reporting agencies, 'you have a credit report if you have applied for credit. This includes instances where you have applied for a new phone contract, credit card, loan, mortgage or hire purchase'.[7] Your

---

6   See www.privacy.gov.au/faq/individuals/q17.

credit score is privately compiled from, and available to, a wide range of subscriber organisations like banks, retailers and other household service providers. It contains personal details like name and residential history, a record of credit applications, details of bank accounts, details of overdue or late payments, bankruptcy and other negative legal outcomes. In the United States, where credit reporting is much more comprehensive, and the range of data collected as well as those who are able to access it is much wider, prospective employers have, for instance, the right to use credit reporting agencies as part of their decision whether to hire you or not. In Australian, in 2012 the *Privacy Act* (1988) was amended to enable 'positive' as well as 'negative' credit records to be compiled on a wider range of individual credit details (Australian Government, Office of the Australian Information Commissioner 2013).

Experian Australia is a branch of a global data company. It offers services to individuals and to corporates. According to its website:[8]

A vast amount of data is produced around the world each day. Every phone call, every purchase, every visit to your website generates data. But how do you begin unravelling and making sense of it? How do you begin to turn insights into action?

At *Experian*, we believe data has the power to transform lives and societies for the better. We specialise in making sense of data in powerful new ways that create opportunities for consumers, businesses and society as a whole.

...

We can help you identify with your customers, from knowing where they live and how to communicate with them, to understanding what motivates them to buy and what they might buy next. We can also provide an insight to the many different forces – social, economic, technological, cultural and political – that shape society, markets and the lives of individuals.

7　See dnbcreditreport.com.au/faqs/index.aspx.
8　See www.experian.com.au/business-services/customer-acquisition.html.

If you are a university student, you may be interested to know that this is a service Experian offers to Australian universities. The 'customers' who universities want to know so much about that they pay companies like Experian are you, with data you have provided to social media sites knowingly or unknowingly for free!

Data organisations in effect share information to build personal credit and payment histories for all of us. Indeed, Equifax (formerly known as Veda), another leading credit reporting agency in Australia, claims the largest consumer credit database in Australia with data on 16.5 million individuals.[9] Data show for instance that more than one in five households misses a regular payment, and this can show up as an adverse impact on your credit history. If you are unsure of your history, you can purchase from Equifax access to your own file (yes, purchase!), pay an annual fee to get email alerts when there are changes to your record, and even pay to have your credit record 'repaired'. A new industry is emerging involved in 'credit repair'; that is, in cases of wrongly attributed credit default (for example, an energy bill that is unpaid because of a change of address), there are commercial services from companies like Credit Repair Australia which will make representation to restore your credit record.[10]

The histories show for each of us the types of credit we have, our credit limits, overdue payments and all inquiries that have been made on our credit cards. Increasingly now lending agencies are using credit scores to set personalised interest rates and charges. If your credit score is good, you will be charged a lower rate of interest or acquire cheaper insurance, or more likely be charged a risk premium if you fall outside of any of the lending criteria. If your credit record has too many strikes against it, you may lose access to financial facilities. Indeed, 18 percent of adult Australians are reported to be 'severely excluded' from financial services. This figure is made up of 1.1 percent of adults who are fully excluded and 16.6 percent of adults deemed to be 'severely excluded' in that they only had one financial services product. Generally, this

9   See www.veda.com.au/insights/nccp.dot.
10   See www.mycreditfile.com.au/ and www.creditrepairaustralia.com/content/
     co/creditrepair.

means they have a transaction account with a financial institution but no credit facility of general insurance (see Connolly 2013).

In the United States (though it seems not yet in Australia) it is reported that Facebook has recently acquired the patent for a system that would enable lenders to use an individual's friendship list (and hence their friends' credit ratings) in deciding whether to grant a loan (McCarroll 2015). Also, prospective employers are getting access to applicants' credit records and using them to make decisions about whether you get a job. If you have a bad credit history you might be denied access to the very employment that would permit you to pay off your debts! (Traub 2013). While Traub's study is from the USA, it is nonetheless significant, and no such study exists in Australia. The study reports a survey in which one in four unemployed workers say a prospective employer has requested a credit check as part of a job application. The study shows, not surprisingly, that this process works to keep disadvantaged social groups out of employment.

So the bottom line for those who say they don't think about finance in a strategic way is: even if you don't think this way about finance, finance thinks this way about you. And it matters!

Everyone is in this web of risk calculation, but not just as a means to shut some people out of access to finance because they are deemed high risk (the 'at risk' or, as one insurer has called them, the 'risky'). Indeed, the rest are graded as tolerable to good risks (the 'risk managed'), and that makes us credible targets for loans and other contracts in the market for risk. In 2016, Wall Street investment bank Goldman Sachs opened its first retail banks specialising in small personal loans. It is all online. Goldman's specialist advantage is its access to big data. Its 'Mosaic Project' uses coders to develop algorithms to gauge the credit quality of each individual borrower (Popper 2016).

In later chapters we will see that financial institutions (attempt to) grade people's risks precisely in terms of probabilities that they will or won't default on financial contracts – especially on mortgages, but credit cards too. But at this introductory stage in our analysis, it will suffice to emphasise that financial institutions want people to trade in the various risks of their daily lives – and it is profitable for them that we do trade. In the process, households finish up absorbing risks, making our lives often more risky.

In later chapters we will also explain in more detail the systematic process that makes risk shifting to ordinary people integral to a capitalist economy as it is currently configured. But the observation itself is not novel. Notably, Jacob Hacker published a book in the United States called *The great risk shift*, although his approach is different somewhat from ours. The International Monetary Fund, in its April 2005 *Financial stability report*, described the world's households as the financial markets' 'shock absorber of last resort'. It is a statement they have never repeated, for they have been widely criticised for it, and probably deeply regret being so open about ever saying it. But events since then, in the form of a GFC and European recession, seem to have confirmed their observation.

What follows: going back to understand the future?

So how did society get into this risk shifting momentum of social and economic change? The simplest way to frame it is to identify the historical change that set the pricing and trading of risk in motion.

From early in the 20th century, and especially the end of the Second World War, governments and employers took responsibility for many life-course risks. Governments tightly regulated finance and employment conditions, they provided pensions, public education, public hospitals, were often the sole telecommunications and utilities providers. Government policy gave priority to the ' affordability' of housing and other necessities. They set economic policy to secure full employment and the affordability of life's basics. Employers provided many people (but predominantly men) with secure, full-time jobs, effectively offering a stream of income until retirement, after which time there was the government's aged pension.

That regime started changing by the 1970s, as the long postwar economic boom came to an end. Change gained momentum and started to impact in social and economic policy in the 1980s with a range of 'pro-market' economic policy changes and the demise of secure jobs. People who disliked the change talk of the rise of 'neo-liberalism'. It was not simply an ideological shift as the term 'neo-liberalism' might suggest, nor did the momentum of change actually follow an orderly path. But risk shifting, while not framed at the time as an undercurrent, was, from today's perspective, certainly its abiding theme.

For our purposes, we can identify three dimensions of risk shifting since the 1980s:

1. Risk shifting from employers to the employees

Employment relations are complex and diverse. They always have been, and we will explore these issues in more detail in Chapter 3. Suffice it here to say that there was a discernible change in employment conditions in the 1980s – away from permanent, full-time, especially male jobs and towards part-time and casual, female jobs in service activities like retail and hospitality. Wages and working conditions came increasingly to be set with explicit reference to the profitability of employers, and, with the intensification of international trade and investment flows, these wages and conditions were being set with an eye to the international competitiveness of Australian-located companies. Accordingly, the setting of wages and conditions themselves shifted from a centralised system, where pay scales had a national framework and minimum wages were set with reference to the requirements of socially acceptable minimum living standards, and moved to the level of the enterprise, where specific commercial circumstances, rather than national standards, are driving employment contracts.

Companies themselves now face more risks in global competition than they did previously and through modern industrial relations and other regulation they can aspire to pass as many of these risks as they can down the line to their workers and service providers, if not also their customers. The move from centralised determination of wages and conditions to enterprise-level bargaining (enterprise agreements) gave employers greater capacity to shift many of these risks. The decline of organised labour at the workplace gave them motive and means for exploiting this capacity.

2. Risk shifting from the government to individuals

In the postwar period, the core question of government was: what can states do to build economic growth and improve living standards? By the 1980s the core question shifted to: what things can be done only by states, and what things can be left to markets? And even within those roles deemed to require the state, the agenda became: how might the state simulate market modes of calculation in organising or delivering its services? Further still, the question became: of those things which must be done by the state, what subcomponents of those roles might be reconfigured as market-compatible (i.e. profitably provided by private companies, or delivered by NGOs)?

Accordingly, we have seen states embrace financial 'deregulation' and labour market 'deregulation' (as they were popularly called, though the term is misleading),[11] policies of free trade, selling off state-owned assets, and so forth.

Critically, there was also a change in welfare policy; from welfare being framed as a right of citizenship to a system of tightly targeted access. It is often called a shift from welfare to 'workfare' with eligibility contingent on verification of employment availability (metrics of job applications, training courses etc.), but also means testing of income and increasingly assets that might be sold or borrowed against. A further iteration in the shift in welfare is the encouragement of private investment in welfare expenditure via 'social investment bonds' (Mitropoulos and Bryan 2016). In relation to such bonds, the then Minister for Social Services, Scott Morrison (2015), crystallised the link between welfare and investing: 'What I am basically saying is that welfare must become a good deal for investors – for private investors. We have to make it a good deal, for the returns to be there'.

For income after work we have seen a shift from a right to state-provided pensions to privately accumulated superannuation (see Chapter 4). While the system is managed privately, contributions are compulsory and access to those retirement savings is controlled by government policy.

Perhaps each of these changes in isolation could be variously justified in terms of promoting economic growth, reigning in government deficits, global integration, or some other rationale. But the

---

11   These terms are in common usage, with a generally understood meaning, though it is patently clear that the labour market and financial institutions remain subject to extensive state regulation.

combined effect is that many risks once covered (insured) collectively via a system of government revenue and expenditure and a socially oriented agenda of regulation started to be turned back to individuals to manage as best they could. Moreover, to manage those risks, financial markets began producing more and more financial products (including advice and insurance), which could be bought by households. Indeed, as we will see shortly in more detail, household financial management has become a frontier of global financial market innovation and profitability.

At a wider level, policies and cultures are being built to make households more financially robust. These policies, often framed by their advocates as necessary state 'paternalism', range from financial literacy to compulsory insurance and savings (superannuation), to conditional access to social welfare and, in the case of some Indigenous communities, direct control over expenditure items. As time passes we see a development and refinement of this risk shifting. The effect of all these changes is a rise of what we can call 'contractualism': that things once deemed rights of citizenship, accessed for free or in a subsidised (or otherwise generous) way, are now subject to contractual obligations, so that 'parties' rights (and risks) are clearly specified. Contracts decree our obligations as taxpayers and our access to government services, and those services themselves are increasingly subjected to 'outcomes-based contracting', where the state's contracting out now purchases a pre-agreed outcome rather than simply a service or capacity.

An individualist philosophy casts this change as a virtue, in terms of freedom from government control, and an industry of financial advisers and insurance has emerged for people to purchase 'wisdom' and management to access this freedom. There was recognition that the management of household finances involves more than a bank account, a credit card and a mortgage: it involves constantly calculating citizens who are financially savvy and sound. A more collectivist philosophy casts the change as a systematic shift in power relations.

3. Risk shifting from financial institutions and markets towards households

This is perhaps the sharpest edge of the risk-shifting process, because it is where we see financial innovation most tangibly in action. As with the other two dimensions of risk shifting, the process is not new, but it intensified massively from the 1990s with the growth of household borrowing, compulsory superannuation, the financial advice industry and a range of new financial products. Banks transformed from local organisations that dealt with household saving and borrowing into global wealth management institutions that brought with them 'opportunities' (framed as both products and services) for households to borrow and invest in novel ways. In the process banking has morphed into wealth management. Central here was the rising need for insurance to cover the contingencies of insecure incomes, and the growth of superannuation, which sees a share of wages compulsorily deducted from wages to be converted to 'savings' by the wealth management divisions of the finance industry. Out of the sales and product distribution departments of life insurance offices, we also saw the rise of financial advising as a 'profession' at this time, but still integral to financial institutions' profit strategies. (The complex, chequered history of selling financial products and 'financial advising' is addressed in Chapter 4.)

Indeed, risk shifting from financial institutions may be said in part to be a consequence of the other two forms of risk shifting for they, in combination, left individuals and their families open to intensified financial calculation and so inevitably exposed to developments in financial markets. The self-employed contractor who has to borrow to purchase their tools or pay for workers compensation or income protection insurance, the retiree who has to manage their superannuation or chooses to buy into a retirement village and the household signing mobile phone contracts are all now participants in financial markets as never before.

Figure 1.1 shows the three risk-shifts as a depiction of different economic positions of households in the 20th and 21st century (bearing in mind that any such diagram inevitably entails simplifications and generalisations).We identify a pattern for the 20th century, though we are describing the period from the 1940s to 1980s. We are borrowing

20ᵀᴴ CENTURY

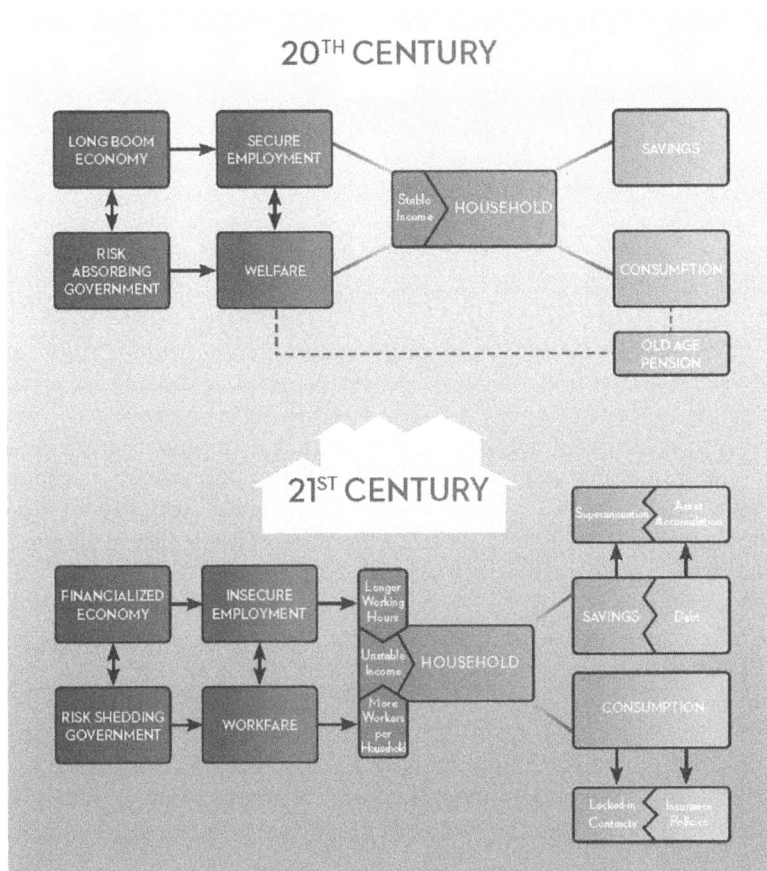

21ˢᵀ CENTURY

Figure 1.1 Households and risk shifting, 20th and 21st centuries.

historian Eric Hobsbawm's depiction of the 'short' 20th century, though his goes from the start of the First World War (1914) to the end of the Cold War (1991). We have also ignored that there are many different sorts of households, that individual households have different experiences, and that we have excluded a range of other issues that could legitimately be included in a more detailed diagram. The reader is asked to treat the diagram as a stylised impression; not in any way as the depiction of a formal 'model'.

The depicted changes between the 20th- and 21st-century in the state, the labour market and household finances are the issues we need to explore in later chapters, to show how people's lives are being reshaped to fit with the calculative requirements of finance.

Why 'households' rather than 'class', gender or race?

We have not so far spoken of 'class'. In part, this is because risks are transferred to rich as well as to poorer people, but the rich have the capacity to absorb risk in a way that lower income households do not. But in part also, we see the word 'class', as it is commonly used, tied to employment: the idea of a 'working class'. Our analysis suggests that a conflict between 'workers' and 'bosses' in the workplace is now too limited a framing of class relations. Financial calculation and risk shifting are seeing people being squeezed by 'capital' not just, or even primarily, in their role as workers, but in all facets of daily life that involve finance or a social logic of risk.

Much is written about social divides and how they drive our understanding of society. Should we focus on class, race, gender, ethnicity, location or age? The apparent answer is that these are all important divides in interpreting how society works, and some are critical in explaining some aspects of finance; others critical in explaining other aspects. Younger people carry much higher debt; Indigenous people face much greater exclusion from finance; women find it harder to get large loans and are often penalised by child rearing in saving for retirement. More generally all of these criteria are relevant in explaining people's engagement with finance.

But our objective is not a comprehensive explanation of people's differential experiences of finance, important as that issue is. We want to explain the calculative logic within finance, and how that logic is used by 'capital' – the financial and business system and those who run it – to create a world in its own image: a world in which monetary calculation and profitability are becoming the ruling criteria of social relations.

Because most people acquire income to fund their lives via work, the status of people as 'workers' (or unemployed or pensioners) is an obvious framework from which to start an analysis, although we will see in Chapter 3 that, with the rise of subcontracting, the concept of being an 'employee' and even a wage 'worker' is itself becoming ambiguous.

The other framework we use is that of 'households'. The idea of households is a difficult one in our context for they are diverse by all the criteria we have just nominated, and becoming more so. They vary, most obviously, by size, age, employment patterns, gender profile as well as income and wealth. So it means that when we present an analysis of households, it is about capturing broad trends of social change, not depicting each particular household's circumstances.

A focus on households as a central economic category is, of course, not new – indeed the origin of the term 'economics' (the ancient Greek word *oikos*) lies in the science of household management. In postwar 'Keynesian' economics, households were cast as consumers who created demand for industry's output and as savers whose deposits in banks were then lent to investors. The world has changed a lot since that model of the economy. From the 1970s scholars in feminism and peasant studies were both focusing our attention on production within the household as a major element of the economy, with household access to and sharing of money a key social and economic issue.

Our focus recognises these latter contributions, but adds two distinctive dimensions: the issue of households and the transfer of financial risk, and that 'production' inside the home attaches to global financial markets through a process of securitisation which sees household payments converted into financial assets.

In the context of a study of financialisation, we focus on households for two reasons. First, the household is a unit of financial administration. One-quarter of households in Australia are reported to comprise just one person, but we can broaden the concept to also recognise wider kinship relations with financial dimensions. Many living costs are shared within households. They may be shared in different sorts of ways, but issues of housing costs and utilities, childcare, education, consumption, and even things like health insurance have a strong collective dimension, albeit that in some households opinions are divided on many matters, including financial strategy.

In important ways, finance is creating a distinctive and contemporary image of households: financialisation is seeing households being shaped by the incentives and penalties that derive from financial institutions and markets. In Chapter 5 we depict households as having to operate like hedge funds, managing loans and risky assets and hedging risks through insurance.

Second, the household is increasingly a unit of policy analysis and risk surveillance. Especially since the GFC, many central banks and financial institutions are addressing household riskiness and its financial management. Some central banks now have new research centres focusing on household finance, and all major financial institutions undertake monitoring of financial viability of borrowers-as-households to oversee the risks on their loans; an issue we detail in Chapter 6. Governments also are thinking about social policy like retirement, education, childcare and unemployment in terms of household income and asset management, including what is now called 'asset-based welfare'.

Yet if risk is our focus, and risk transfer and risk management is the centre of our analysis, we need to be clear that the 'household' is a limited category. It works as our first port of call, and where appropriate we indicate where there are significant differences between households, especially in wealth and income, which themselves link to underlying issues of age, relationship status, race and location. The trouble is that there is no other social category that maps directly onto risk, and the data that are available to us for that purpose is household data.

But it is more than a matter of data convenience. The objective of this book is to get inside the financial logic of capital, so as to work out ways to challenge its trajectory. Some critics may say that if you get too much inside its logic you start to take on its logic. That is a risk we have to take, for we believe that to stand outside and make critiques of financial greed, inequality, 'deregulation', 'commodification' and even 'neo-liberalism' is not a sufficient foundation for strategic challenge. So we will use the category of 'household' cautiously. Those who might prefer a greater focus on 'class' or gender or race, etc. are welcome to make that addition, but our prediction is that it will be an addition to rather than a refutation of our analysis.

Conclusion

Surveys show that 41 percent of Australian households describe themselves as risk averse, and only 8 percent (mostly high income earners) report a high tolerance for risk (Black, Rogers and Soultanaeva 2012). But it is this generally risk-averse population that is now absorbing more and more diverse types of risks; transferred from governments, employers and financial institutions. Each process accentuates a different facet of individual life: as individual citizen, as worker, as householder and as wealth manager.

There is no single story here, for each person has different roles and positions. They absorb different types and degrees of risk and have different capacities to absorb them. But there is a common theme, across all roles: most people prefer safety to risk and volatility. When people are asked to decide how much income they will be prepared to give up to avoid or insure against downside risk (losing their job, their superannuation, their house and car) evidence shows that most people will give up a lot to buy a promise of safety in these domains. Indeed, Reserve Bank Governor Philip Lowe has contended that as workers we have become too risk-averse. 'People value security and one way you can get a bit more security is not to demand a wage rise' (Greber 2017). He said that we were too afraid of losing our jobs and had lowered our expectations about pay rises as a consequence.

But what we'd like or need, and what employers say they can afford, are different matters. Safety comes for many at a very high price: lots of insurance contracts, expensive financial advice, low yields on the capital guaranteed option in superannuation. In a low income growth environment, people simply can't afford to insure against all possible risks. So they are stuck as reluctant gamblers on themselves: whether to buy a house and if so when and where; whether to have fixed or variable rate loans; which sort of health insurance; whether to have comprehensive car insurance; which superannuation package, which employer and what sort of work contract to take? Many risks and no clear answers.

Readers may have noted that when we talk about the shifting of risk, exactly what gets shifted, how and who it gets shifted to is not fully explained. A deeper consideration of this process is considered in the following chapter, but here a few points of conclusion need to be noted.

First, the risks that are being shifted can have an upside as well as a downside. Some people benefited when employment contracts became deregulated; some subcontractors have made a lot of money. Some people are grateful that they took out more and more insurance, and many have got into the housing market and have benefited from price rises, so far. But many have not and, we will argue, the logic of risk shifting is that there will always be far more people who lose than who win. As with poker machines, individuals may win, but overall it is designed so that in aggregate the gamblers lose. That proposition, applied to wider social experiences of risk and uncertainty, will take time to validate – indeed to Chapter 6 – but it is, we believe, a critical dynamic of social change.

Second, when we talk about who risk is transferred to, we have talked sometimes about individuals, sometimes about workers and sometimes about households. How we identify the specific recipient depends on the specific risk and the context. Our point is that the process of risk shifting is systematic and whether it impacts on people as social individuals, as workers or as households, it is all part of the same process, albeit those different individuals carry different exposures to each of these domains of risk shifting. In particular, in the change we are projecting, it is younger people who are the greatest victims. No matter what their class, race or gender, compared with their parents, they face more insecure jobs, more expensive education and housing, fewer subsidised government services and the need for more self-funding in old age.

So the political question is: how do we tie together these various experiences of growing risks relating to work, to the purchase of contracts for loans, utilities and insurance, and that follow from restricted access to government services, such that they are all seen as part of a general process? It is an issue to which we return in our final two chapters. Our first task, addressed in the next chapter, is to explain how these different risks are all tied together by financial calculation, and how many of them pass through financial markets.

2
Risk and the intrusion of finance into daily life

To think of all the different sorts of risks we face in our daily lives as in some way connected, we need to have an overall idea of risk that covers them all. Risk in general is not an automatic way of thinking. Indeed we are encouraged to think about risks as discrete: the chance of breaking your leg is different from the chance of getting laid off at work, or of your house burning down. We insure against them with different policies. So to argue that there is a single momentum, we need to build an understanding of risk as a social concept: an understanding that helps us to frame the connections between different risks.

Risk itself is now a highly technical matter, or at least it has become so in the hands of financial analysis. Our task is to present a cut down version of this technical analysis, for, once we get inside the heads of financial analysts, we will see how they put prices on risks and connect different risks. Getting to their framing of the issues is the only real way to challenge them.

So in this chapter we build from some basic, common-sense notions of risk to some more complex risk products like financial derivatives. They are not that far apart!

Some risk basics

While we commonly think of risk as something dangerous, in financial hands it is a calculative device that links to probability theory: 'odds' in the language of gambling. If you think of high school probability theory, there are some pretty basic, but sensible, propositions there. The probabilities involved in tossing coins and turning cards tell how likely events are to happen, and it is then but a short analytical step to know how to bet on any outcome in two-up or a game of poker. Finance and risk are immediately tied together.

But, of course, the issues get more complex, and pretty quickly. First, outside the casino (or the classroom) there is something unclear about probability because the world is not as clinical and straightforward as coin tossing. There are odds on horseracing, but people will disagree on probabilities, horses can have lucky or unlucky runs, and it is possible that owners, trainers or jockeys may have different incentives than winning every race. Second, a critical assumption of casino odds is that each toss of the coin or turn of the card is independent of the previous toss and turn. But in the social world, events aren't independent or at least not fully independent, but are linked in complex ways we can at best intuit, but can't measure. Hence, and third, in the world beyond coin tossing there is uncertainty as well as risk. Risks we can calculate (they are the subject of odds and probabilities); uncertainties are ... uncertain, and in the social world there are always contingencies that could not be predicted or foreseen. Whenever you trade a risk some uncertainty will come with it. Former US Secretary of Defense Donald Rumsfeld made famous the idea that there are known unknowns and also unknown unknowns. We should never get too confident about our ability to predict the future. So we live with uncertainty, both socially and in financial markets: we can be lucky and unlucky and there are good and bad calculators of probabilities. (For most of our analysis, we will talk about risk as if it includes risk and uncertainty combined, but we will note when we want to differentiate them.)

This basic framework for thinking about risk, probability and odds sounds fine. But, you might say, it applies when you go to the TAB (betting shop) or the casino, but it is not central to daily life. People choose to go to the TAB or the casino, but for the rest of the time the contrived world of formal risk calculation does not apply.

Well, we think that's not right. Probabilities abound, although with most of them no one bothers to do the calculations. There is a probability that you'll forget 'bin night', or that you will find a parking spot within the next two minutes or that you'll actually lob that screwed-up ball of paper in the waste basket. It's just that no one (we hope) bothers to collect the data needed to make the estimates.

The reason no one bothers to collect such data is that nothing significant rests on the outcome. But what we find with the rise of financial calculation is that more and more data are being collected and analysed because someone wants (that is, finds it profitable) to put a price on these risks. So more and more aspects of daily life get counted, and the technology is there to do it. We now know details about how people spend their money, how they use their mobile phones, how reliable they are in paying the rent and the mortgage, and what the connections are between job loss and mortgage default, or relationship breakup and credit card debt. We know from household financial data how much alcohol people drink and what sorts of food they buy: data valuable to the pricing of health insurance. It's all recorded. When you ring organisations like banks, insurance companies and utilities providers, the recorded message that greets you will invariably mention the company's privacy policy. Actually, it's their sharing policy: warning you that much of your data is being sold to or shared with other like companies, or that they will access information from other financial service providers before offering you a contract. Combined, they are developing a detailed profile of your personal and financial life.

Actually, this isn't all that new – think of life insurance and car insurance, where these data have been used for decades. The life insurance companies want to know where you live, your occupation, if you smoke or drink, what your family illnesses have been, what sports you play, and so on. Car insurers want to know where your car will be parked, who will drive it, what their driving record is. These companies have, over many years, developed probabilities (risk ratings) about the connection of smoking to life expectancy, and the connection of where your car is garaged to the likelihood of theft. These are familiar processes of risk calculation, and your insurance costs vary with the answers you give.

In Chapter 1 we identified the mid-1980s as a turning point in social and economic policy as well as in finance. Specifically in relation to finance, the mid-1980s relates to the rise of financial derivative markets and rapid increases in cross-national flows of finance and investment. In Australia it relates to 'financial deregulation' which saw the floating of the Australian dollar, the dramatic reduction of restrictions on flows of finance in and out of the country and the granting of licences to foreign banks. What has been happening more recently – say the last 30 years but especially the last ten years – is that more and more risks are being calculated with more precision and turned into more and more products that trade risk. Initially they were being calculated in the world of business; increasingly they are about ordinary people's daily activities. These risk calculations are increasingly personal and individual. We see the last decade as the era of the intensive development of new financial products targeted at households.

This trend is important for our understanding of social and economic change for two sorts of reasons. One is that monitoring of risk turns us all into risk calculators and traders, whether we like it or not. Second, financial calculation does not simply describe what we do; it changes and shapes what we do.

Financial market imagination: turning ordinary things into risk products

To get a handle on how risk calculation is being expressed in our lives, think of betting on sports. It may not be the best place to start, because we think of sports betting as leisure and optional (or perhaps wasteful and morally questionable), and not integral to daily life. But, because it is familiar, we can temporarily push our perspective simply by heading in this direction.

Sports betting has always been a domain of probabilities (but emotions too). For centuries, odds have been offered and money changed hands on the basis of outcomes of contests. But there is a change. It will be apparent that sports betting is becoming more elaborate. More and more aspects of a game are now the object of bets, not just the final score: scores at various points in the game; the performance of individual players; which player will be the first to perform some act; what the total score will be; and the 'spread' of scores between the competitors. You can now also exit from many bets during the contest (at the current odds – less a fee). So a single contest, which once involved a single issue (who will be in front at the end of the contest), can now be unbundled into a stream of attributes or outcomes, and turned into a range of simultaneous betting contests.

The same is true of everyday life. Just beyond sports betting lies the world of high finance, using essentially the same mode of thinking applied to a vast array of new contexts and new uncertainties that might be reconfigured as tradeable risks: risks that are being 'created' by looking at everyday things with an eye to creating a new risk product. In relation to households, we see insurance products for all sorts of things – not just health, the house and its contents and car, but insurance on income, house prices (not just houses), trauma, divorce, funerals, pets, holidays, hole-in-one insurance (for golf day prizes and even for when you have to shout the bar), weddings, parties, anything. For example, the National Hole-In-One Association (NHIOA) has offices in Melbourne, Dallas and London. The website says that NHIOA offers an insurance policy that allows you to organise a golf event and to 'offer a prize worth up to $1,000,000. If one of your participants should have an Ace in the event, the NHIOA will pay for the prize'. On individual insurance for golfers who score an ace and are obliged to shout drinks for all in the bar, UK insurer Golfplan offers three levels of insurance to cover the costs.[1] Also in the UK, the department store John Lewis has an insurance division that offers a range of novel risks to trade. These include wedding insurance, in case any member of the wedding party is ill, or the wedding cake either goes missing or gets damaged; pet insurance, including not only vet costs, but a payout if you have to cancel a holiday because your pet is unwell; and 'event' (party) insurance if the hire equipment gets damaged or the caterers or

---

1   See www.hole-in-one.com.au/about-us and www.golfplan.co.uk/golfplan-cover-prices/.

band fail to turn up.[2] Financial market actuaries have worked out that an increasing range of life's experiences or events can be calculated as risks and then traded as insurance policies and financial securities.

There are some pretty strange risks traded in open markets, too. For a brief time in 2003 the US Pentagon ran a market where you could bet on the probability that key political leaders would be assassinated (Hulse 2003). Someone at the Pentagon figured that if people really had inside information on plans for assassinations, they would likely bet money on it, so the 'terrorism futures market', as it came to be called, was thought to be a means to draw out 'secret' information. It was shut down after three days, under storms of protest about financial bad taste, but it illustrates the sorts of imagination being applied to the invention of financial products that trade risk.

The Chicago Mercantile Exchange (CME) – the biggest financial exchange in the world – started life as the Chicago Egg and Butter Board, trading agricultural outputs. It has evolved extensively. You can now trade in measurements of future weather, including the Australian weather (temperature, rainfall, snow, the likelihood of frosts), and you can trade in house price movements in many different cities and suburbs, as well as standard things like stocks and bonds, interest rates, currencies and raw materials – both current and future prices. People trading these products are engaging the risks of price or other appropriate measures (like temperature) changing in a certain direction. The calculation of risk or probability then tells them how much they should pay/charge to buy/sell the risk of change in the measurement.

In developing these novel sorts of products, all you basically need is a capacity to measure in a way that, at least in principle, cannot be manipulated, and people who will be inclined to take each side of the bet – someone who will put money on more than 40mm of rainfall next July, or the ruler of a particular Middle Eastern nation dying by June 30, and someone who will put money on there being less than 40mm, or no death. At one level, it might be no different from sports betting – although note that farmers and construction companies, unlike most sports punters, all have innate risk exposure

---

2   See www.johnlewis-insurance.com.

to rainfall, as do the US State Department and oil companies to an assassination in the Middle East. The farmer who bets on low rainfall may be astute, for if the rain falls the crops grow and the revenues come in, but if the rain doesn't fall they have no crop to sell but they win their rainfall bet. They have 'hedged' their income in the financial market. The construction company may bet on rainfall, as a hedge on the time when construction must stop due to the weather. This is a more 'basic', and some might contend honourable, motivation for 'betting' than sports or assassination betting. We can see why it might be 'sensible' that these strange items are traded on the CME. Indeed, this is where our comparison with sports betting is stretched to its limit, or starts to break down.

There are many other innovations, which we will raise at a later time when they become critical to our argument. Our point here is just to note the remarkable development in financial markets has been the imagination which has turned such things as the weather, weddings, holes in one, house prices and espionage into risks to be priced and traded.

So you may think of insuring your own wedding, or if you run a construction company you may place bets on the weather. If you run an airline, you are interested in the price of oil, so you may place bets on future oil prices (or indeed on political assassinations). That all makes sense for the risk averse.

But what if, in financial markets, you can bet on other people's risks; not just on your own? That is, investors may not be just insuring themselves, but placing 'bets' on other people's risks, to be held as part of an asset portfolio made up of diversified risks. They may look to hold bets on oil prices and snowfall, along with stocks and bonds. This is what professional gamblers do when they bet not just according to which horse or team they think will win the race, but which odds at the bookmaker look like a good deal. Investment banks and hedge funds do this same calculation, but over different sorts of risks. There, an investor is looking to find the best buys (under-priced assets, whatever they may be) and to diversify their risks so that when one part of the market falls another may rise. And as financial market traders buy and sell these bets (assets) as their prices change, all different odds (prices) on all different sorts of events and forms of capital are being compared as good or less good investments. When people are choosing what risks to buy and sell according to prices and probabilities, we are in the world of the pricing and trading of risk! Moreover, we have created the idea that all risks have something in common: they are products to be bought and sold and all increasingly priced relative to each other.

Derivatives: a complex ingredient made simple

There is one more layer we want to add to this risk story: the idea of financial instruments called derivatives as primary instruments of risk trading. As we will see, in the very design of derivatives will be the means to actively trade exposure to risks as the odds change, so they are the tools of connecting all risks to each other. Moreover, as our argument develops, we will show that a growing range of workplace and household decision-making and social policy and practice are being reconfigured around what we call, following Martin (2015), 'the derivative form' or a 'social logic of finance'.

Derivatives sound complex – and indeed many of them are – but their idea is ingeniously basic. So we ask the reader to put aside the connection of derivatives to financial crisis and complex mathematics, and think about the *idea* of derivatives, for they are a key ingredient to understanding risk. Indeed, we have already been describing derivative processes in this chapter without naming them.

The essence of a derivative contract is that you own exposure to the performance of an underlying 'asset', but you don't own the underlying asset itself. A simple form of a derivative which will be familiar is a bet on the horses. When you place a bet on a horse race you own a financial exposure to the performance of a horse (the underlying asset) in a particular race, but you don't own the horse itself. The same is true of an oil derivative: an oil futures contract gives you exposure to the price of oil in, say, three months, but not ownership of oil. If the contract says you can 'buy' a barrel of oil for $150 in three months, and the actual price turns out to be $160, you've made $10 (strictly, it is $10 less the price of buying the futures contract). But, unless you specifically arrange it, you don't actually buy the oil: there is simply a cash settlement on the price difference. So you have profited from exposure to the market 'performance' of a barrel of oil, but without ever owning a barrel of oil. The same applies definitionally to weather derivatives – since of course you can't own the weather, but you can own a dollar exposure to changes in some aspect of the weather (temperature, rainfall, frost, etc.). You can buy (or sell) a contract that gives you a payout if the temperature or rainfall gets above or below a certain average level in a particular city or region. It is profit from changes in price or some other measure (like temperature), but without ownership. And it applies also to those securities backed by mobile phone bill payments: owners of the security hold exposure to the monthly bill payments; they don't own the phone or the phone contract itself.

A consequence is that, compared with buying an underlying asset, trading derivatives keeps you 'liquid': able to buy in and sell out of positions on an asset without the legal complexity, time and transport of buying and selling the asset. Liquidity means being able to convert one asset to another without a significant cost of trading. This is how all different risks can be compared, and in the process create an overall price for risk.

The essence of derivatives, therefore, is that they exist to trade risk, often with rapid turnover. They put a price on the probability of something (often price, but it could be temperature) going up or down and they permit easy (fast, cheap) trade in risks associated with that change. People decide to buy and/or sell derivatives according to whether they want to take on risk (in expectation of making a profit) or sell-off risk (in expectation of avoiding a loss) or, by locking in some predictability about future prices, to avoid exposure to volatility in price and index movements.

The next feature of derivatives follows logically. It is far cheaper to buy an exposure to the performance of an asset than to buy the underlying asset. Placing bets on horses is far cheaper than buying a racehorse (unless you gamble very large amounts of money) and the same is true of derivatives on currencies, interest rates, stocks and bonds. So for a (relatively) small outlay you can take a highly 'leveraged' position: by owning an exposure but not the underlying asset you can win a lot, but also lose a lot; indeed more than the value of your initial investment. It is this capacity for high leverage that sees derivatives condemned as dangerous.

Really, derivatives are as simple as that, but if you would like more details on types of derivatives, see Appendix 1. The complexity in derivatives arises in relation to variations on the contractual terms and how they get priced and traded, how they get combined to form multiple risk exposures, and whether they are making global markets more stable or speculative. These are indeed important questions, but at this stage we are not looking to make such judgements. We here simply note two aspects of derivatives:

1. Derivatives are products developed and used to price and trade risks in highly liquid markets, and through them the trading and importantly transfer of risk has become an increasingly conspicuous and precise process over the last 30 years.
2. Derivatives create exposures to the performance of certain aspects or attributes of an underlying asset or future event. The effect is that one underlying asset or event can be seen to embody a range of risks, each of which can be priced and traded discretely.

The imagination of financial calculation is to break down underlying assets into more and more discrete and measurable risks, and to break down these risks into subcomponents, with each of these priced and traded.

This latter point may sound complex, but we have already raised it in the context of how many different things you can bet on in one sporting contest. Think of it in relation to mobile phones or health insurance and these insights become integral to daily life: in a mobile phone contract, you are not purchasing a single thing; or, to put it another way, a whole range of things and services go into providing the phone. If it is possible to disaggregate any or some of the 'exposures' you are purchasing, then each can be priced: how much you text relative to call, how much internet access you use, your use of local compared with long distance calls, calls to mobiles compared with landlines, use of 1800 numbers, the 'apps' you download, maybe the mobile phone itself, etc. These are all being calculated in the contract you are offered, and you are in turn asked to calculate your risk of exceeding the limits on each of these, compared with the costs of paying a higher monthly fee. It is the same basic logic of derivatives.

In health insurance the same thing applies. Do you take out insurance for spectacles? How much hospital and dental cover will you need? What proportion of a medical bill do you want to lay off to the insurer, and what percent are you prepared (and can afford) to pay directly? These are all complex calculations based on the disaggregation of you as an individual into a spectrum of attributes and risks. And you have to choose which risks you will carry, and which you want to sell off via insurance.

In summary, it is the mindset of derivatives that is the driver of financial calculation: the mindset that looks to dissect or unbundle things into subcomponents, and create means to 'take a position' on those subcomponents. Increasingly there is a technical capacity and incentive for the finance industry and others to dissect work, products, household expenditure, and potential events that may impact on households in this way. This is the essence of what Randy Martin (2002) has called the 'financialization of daily life'.

Conclusion

Our opening propositions about financial risk can now be made more precise. People are being framed socially and economically as a set of increasingly precisely-defined risks. They are being required to manage more and more of their lives by identifying the risks they face and determining which to hold and which to sell off. They are, in a sense, asked to become a sort of hedge fund of their own lives (a theme we develop in Chapter 5).

In Chapter 1, we identified three dimensions of risk shifting: from employers to workers, from states to individuals, and from financial institutions and markets towards households. We can now give those three dimensions a deeper commonality, as a logic of financial calculation, although a more developed argument will be given in later chapters. What we will see, as the analysis unfolds, is that more and more aspects of daily life at work and at home are being subjected to financial calculation. We are used to hearing about governments and government debt being rated for their risks. And we are used to hearing about companies and company debts being rated for their risks. In order to build a risk profile, finance collects a lot of information about attributes of government finances and corporate activity. But it is households that are now also being subject to the same sorts of calculations of their riskiness across a range of attributes. Finance is therefore also now very interested in our incomes, expenditures, jobs, health and even our height and weight if they are found to be linked in some way to our riskiness of, say, paying a car loan or mobile phone contract or to setting premiums on health insurance. It is sold as 'personalising' our insurance policy or phone contract, but it is ultimately about building a more complete risk profile of each of us.

According to one financial services firm, Experian (2010: 3), it used big data to help build risk profiles of customers of mobile phone and telephone providers:

> Customers are finely segmented according to a wide range of variables to create an accurate profile. Using behavioural scoring, each customer is assigned a risk score according to their account and delinquent behaviour, which is used throughout the collections activities to drive the most appropriate strategy according to the level of risk and value.[3]

We have to look at this spread of risk across the social world. A corollary is that where risk and risk products go, measurement and quantification has already taken hold. So finance is changing the world not just by trading its risks, but by creating an economic culture in which more and more things are measured, to be framed in the language of risk. We are also being asked to think about more and more aspects of our lives in financial terms.

Somewhere in there, by the end of our analysis, we aspire to find the space to push back against this financial domination of daily life, and to do so via an understanding of finance, not a moralistic rejection of it. At this point of the analysis, though, that looks like a near impossible agenda. Let's wait and see.

---

3   This issue is explored in detail in Chapter 6.

3
Financialised work: re-thinking employment through finance

The nature of work and employment in Australia is changing before our eyes: indeed faster than we can analyse it! There are many ways of understanding those changes. Our proposition in this chapter is that issues of work and employment are being framed more and more in the language of finance and risk, focused on issues of liquidity and trading risk exposures, increasingly like a financial derivatives market. Yet current public debate about work and labour markets is of a different order: it is about issues of standard versus non-standard work, regulation vs deregulation, incomes of workers vs affordability and costs to employers, and security of jobs vs flexibility in labour costs.

To be sure, those debates are important. A federal election was lost by the Liberal and National Party government in 2007 because its 'Work Choices' legislation pressed for deregulation to achieve lower labour costs and workplace flexibility. The ACTU campaign on 'Your rights at work' was highly successful in arguing for the maintenance of close regulation, a minimum wage that is closer to a living wage and working conditions that protected workers' rights to stable and fair working conditions. But even in the decade since that battle, the terms of debate have changed.

Successful as that ACTU campaign was, we see a continued momentum towards employer demands for flexibility in wages, employment conditions and even in the very nature of 'employment'. We are moving towards a society in which conventional notions of 'employment' are changing, and the process of paying people for work, be they employees or independent contractors, is increasingly conspicuously about risk/return calculation and systematically shifting risk onto workers. What makes a contract of work different from any other common law contract – the issues that make work 'social' – is being wound back and work itself (in the name of 'flexibility'), is being moved towards what finance calls 'liquidity'. In the world of work, we are each becoming bits of liquid capital and priced like mini profit centres.

Our proposition is that this shift is critically about the way in which financialisation is manifesting in work and employment. Financialisation involves both a discipline on employment costs and a calculative reframing of employment practices. But, more than this, financialisation is changing the nature of 'work' itself. The rise of what is now called the 'gig economy' – driving your private car for Uber or renting a room in your home on Airbnb – is changing what we mean by 'work', where it occurs, and how we 'earn' an income.

So in this chapter we will first frame financialisation as a growing discipline on employers and 'employment'. We then reframe this as the demand for labour as a form of liquid capital, and how the calculative logic of finance is changing the terms of labour market debate.

Finance as discipline: shareholder value

Finance as discipline involves the proposition that financial markets demand firms produce higher reported profits and hence a reduction in all production costs. Labour costs are often the focus here, for these costs can be negotiated in a way that other production costs often cannot be.

We could say that this pressure has always been present as part of capitalism, but financialisation in the last 30 years has intensified the pressure. The change is called the imperative of 'shareholder value'. Essentially, shareholder value is the influence placed by shareholders, or the institutions that represent owners (and in some cases lenders), on corporate managers, pressing them to cut costs and invest shorter-term in order to get higher profits and declare higher dividends for shareholders.

What has changed in shareholder value is the way that shareholders exercise their power. Although many individuals in Australia personally own shares (more than you'd think)[1] it is superannuation funds that now do most of the investing and, while there are many such funds, the actual investing is generally delegated to a relatively small group of large fund managers like Commonwealth/Colonial, Macquarie Bank, State Street and Vanguard. So there is a lot of concentrated influence at company AGMs. Total funds under management in Australia is more than 2.5 trillion dollars (ABS 2018). The top ten fund managers control over 55 percent of these funds; the top 20 control 75 percent (Austrade 2010). Superannuation funds contribute 56 percent of those funds (Price and Schwartz 2015). A concerted pressure on corporate performance follows, demanding high and rising share prices and high dividends. Delivering that sees employers seeking round after round of cost cutting.

The paradox, of course, is that workers are on both sides of this pressure: as shareholders via superannuation they want higher profits; as employees they want higher wages and better working conditions. They want to intensify and resist exploitation at the same time. Movements for 'ethical investing' are an attempt to grapple with this paradox, albeit that it can never be resolved.

Changing forms of employment

The competitive pressure that came from the 1980s with the rise of shareholder value (together with globalisation and shifting agendas in government regulation) has been central to the shift away from nationally bargained standards and secure jobs as the 'standard' form of paid employment to what is often termed 'flexible', 'internationally competitive', but 'precarious' and 'non-standard' employment relations (Lansbury 2000; Shaw 2004; Kirby 2005; Stewart 2007; Brown 2013).

---

1   Thirty-six percent of adult Australians have some share ownership through direct holdings or unlisted managed funds (that is, not including superannuation) (ASX 2015). The figure was as high as 44 percent in 2004.

This change is well documented, but it nonetheless warrants noting here. For most of the 20th century, the benchmark of employment was full-time jobs with security of tenure, conditions like holiday and sick leave and a wage sufficient to support a family. It was referred to as 'standard' or 'permanent' employment. It doesn't mean everyone enjoyed these conditions: many, especially women, had lesser conditions; some, especially professionals, had more. But this norm was the way the wage system got talked about and wage levels and conditions determined.

Things changed dramatically in the 1980s. With the aim of cutting labour costs, adding flexibility, and meeting international competitive norms, standard jobs went into relative decline and we saw the rise of part-time, casual and self-employed (or subcontracted) work. These forms of work are growing faster than standard full-time ('FT paid leave') jobs, as seen in Figure 3.1.

Over 24 years from 1992 casual employment (full-time and part-time combined) has grown by 200 percent, while 'full-time paid leave' (a proxy for 'standard') employment has grown by just 40 percent. 'Part-time paid' leave has grown fastest of all, by 300 percent, though from a low base; much of it female employment.

This dramatic change has been referred to as the rise of non-standard forms of work and employment, but it is, we believe, not a helpful framing. The trouble with the 'standard'/'non-standard' dichotomy is that it invokes a standard of a past era. We are already more than 25 years on from that era, and to continue to invoke full-time permanent jobs with paid leave and other benefits as a norm must be seen as a case of analytical nostalgia. Part-time and casualised employment, as well as self-employment and subcontracting, are becoming part of the new norm. In this context, some are arguing that the way employment data are collected is outmoded, for it is stuck with old categories and does not take on the real significance of increasingly flexible work and people having multiple jobs (e.g. Lewis 2017).

So our proposition is that to understand the contemporary nature of work and employment change we need to stop focusing on a deviation from a postwar employment ideal and analyse work in terms of the current underlying drivers of change. We have to make strategic sense

3 Financialised work: re-thinking employment through finance

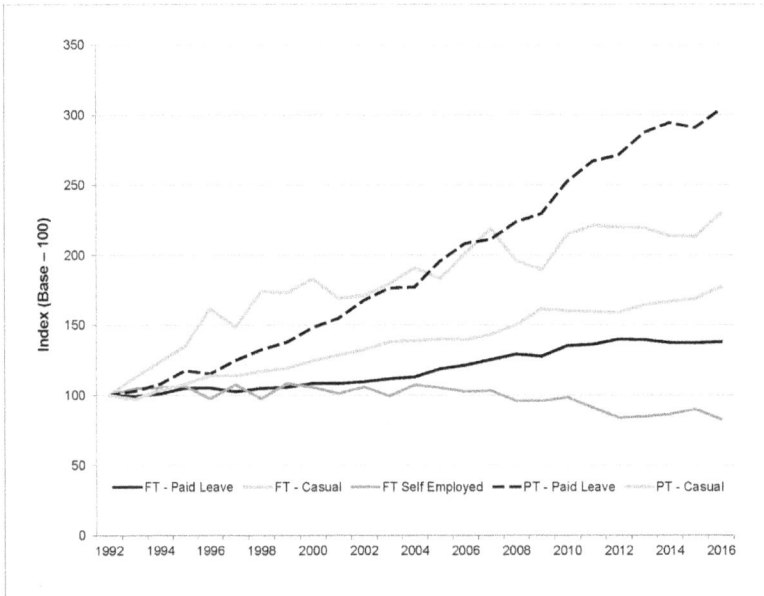

Figure 3.1 The growth of different forms of employment, 1992–2016, base index 1992 = 100. Source: ABS, Labour Market Statistics, Cat. 6105.0, July 2016.

of a present and future where work is less secure, the number of hours worked per week less predictable, and hence income more volatile.

In this future, the world of work is more precarious: it is seeing the rise of what Standing (2011) has called the 'precariat'. Following the work of Jacob Hacker we frame it as risk shifting. Hacker (2005, 2008, 2009, 2011) has written extensively about risk shifting in the United States, centred on the labour market, but moving beyond it too. He has shown that as a result of economic restructuring, and particularly the greater risks now being borne by American workers, households are experiencing much greater volatility in their incomes, and as a consequence become much more financially unstable and fragile. How companies (and indeed individuals) do and do not profit in this changed environment is what the future of work and income will be about.

But before we frame this future, let's look at what has been happening, using the framework of finance and risk shifting.

'Permanent' employment

We are not announcing the disappearance of 'permanent' work. Figure 3.1 shows that this type of employment has not disappeared. It is not even shrinking. It has just been growing less rapidly and most of the growth of permanent employment has been in part-time work – a trend desired by some employees, though surveys show that most would prefer those jobs to be full time.

Yet the terms of 'permanent' employment are changing. The first notable change is that people in full-time work are now working longer hours, often without extra payment. Evidence shows a growth of unpaid overtime. It is not easy to compare hours by forms of employment because of data limitations, but an Australian Bureau of Statistics survey in 2007 found that people who are on contracts with paid leave entitlements (the indicator of permanent employment) are much more likely to work extra hours (53 percent) than (generally) casuals who work without paid leave entitlements (22 percent).[2] Consistent with this finding, a large study of working arrangements in Australia by the Workplace Research Centre at the University of Sydney has found that around half of full-time workers report regularly working some overtime every week. In 2010, for instance, a quarter of full-time employees reported working between 41 and 49 hours per week. A further quarter report usually working more than 50 hours a week. The survey respondents also reported that an increasing amount of the overtime being worked was unpaid. As a consequence of the pressures on workers to complete jobs, often with too few staff to support the job, Australian workers in full-time employment now work some of the longest hours in the developed world. An ACTU (2011: 36) survey estimates that 47 percent of overtime in Australia is unpaid. The highest rates of unpaid overtime are among the lowest and highest paid workers. The former lack the power to say no; the latter have received

2   ABS 6361.0 – Employment Arrangements, Retirement and Superannuation, Australia, April to July 2007 (Re-issue).

the highest price for the employer's claim. Permanence, it appears, comes at a real (if implicit and often hidden) cost.

Second, the range of conditions that attach to enterprise agreements of permanent employees has been dramatically circumscribed to very workplace-specific conditions (and now referred to as 'allowable matters').[3] The content of registered (workplace or enterprise) agreements does not have to be restricted only to 'allowable matters', but the 'no disadvantage' test can only be used against Award allowable matters and the industrial umpire (the Fair Work Authority) can only hear issues restricted to 'allowable' matters. Indeed, in order for registered agreements to comply, they can no longer include 'prohibited content' – matters not seen as pertaining to the employment relationship (e.g. deduction of union dues, leave for union delegates and representatives). Increasingly the beneficial conditions traditionally attached to permanent employment (things like various forms of special leave, shift and other allowances and loadings) are being narrowed, more tightly monitored (especially the policing of concessional leave) and also traded off against wage increases. Rights to payment during periods of ill health, to various sorts of leave and to termination payments have all also narrowed in recent years. In 2015, the Fair Work Commission gave employers the right to demand that annual leave be taken, reducing the capacity of workers to build a 'leave safety net' (FairWork Commission 2015). Similarly, the terms of access to workers' compensation were narrowed in NSW in 2015, with the onus of proof and legal costs shifting increasingly onto workers (Simpson and Davies 2015). In 2015 the reforms were partially wound back.

An ACTU survey of 40,000 workers reports that 28 percent of workers feel pressured to attend work when sick (2011: 40). Indeed, sick leave itself has been decomposed, in the style of the derivative, into various employer exposures and there are now management consultants like iHR and Direct Health Solutions (DHS) who specialise in 'absence management solutions'. DHS describes itself as 'the Leader in Positive Absence Management & Organisational Wellbeing in Australia':

---

3   For the list of allowable matters in Industrial Awards see airc.gov.au/awdsimp/asinfo/20matters.html.

We enable organisations to *reduce absenteeism by up to 40%* and enhance employee performance, delivering a positive *Return on Investment* and a self-funded health benefit for all employees. (www.dhs.net.au/; emphasis in original)

Their agenda, in essence, is that if leave is decomposed into different causes, those causes can be better targeted for 'improvement' and better risk-managed. In this context, the achievement in the mid-1990s of new sorts of leave categories like carers' leave and family leave may be seen not just as a success for workers with family responsibilities, but also as a device to take these morally affirmed sorts of leave out of the category of 'sickies' and hence further socially discredit the residual category 'sickies'.

In effect, workers in permanent employment increasingly have to buy (via extra hours, diminished conditions or lower real wage growth) those provisions that once were part of standard conditions. In financial language, we could say that the 'benefits' traditionally associated with permanent employment are now being thought about and even priced like financial options: in effect, employees are now explicitly buying the conditions that differentiate permanent employment from others. Conversely, there is also evidence of workers selling these options (conditions) as a means to secure a pay rise.

Casual employment

Casual employment is where a worker is purchased for a specific task or duration. There is no presumed continuity of employment, and often even the hours per week vary, so annual income is likely to be lower and more volatile. Campbell and Burgess (2009) note that 'the basic (historical) definition of a casual employee is to be found in the common law, where casual employees are presumed to have a contract of employment that is of so minimal duration as to barely exist'. That is clearly no longer the basis of the modern casual employment experience, and instead is more about paid employment with minimal additional rights apart from pay. Not surprisingly, therefore, 30 percent of casual workers in Australia say they would prefer to work more hours.[4] This is especially the situation for younger workers, who increasingly face casual employment not as just a starting point in employment but as a long-term, if not a lifelong, condition, often doing the same work as permanent employees. Indeed, for many younger workers, at the frontline of these changes, it now takes almost five years from leaving full-time education to securing a full-time permanent job (compared to one year in 1986). In 2014, almost 60 percent of 20–24 year olds were employed in casual or part-time forms of work, and this proportion has increased by 10 percent since 2008 alone (Stanwick et al. 2014).

In comparison with permanent workers, casual workers' incomes are much more unpredictable. ABS data show that 47 percent of casual employees report that their earnings vary from pay to pay, compared to 16 percent of other employees (cited in Stacey 2013). Casuals are employed only when there is work to be done, and so carry the risk of ebbs and flows in the volume of work. They conventionally receive no holiday, sick leave and other employment conditions and lack protection from unfair dismissal (Pocock 2008). As 'compensation' casual employees are normally entitled to an hourly loading, generally around 20 percent, but whether this is paid or not is uncertain, and depends very much on enforcement, and is especially unlikely where payment is cash-in-hand.[5] The February 2017 Fair Work decision to cut Sunday and public holiday penalty rates in certain industries, for all its negative reception, did 'widen' the compensation for casual employees.

Self-employment

In a parallel development, we have seen people once employed on wages now working as self-employed, so-called independent contractors. As self-employed people earn profits as well as wages, their rise distorts and blurs aggregate figures about the share of national income going to wages and profit. The Australian Bureau of Statistics defines these contractors as:

---

4   ABS 6361.0 – Employment Arrangements, Retirement and Superannuation, Australia, April to July 2007 (Re-issue).

5   The notion of 'compensation' is formally acknowledged by the state. See, for example, www.fairwork.gov.au/industries/clerical/classifications-and-categories/pages/casual-employee-entitlements.aspx.

People who operate their own business and who contract to perform services for others without having the legal status of an employee, i.e. people who are engaged by a client, rather than an employer. Independent contractors are engaged under a contract for services (a commercial contract).[6]

In 2014, some 1.1 million people (over 9 percent of workers – mainly older men) were classified by the ABS as independent contractors, although there is reason to doubt that these data actually capture the extent of independent work performed in addition to employment, such as contracting to Uber after working hours, or working through platforms like Airtasker.

Compared with a formally constituted employee, an independent contractor is considered to have greater control over their own work practices and hours worked (although in practice this becomes a moot point because they report working longer hours and are more likely to work on weekends). In one account of this test, 43 percent of contractors reported having no authority over their work; 47 percent work 40 hours or more in their main job (ABS, Forms of Employment, April 2013, Cat. 6359.0). Waite and Will (2001), observing at a time when independent contracting had already reached 10 percent of the workforce, found that a quarter of all contractors should be deemed 'dependent' contractors as their work arrangements were similar to those of employees. In return for this nominal independence, a contractor must bear a range of risks once borne by the employer, such as: (dis)continuity of work; ability to perform tasks due to things like weather, availability of materials, etc.; liability for such things as remedial work, workers' compensation, and public liability (thus requiring a range of insurance policies); and they face the risks of non-payment of income. They receive no employer contributions to superannuation, no paid annual leave, sick leave or other such benefits.[7]

---

6   ABS, Characteristics of Employment, Australia, August 2014, Cat. 6333.0.
7   These points are derived from the Fair Work Ombudsman's explanation:
    www.fairwork.gov.au/resources/fact-sheets/workplace-rights/pages/
    independent-contractors-and-employees-fact-sheet.aspx/.

Companies may seek to reduce their overall risks by simply reclassifying work as being independently contracted rather than done by employees. This is the practice known as 'sham contracting'. For instance, in 2012 some 200,000 people classified as independent contractors were performing work as labourers: an unlikely occupation for 'self-employed' people (ABS, Forms of Employment, April 2013, Cat. 6359.0). In industries like construction the use of independent contractors (typically requiring an ABN) is common. Estimates vary, but at least a quarter, and as much as half, of these contractors may effectively be disguised employees. It is hardly surprising, therefore, that in the construction industry around 40 percent of the union (CFMEU) members are subcontractors.[8] While formally independent, they are in every practical sense worker/employees and many seek the protection of union membership.

A consequence is that unions with such members reach beyond a constituency of 'employees' to take on the role of protecting independent contractors against the consequences of their work-based risks. One example here is the insurance company Coverforce, established in 1994 'as a specialist provider of income protection and ancillary workers compensation insurance, to workers in the Australian construction industry' (see www.coverforce.com.au/history.php). The construction industry union (CFMEU) and manufacturing union (AMWU) are partners in Coverforce and its senior management team includes former and current union office bearers.

The Fair Work Ombudsman defines sham contracting as:

[W]here an employer attempts to disguise an employment relationship as an independent contracting arrangement. This is usually done for the purposes of avoiding responsibility for employee entitlements.[9]

It is formally illegal, but hard to prove. Under the sham contracting provisions of the *Fair Work Act 2009*, an employer cannot contrive

---

8   Estimate by Assistant National Secretary, CFMEU, provided to the authors.
9   See www.fairwork.gov.au/resources/fact-sheets/workplace-rights/pages/independent-contractors-and-emplyees-fact-sheet.aspx.

an employment relationship to be an independent contract. But as a leading Australian labour law academic Professor Andrew Stewart (2005: 5) has observed:

> The reality ... is that any competent lawyer can take almost any form of employment relationship and reconstruct it as something that the common law would treat as a relationship between principal and contractor (or contractor and subcontractor), thereby avoiding the effect of much industrial legislation.

Self-employment and subcontracting is not just about converting extant wage jobs into contract work. The rise of the so-called gig economy or sharing economy is seeing new technology-based jobs, especially jobs that emphasise phone apps and other peer-to-peer technology. One example is taxi-driver-like jobs with Uber. Another is handy-person jobs, like repairs or running errands, administered through companies such as Airtasker or Expert360. There are also 'gigs' for professional independent contractors who take positions for the duration of a specific task.

It is apparent that this trend, on a significant scale, is so new that such work is yet to appear strongly in official data on subcontracted labour. Minifie (2016: 33) estimates that only about 80,000 Australians work on peer-to-peer platforms; one-quarter of them for Uber. But it may well soon, and with significant impact on our understanding of 'employment'. The Productivity Commission (2016: 69) has noted:

> On-demand or 'gig' employment provides benefits for some workers, with increased flexibility of employment, ability to supplement or smooth income, and by making it easier for some demographic groups to find work. However, there is concern in the community that gig employment may, in the future, represent a major shift in employment relations, with workers bearing more risk associated with insecure employment. The size of any shift is uncertain at this stage, particularly as the gig economy is still in its infancy.

We should note the significance of this statement. The Productivity Commission is pointing to new developments that could change our whole conception of work and employment. This is an issue we will take up shortly.

For now, we note that the outcome of all the above changes is that, consistent with the discipline of shareholder value, labour costs in Australia have been falling. Figure 3.2 shows that since the mid-1990s real wages (that is, wages discounted for inflation) have grown 23 percent, while labour productivity (LP) has grown 59 percent. As a result, real unit labour costs in Australia (effectively the measure of the costs of labour in production) have fallen 9 percent since 2000 alone. These gains have particularly gone towards profits, although international competition has been an issue too. According to the ABS, 'the profits share [of national income] recorded since the late 1980s are at a distinctly higher level than those reported at any time since 1959–60' (ABS 2015).[10] However, with the growth of self-employment, what constitutes a 'wage' and 'profit' have changed dramatically over this period, so a precise meaning is increasingly hard to identify.

Financialisation as calculation

The various forms of risk shifting we have depicted as changing forms of 'employment' all fit within a financial logic which itself is evolving.

That logic makes the contracting of work look more and more like a common law contract akin to those used for non-labour inputs into industry. This is a profound shift.

For the previous 175 years, from the British and European Factory Acts of the 1840s, labour market laws have been about recognising the need to make employment comply with social minima of living standards, safety, fairness and dignity. In recent times this social agenda is retreating, as emergent forms of work create a disconnect with living standards, and financial discipline sees employment options stripped out of employment conditions. The new objective, it seems, is to make labour look, as much as possible, like just another production input.

While the distinction between workers and other production inputs can never disappear, increasingly the employment agenda is

---

10   See Cowgill (2013) for an important discussion of trends in wage share.

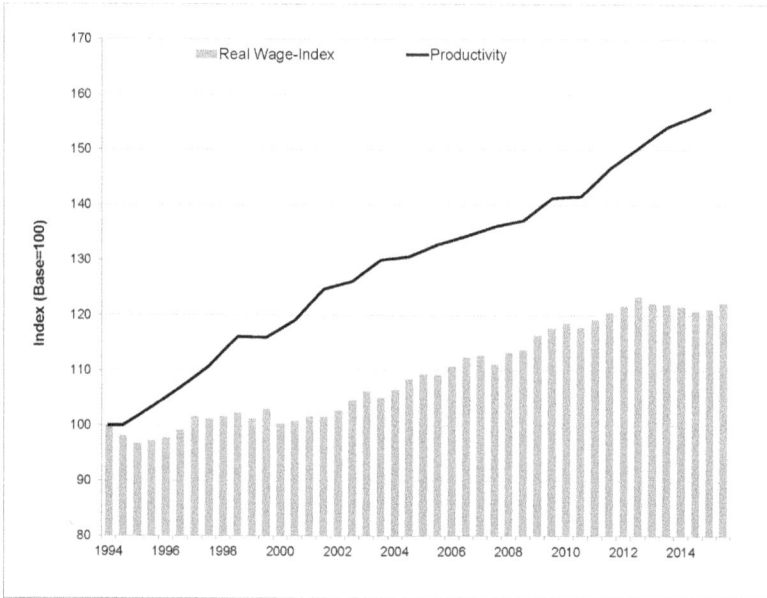

Figure 3.2 Labour productivity and real wage growth, 1994–2015. Source: ABS Consumer Price Index 2015, Cat. 6401.0; ABS Average Weekly Earnings 2015, Cat. 6302.0; ABS Australian System of National Accounts 2012, Table 13: Productivity in the market sector, Cat. 5204.0.

about risk management – to reduce an employer's *exposure* to the *consequences* of the distinction between its labour and non-labour inputs. (Note that this is a framing in the language of financial derivatives: about trading exposures to performance.) Among labour lawyers, there is understood to be an emerging blurring of labour and contract law, or what some have called a growing contractualism of labour law (see Fudge 2006). The growing 'contractualism' of industrial relations, including common law regulation of labour along commercial lines, has been noted for many years.[11] Our contention is that this is not just a re-commodification of labour but its financialisation as well.

We cannot know how quickly or how far this blurring will go, but it does have policy credibility. Cass Sunstein (2001) has advocated that most labour laws should be written like common law contracts (i.e. not be labour-market specific) and be subject to 'opt-in' rather than 'opt-out' clauses. In the style of financial derivatives, this frames worker-specific contractual conditions as financial options that workers must purchase with part of their wage. Sunstein's agenda involves decomposing the employment contract into a menu of tradeable attributes in which the worker can (for a price) buy in to or sell out of.

Sunstein was head of the US Office of Information and Regulatory Affaris in 2009–2012 and was described by the *Washington Post* as President Obama's 'intellectual mentor' (Fahrenthold and Wilson 2012). He also advised the UK government. The British Conservative government Cabinet Office established the Behavioural Insights Team.[12] It is often called the 'Nudge Unit' after a popular book called *Nudge: improving decisions about health, wealth, and happiness* by Richard Thaler and Cass Sunstein (2008) – academics who blend law, economics and psychology. In essence, they use insights of psychology to design incentives in policy. They believe their policy framing helps people make better, clearer choices. Thaler and Sunstein refer to it as libertarian paternalism.

As explained succinctly by McGaughey (2015: 29):

If workers 'wanted' to, why not let them give up of the right to a fair dismissal (to the extent it exists)? If workers 'chose', why not let them waive the right to not be discriminated against on grounds of age? Why not permit contracting out of the right to paid holidays, or parental leave? Even more, why not let workers opt out of the right to join a union, or the right to have no labour organisation dominated by an

---

11   See, for example, Campbell and Burgess (2001) for an early review of these developments, and Frade and Darmon (2005) for the link between corporate reorganisation and labour re-commodification.
12   See www.gov.uk/government/organisations/behavioural-insights-team/about. In 2012 the UK 'Nudge Unit' was employed to advise the government of NSW. See www.bbc.com/news/uk-politics-19656595.

employer? And, as sometime co-author Christine Jolls has added, why not throw in an opt-out from the minimum wage?

In the Sunstein vision, the sole criterion for work contracts becomes the price that has to be paid for the performance of work, consistent with profitability of the company; any extra conditions/protections have to be 'purchased' by the worker as part of contract negotiations.

This could well be the financial agenda that lies at the core of the push towards so-called non-standard employment conditions in Australia. Accordingly, achieving a 'living wage' or 'work–life balance' ceases to be a social issue and instead becomes the responsibility of the workers themselves to manage.

This momentum is evolving further with the rise of work in the 'gig' economy (Productivity Commission 2016). Significant here is that the gig economy is not just about self-employment and subcontracting, but that platforms like Uber and Airbnb change our conception of 'work'. Driving your own car as a taxi, or renting out a room in your house as a motel, breaks down the distinction between work and home, transforming the domain of the personal into the domain of business; of 'capital'. In order to produce a semblance of financial stability, we become entrepreneurs of ourselves, breaking our lives down into a range of possible commercial applications, and contracting ourselves into the market in ways different from, and largely unprotected by, conventional labour law.

Moreover, decomposition of ourselves into a range of business opportunities is being increasingly framed not simply as a choice for the entrepreneurially minded individual, but as a credible and possibly essential strategy to compensate for the uncertainty of work and income that comes with a casualised economy (Productivity Commission 2016: 78; JPMorgan Chase Institute 2016).

There is also a new notion of 'employment' here. Labour market intermediaries (LMIs) are the collective term for labour hire, temp and training agencies and recruitment firms. Uber is just the latest of these. These organisations perform aspects of the 'employment' function – recruitment, training, verification of skills and qualifications, supply of temporary workers, payroll, and so on[13] – and in the 'gig economy' they oversee peer-to-peer transactions. They are not new, but they have grown rapidly in the past 20 years as they become devices for the dual objectives of making the labour market more liquid and unbundling production risks and shifting them between clients. Brenner (2003: 625), for instance, notes that an important function of LMIs 'stems from business desires to shift economic risk and reduce fixed labour costs, including training costs'.

LMIs performing services for the government are paid to make different parts of the labour market and non-labour market more liquid. By shifting the risk of employment service to intermediaries, the state has shifted some of the risk (though not the cost) onto LMIs who get paid by getting people who are unemployed or not in the labour force 'job ready'. They make 'illiquid' labour 'liquid'. For more on these roles, see, for instance, Harrington (2006: 2), who observes that: 'given the contingent relationship that potential employees – even executive talent – have with LMIs, the risk is largely transferred to the employment seeker ... The major reasons for LMIs' existence is to reduce producers' long-term liabilities to workers and to ease the flow of information between and about job vacancies and job seekers.'

The continual demand of both formal employers and LMIs is for more and more rounds of labour market regulatory reform. The goal is to achieve ever-higher objectives of labour market liquidity to get labour costs and conditions better and more quickly aligned with a firm's changing business model. As the pressure to deliver 'shareholder value' is relentless, so too the demand for growing levels of flexibility is continuous. This is a point clearly made by *Australian Financial Review* journalist Matthew Stevens (2013):

In the 1990s ... for employers, enterprise bargaining was more an opportunity than a threat. Today, enterprise bargaining is more a threat than an opportunity. For most employers, the goal now is to

---

13   In November 2011, there were 605,400 people (5 percent of all employed people) who found their job through a labour hire firm or employment agency; 56 percent were males. Twenty-three percent of those recruited this way stayed labour hire workers: they were paid directly by a labour hire firm or employment agency (ABS, Forms of Employment, Australia, November 2012, Cat. 6359.0).

reduce, as far as possible, the higher cost/lower control demanded of them in negotiations. [Employers] are often stuck with an existing enterprise agreement with obligations which might have made commercial sense five or 10 years ago but not today. And unlike other commercial agreements, enterprise agreements can only be replaced (by another one through collective bargaining) or terminated by the Fair Work Commission (but only in rare circumstances).

Some years on from Stevens' observation we can see that these 'rare circumstances' are becoming more common, as more and more employers apply to have enterprise agreements terminated because the agreed terms are considered incompatible with corporate profitability. One such case was explored by ABC journalist Stephen Long in relation to the Griffin Coal Company and its mine in Collie, Western Australia.[14]

In noting this financial momentum of change, we should not confuse it with a process called simply 'deregulation', as if the state is renouncing responsibility for labour market outcomes. The Fair Work Commission continues to oversee employment in a way that ensures there will always be some minimal innate protections for workers. But the state is also active in prompting the financial calculative agenda, especially through the connection of employment to the welfare state.

Welfare to workfare

In the era when permanent employment was the social norm, the state's minimum wage, industrial arbitration and full employment policies effectively set minimum living standards. The state's welfare policy was directly tied to employment policy. Stephen Castles called it a 'wage earners welfare state', because paid work effectively provided a range of social conditions and protections that allowed Australia to have a small government welfare sector by international standards (Castles

---

14   See 'Shifting the risks of doing business from companies to workers', *Lateline*, ABC Television, 10 August 2016.

1985, 1994). In a similar way state regulation (and provision) of land and housing ensured that access to home ownership was affordable and general, a welfare system run via the labour market. Here Castles can be seen as developing on the idea of Titmuss (1956) that welfare (what we might term social risk sharing) can occur through state expenditure or through regulations in the labour and housing markets, and elsewhere.

But from the 1980s the rise of what became known as 'workfare' saw state policy (itself increasingly contracted out to private service providers, see Considine et al. 2015) maintain the close connection of welfare policy to labour markets. As employment became less secure, welfare attached to employment (and unemployment) in new and highly targeted ways. Framed alternatively as 'mutual obligation' and sometimes as 'self-reliance' or 'new paternalism', there remains a system of unemployment benefits and income supplements, but now with the contractual requirement that the unemployed or low income person repeatedly prove their attempts to secure wage income and with tighter eligibility criteria (combined with heightened scrutiny requirements), increasingly delimiting rights of access (including by changing measures of poverty) (Farnham 2013).

Since the 1980s, Australia has had the most targeted welfare system in the OECD. Based on data from the mid-2000s, Whitford (2013) reveals that Australia leads the OECD in a number of criteria of targeting, notably: percentage of GDP spent on income-tested benefits (Australia's percentage is twice that of its nearest 'rivals'), and the ratio of benefits received by poorest quintile to benefits received by richest quintile (Australia is six times the OECD average). As we will see in later chapters, government policy is also redefining the conditions of access to welfare not simply in terms of a lack of labour market income, but also a lack of assets that could otherwise be sold or financialised to supplement current consumption. This is known as 'asset based' welfare but another way to frame it is the culture of shareholder value being implemented within the state.

In this financialised reframing, welfare shifts from a right of citizenship to a quasi-commercial relationship (in a double sense in that it is framed in terms of 'mutual obligation' and that increasingly also the 'face' of welfare is a private sector/commercial organisation). With it all comes the purported need to monitor and surveil workers by reports, inspections, performance targets and spreadsheets: to make people as workers predictable, compliant and accountable for as many work-related contingencies as possible.

We are also seeing welfare being framed by reference to risk, with the unemployed deemed 'at risk' and in need of 'risk management' (this development is coming closer to reinventing the 19th-century Victorian moral distinction between a deserving and an undeserving poor). With employment and life risks now cast as individual rather than social, welfare policy has sought to decompose the disadvantaged population to identify its specific 'failures' that require remediation. For example, the Department of Education, Employment and Workplace Relations (DEEWR 2012) utilises a 'job seeker classification instrument' that streams the unemployed into four risk categories (tranches) according to their predicted difficulty in finding employment. This tranching, based on 18 personal attributes, determines the price paid to private employment agencies which are contracted to make the unemployed 'job-ready' (liquid in the market for paid work) and then actually employed. Here is clear application of a 'derivative logic' to unemployment.

The alarming point is that the 18 personal attributes are depicted as descriptions of an individual (suggesting personal responsibility), yet they mostly define degrees of disadvantage in social background![15]

Conclusion: shifting risks and shifting norms

A century on from the Harvester Judgement, with the growing commercialisation and contractualism of labour law, an employment debate that was once about fairness, equity, security and a living wage is now increasingly about flexibility, risk trading and employer

---

15 The 18 criteria are: age and gender; geographic location; work experience; proximity to a labour market; job seeker history; access to transport; educational attainment; contactability; vocational qualifications; disability/ medical conditions; English proficiency; stability of residence; country of birth; living circumstances; Indigenous status; criminal convictions; Indigenous location, and personal factors.

profitability. The nature of the employer–employee relationship is becoming increasingly 'complex and ambiguous' and even the general concept of employment (rather than work per se) is becoming anachronistic (Rubery et al. 2010). This condition, not some historical ideal of 'permanent employment', is the new norm, and its expression is the pricing and trading of worker risks.

Using the framework of risk transfer is not itself the point of concern. There are plenty of ideas and European practices that focus on state policies for smoothing the risks that are implicit in labour markets, and especially the shift between employment and unemployment. An important source of research in this area has come from the transitional labour markets (TLM) research (e.g. Schmid 2006; Schmid and Gazier 2002; Gazier and Gautie 2011). The idea here is that the way risks associated with 'transitions' into and out of the labour market are allocated has critical effects on the outcomes of employment in terms of living standards and economic security. Moreover, there is also an appreciation that these risks extend beyond the formal labour market itself. Gazier and Gautie (2011: 5) note:

> A TLM perspective makes it necessary to take into account the whole employment and social protection regime. TLMs depend on the ties connecting the economic (employment), social (social protection in a wide sense) and domestic (family) spheres.

The change we see in Australia is the individualisation of these risks. Increasingly, it is up to workers themselves to put together, individually or in households, combinations of forms and durations of work that secure a 'chosen' level of income, a 'chosen' work–life balance and a 'chosen' level of employment risk. The state only really enters, via the welfare system, to supervise those who have failed to secure sufficient employment or viable income.

Yet this is not simply a 'race to the bottom' in wages and working conditions, as we might conclude if our analysis of financialisation were to stop with pressures to deliver shareholder value. Instead we address the risk sharing and shifting arrangements that are embedded in the labour contract. Viewed this way, financialisation becomes framed as the process of risks being unbundled, to be presented and priced as a series of financial options (the purchase/sale of employment 'rights').

The pricing and trading of these employment options will lead to a range of diverse outcomes. It can lead to outcomes we now call 'casual' or 'self-employed' or to full time with annual leave provisions (i.e. the hallmarks of 'permanent' jobs), or indeed to composite, 'fluid' classifications: it depends on the employment options bargained and the trade-offs agreed. It can even lead also to different pricing of each employment option, where the price will probably be related to employer profitability. Indeed, there is emerging evidence that growing wage inequality is critically explained by who you work for, not just what job you do (Furman and Orszag 2015).

This scenario comes from framing work and employment through the lens of finance risk trading and the 'derivative logic' we introduced in Chapter 2. We are not claiming an inevitability about the future universal imposition of that logic in work relations in Australia. Work and employment are too contested an area to make any definitive predictions. We are simply contending that a financial way of thinking is revealing more about the emerging trends in employment and work than can be found in analyses that posit the rise and rise of 'non-standard' employment.

If we are to push back against risk shifting in relation to work, we are more likely to be successful if we critically engage that derivative logic than if we simply advocate a return to a past era of 'standard' work contracts. But, and this is one of the book's decisive interventions, we want to show how unbundling risks and shifting them is not confined to the world of paid work, but can also be seen in the wider working lives of people.

4
Finance beyond work: debt, superannuation and securitisation

The financialisation of daily life is changing the economy and the way we live. In Chapter 3 we saw this change depicted in the domain of work. But the experience is not solely, or even primarily, in that domain. There has also been a remarkable change in the relation between households and capital (financial institutions and industry), and between citizens and the state. In this and the next two chapters we address this relation beyond the workplace, and how the rise of financialisation has demanded us all increasingly to become autonomous, calculating subjects, operating actively in financial markets to manage life-course risks and to access, through financial markets, services and protections that used to be provided by the state by virtue of citizenship.

This required process of active financial participation by individuals and households is being experienced as increasing costs, volatility and uncertainty. More than this, we contend, it is a historically significant turn, leading to a systematic shifting of risk onto households, especially those of middle and lower incomes and wealth.

Along with workers producing for capital an output surplus in production (workers create more in outputs than they can purchase with their wage), households are now also producing a risk surplus in finance (the risk that comes into households is greater than the default risks on their contract payments and mandatory savings contributions).

In effect, the significance of this historical turn is that labour and its households is now being expected to underwrite the profitability of employers at work, and the profitability of finance and financialised services beyond the workplace.

To open this argument we start with a contrast of the 20th and 21st century version of the economic relations between capital and households, before explaining the elements of the new version. The contrast is, of course, highly simplified and stylised: it highlights what are changing and emerging rather than attempting to explain all details and complexities. In reality, also, the turning point is not the millennium but from the 1980s (because as historians have long understood, an arbitrary year like 2000 may be an important calendar event, but rarely separates historical periods). We are here in the tradition of historians who refer to long and short centuries. The 1980s turning point is consistent with the way we have depicted change in earlier chapters. With that qualification, let's continue and see what it helps to reveal about our recent past.

Relations between capital and households in the 20th and 21st century

A century ago, with the development of mass production of the Model T Ford in 1908, Henry Ford famously said: 'I will build a car for the great multitude ... It will be so low in price that no man making a good salary will be unable to own one' (Lacey 1986: 87). One of the key innovations of low cost, mass production was that an employer could rely on workers themselves to purchase its output and still make handsome profits for owners.

Australia lacked the scale of production to secure a balance between labour and capital in this way. Instead, a combination of industrial bargaining and state regulation was needed to incorporate labour as consumer as well as producer. The 1907 Harvester Judgement formalised the concept of the 'living wage' as one based on 'the normal needs of the average employee regarded as a human being living in a civilized community' (Higgins 1907). In many ways the Harvester Judgement institutionalised the living wage as one that calibrated the wage to a standard of 'frugal comfort', which we would identify as later constituting the poverty line (Bryan 2008). In so doing, the state's encroachment into labour-management relations (to regulate wage bargaining and industrial disputation) also averted a challenge to profits both as a potential claim for labour and as a category of property. Although the concept of a living wage was always a contested and fragile balance, it was, like Henry Ford's agenda, designed to see profitable production reconciled with workers' capacity to afford a reasonable living standard (a 'living wage').

Over time, at the aggregate, national level, this balance between households and industry developed a further dimension. Not only would workers purchase output, they would pay taxes and save a little too. Banks would aggregate individual savings so as to create loans to industry and to households. But there was a clear cultural difference between household and business loans. Business borrowing was part of a well-run business, but 'responsible' households borrowed for only specific purposes, to bring forward in time the acquisition of key consumption items like a home or car. The responsible household paid off its loans as quickly as possible. Housing was only a temporary reason to borrow, and for households to *rely* on credit was the sign of poverty and/or poor financial management, usually involving recourse to payday lenders and shop credit.

This profile was changing from the late 1940s, with the rise of hire purchase, but here too the debt was generally linked to the acquisition of an asset or consumer durable, and the goal was to get the loans paid off quickly, lest one was seen to be 'living beyond one's means'.

All that has changed. Flint in Michigan, the site of Henry Ford's first factory, is now a city without industry and in dire poverty, because the manufacture and purchase of cars is now globally distributed. In Australia, as in Michigan, the notion of a job as secure and providing a living wage sufficient to generate a market for local output has given way to 'flexible' work, where hours and income are often uncertain, and with no guarantees of living standards.

Instead, a new kind of arrangement is opening up, where individuals can no longer afford to see themselves merely getting by as hard-toiling 'workers'. They are now required to see themselves as risk-savvy acquirers of assets and even accumulators of capital. Here, borrowing occurs not to bring forward consumption but with the intention to acquire assets which will appreciate in value and/or generate an income (or yield) in addition to that secured from working. In relation to housing, for example, housing policy expert Judy Yates (2007: 6) notes a decisive change:

> The dream of home ownership in the 1950s and 1960s ... might be seen as a fairly modest dream. It was a dream of shelter, security and stability and was made possible by affordable housing.
>
> By the mid-1980s, whilst access to home ownership was becoming more difficult, the introduction of a capital gains tax that exempted owner-occupied housing also made it more desirable. For those who could access it, home ownership became a tax-advantaged hedge against rampant inflation ... Under such circumstances, the Great Australian Dream became a dream of more than shelter, stability and security. It became a dream of an investment opportunity – and a driver of inequality.

The change between a (stylised) 20th and 21st century is shown in Figure 4.1. There is no reference to rent, taxes or welfare, etc., which are clearly important but do not determine the general nature of change. Similarly, there are other players, financial products and institutions involved in lending, investing and financial markets, but our focus is change in relation to households. Figure 4.1 highlights that the 20th century was dominated by the 'work-to-consume' process, with 'borrow-to-bring-forward-consumption' a second order relation. It appears as a linear process. In the 21st century, the 'work-to-consume' relation remains (it is essential to capitalism), but a circular process of capital accumulation emerges: a new spectrum of financial flows which we have termed 'save-by-investing' and 'borrow-to-acquire wealth'.

In the 21st-century arrangement, debt is not something to be paid back as quickly as possible, but more a business-like rolling line of credit to bring forward the purchase of assets (like housing), or to smooth increasingly volatile income–expenditure patterns. Indeed, most young people will enter the full-time labour market in debt (student fees etc.). Whether it should be paid off or loaded up is not so much anymore a moral question of self-reliance, but a calculative,

20ᵀᴴ CENTURY

21ˢᵀ CENTURY

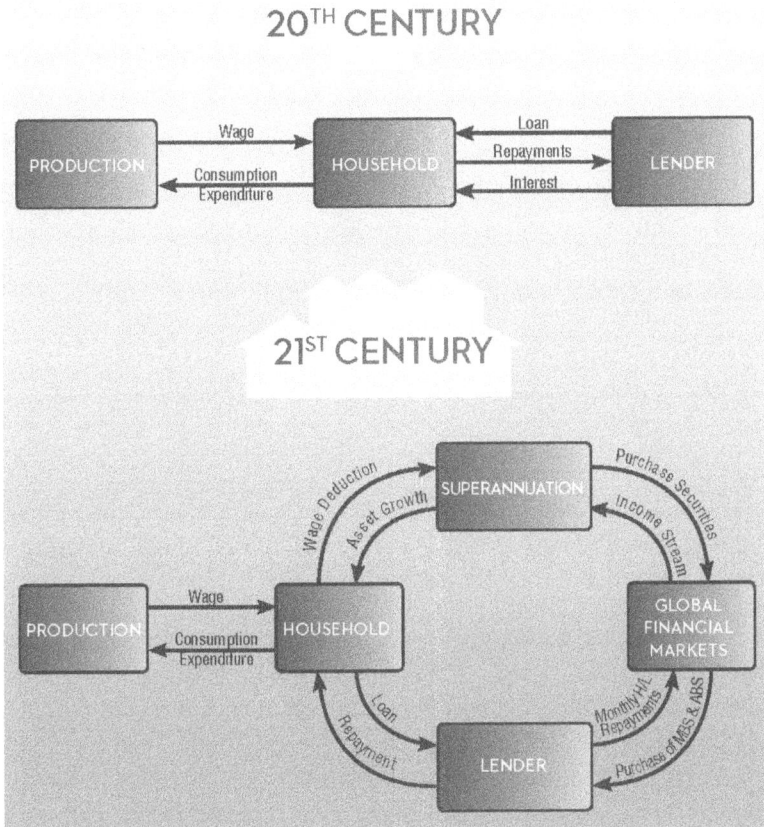

Figure 4.1 Stylised flows between capital and households then and now.

strategic question of what is good family business. In behavioural economics this is referred to in terms of individual attitudes to, and appetites for, risk, and in terms of calculative skill (and luck).

Moreover, this new requirement for labour to be financially savvy is incorporating ordinary people into financial markets in ways compatible with a globalised, financialised economy. Superannuation and a process called securitisation (to be explained shortly; shown in Figure 4.1 as MBSs and ABSs) are central links here. Workers' superannuation contributions are not just expected to replace some or all of the age pension. They are providing a large pool of savings that is in turn creating increased demand for financial assets, and an increasing variety of household payment streams are being wrapped up into the securitised assets that superannuation funds purchase. This is the new financialised 'loop' expressed in Figure 4.1, coming into and out of households.

We will see as the chapter unfolds in more detail how this new household financial loop has developed. But first we must look at each of the components in turn: debt, superannuation and securitisation.

Debt

Some people say of the last 30 years that the effective loss of a state-backed living wage supporting household purchasing power has been temporally resolved via debt. The argument goes that with incomes relatively insecure, and in the past few years scarcely increasing, people have borrowed to fund the continuity of living standards: to balance out the more volatile patterns of weekly income and consumption households now experience, and even hold off the need to reduce consumption. It is more a US story than an Australian one but, individually and collectively, it is clear that a process of debt-funded consumption is unsustainable.

However, for most households in Australia, the experience of debt is quite different: borrowing has been about asset acquisition – especially housing – and only in a minor way about consumption. This process of borrowing-to-acquire-wealth is a major cultural shift. Home ownership has changed from being just a secure form of tenure and affordable place to live into also being an asset class, and hence a means to acquire (or possibly lose) wealth (Allon 2008).

In the last 30 years (roughly since the loss of secure 'standard' employment commenced) bank advertising has pushed housing as well as personal loans, and a growing range of home renovation and other investment infotainment television programs show how income and capital gains are to be made in residential housing price speculation. Owning stuff looks like an easier way to become wealthy than just working for wages. An 'ownership' society was held out as some compensation for the more and more precarious circumstances of work and welfare, and the growing gap between the rich and the poor. Poorer people could adopt the wealth-generating strategies once considered the domain of the rich.

So the key economic question has shifted from the 20th-century one of whether wages were high enough to keep households from poverty, and to ensure consumption demand for producers, to one of whether asset prices will grow fast enough to keep household debt and assets in line and how to keep households paying debt and fixed commitments to lenders and other creditors. In this context, according to the Reserve Bank of Australia's (RBA) current Governor Philip Lowe (2017b), the threat to stable demand in the economy comes not from low wages per se, but from the risk that people may have to choke off discretionary spending to meet financial contract commitments. Similarly, the risk to financial systems no longer comes from the risk of runs on savings banks, but from the risk of mass default from households.

What is the current answer to this key question about asset prices relative to debt? In mid-2016, total household debt in Australia was $2.24 trillion. That is equivalent to around $90,000 for every person living in Australia. It is the highest it has been in the previous 25 years and among the highest personal debt levels in the world. Is this a problem? There is no simple answer.

RBA data[1] show that, as a national average, household debt as a proportion of household income was around 40 percent during the 1980s. It then grew rapidly. As Figure 4.2 shows, between 1992 and 2017 there was long-term growth in household debt from 65 percent of income to 180 percent of income, with growth pausing only in the context of the GFC, before resuming. This widely cited evidence of growing indebtedness is actually a pretty limited measure, for it compares a stock (debt) with a flow (income). It also ignores the assets of households that 'offset' the debt: especially the value of houses and of superannuation. With superannuation understood as a deduction from

---

1   Figure 4.2 is from RBA (2017). Figures 4.3 to 4.6 are all taken from RBA data presented in Lowe (2017b).

Figure 4.2 Housing prices and household debt. Sources: ABS, APM, APRA, CoreLogic, RBA (http://bit.ly/2FPncPt).

wages, in significant ways growing household debt can be interpreted as a means to access in the present that locked-in superannuation (albeit at the significant cost of interest payments), in expectation that the debt will be paid off at retirement by drawing down accumulated superannuation.

Most credit was used to buy houses (about one-third of Australian households carry some housing debt) and it is therefore not surprising that household debt relates closely to house prices, though there was also significant growth in credit card debt, as well as car loan debt and increasingly student debt (ABS 2014).

For some analysts, this high level of household debt is a sign that many Australians are financially fragile. Some of these analysts found easy headlines by predicting a crash, though the RBA was always far more sanguine. But by 2017, the RBA, which had been reluctant to raise the spectre of a housing bubble, finally raised concerns about growing household debt, though its concerns are far from alarmist. According to RBA Governor Philip Lowe (2017b):

> In terms of resilience, my overall assessment is that the recent increase in household debt relative to our incomes has made the economy less resilient to future shocks. Given this assessment, the Reserve Bank has strongly supported the prudential measures undertaken by APRA. Double-digit growth in debt owed by investors at a time of weak income growth cannot be strengthening the resilience of our economy. Nor can a high concentration of interest-only loans.

This growth in debt levels may sound shocking, but consider the following five alternative framings:

1. With debt so closely attached to housing, and house prices growing steadily, debt has generally generated good returns (returns higher than the cost of the debt). ABS (2014) data reveal that borrowing to buy a home has been a good investment: 'Despite the rise in the debt-to-asset ratio, average equity in homes increased in real terms between 2003–04 ($280,000 in 2011–12 dollars) and 2011–12 ($314,000), contributing 19% of the real increase in their overall wealth'. So while debt-to-income ratios have grown rapidly, debt to asset ratios have grown quite slowly. Moreover, interest payments as a percentage of income (debt servicing capacity) has fallen from a peak of 13 percent in 2008 to below 9 percent in 2017 – largely a combination of lower interest rates and increased savings rates. But all that could change if house prices were to fall dramatically or interest rates increase, even by just a percent or two.
2. Since the GFC, borrowers have become more cautious about debt. Many households have maintained the higher repayments associated with previous higher interest rates to create a repayment buffer. This early loan repayment then becomes a form of de facto savings. Figure 4.3 shows RBA estimates that in 2017 half of borrowers are six months or more ahead in their repayments; almost a quarter are four years ahead.
3. Significantly also (for the risk of household debt to finance), national averages hide wide disparities across income (and age)

Share of loans by number

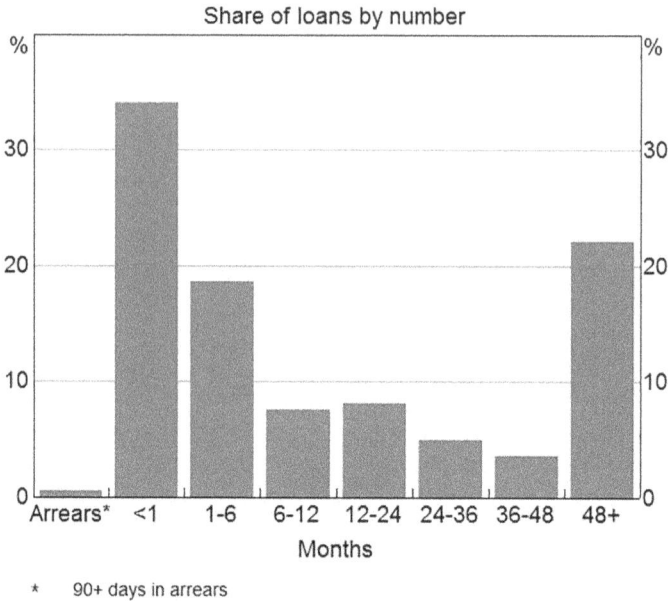

* 90+ days in arrears

Figure 4.3 Mortgage repayment buffers. Sources: RBA, Securitisation System.

levels, and it seems that most of the growth of borrowing has been by those most able to afford it. We will introduce quintiles in more detail in Chapter 5 (see also Appendix 2), but for now think of the fifth quintile as the 20 percent of households with the highest incomes and the first quintile as the 20 percent of households with the lowest income, etc. Figure 4.4 shows that most debt is held by the highest income households with, *prima facie*, greatest capacity to repay the loans. The lowest debt-to-income ratios involve those with the lowest incomes. (The latter includes retired people with low income, but who may hold significant wealth which could be cashed in to pay down debt. So we need to be wary that wealth as well as income needs to be considered in relation to debt. We will explore this in detail in Chapter 5.)

4. We can see another perspective on disparities within national averages when we look at the different ages of borrowers. Figure 4.5

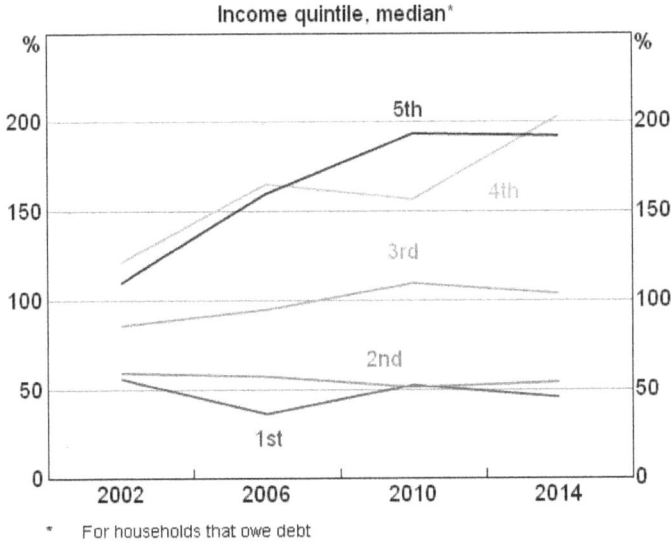

Figure 4.4 Household debt-to-income ratios. Source: HILDA Release 15.0, RBA.

shows that heaviest debt levels are in more middle-age households. Several years ago Finlay (2012: 25) summarised this neatly, and not much has changed since then:

> Debt peaks for 35 to 44 year olds then falls to zero for those aged 65 years or older. This accords with intuition, with young households taking on debt to fund their education and purchase property, before paying down the debt over their working lives. Unsurprisingly, those who own their home with a mortgage are far more indebted than those who own their home outright or those who rent.

5. Despite all this concern about mounting debt, Australian households, in aggregate, are net savers, not borrowers, made up predominantly of bank deposits and net equity in reserves of

Age of household head, median*

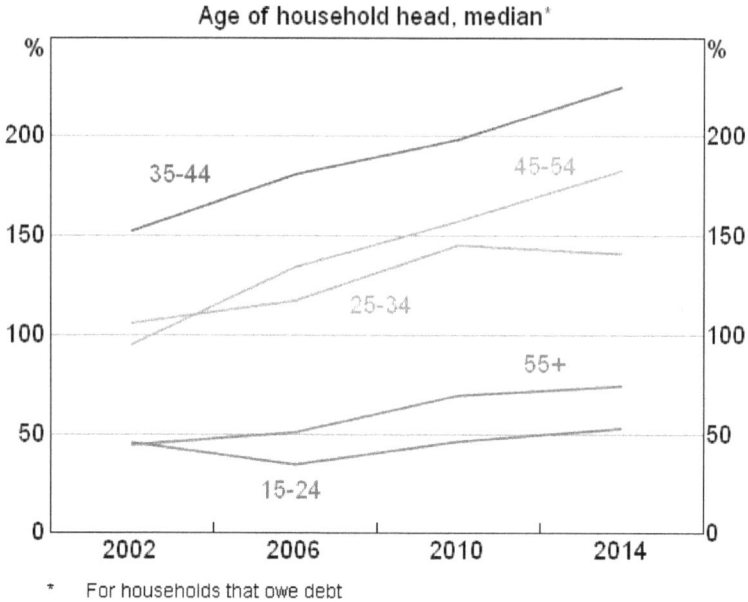

Figure 4.5 Household debt-to-income ratios. Source: HILDA Release 15.0, RBA.

pension funds. At the end of 2016 households were net lenders of almost $6 billion (ABS 2017). Figure 4.6 shows that, on average, net wealth now equals about 700 percent of disposable annual income – more than before the GFC.

These five alternative framings do not sum to an argument that household debt levels are thereby in some absolute sense 'safe'. On the contrary, our proposition is that an appreciation of debt levels is more complex than is commonly argued. It is not debt levels per se that are cause for concern, but debt in two contexts. The first is debt in the context of repayment risk: in particular risks of changes in interest rates and of house prices, and of household income. Debt is different (more concerning) in a situation where interest rates are more likely to rise than to fall, where house prices are more likely to fall than to rise, and where household income is more volatile than more stable.

Per cent of household income*

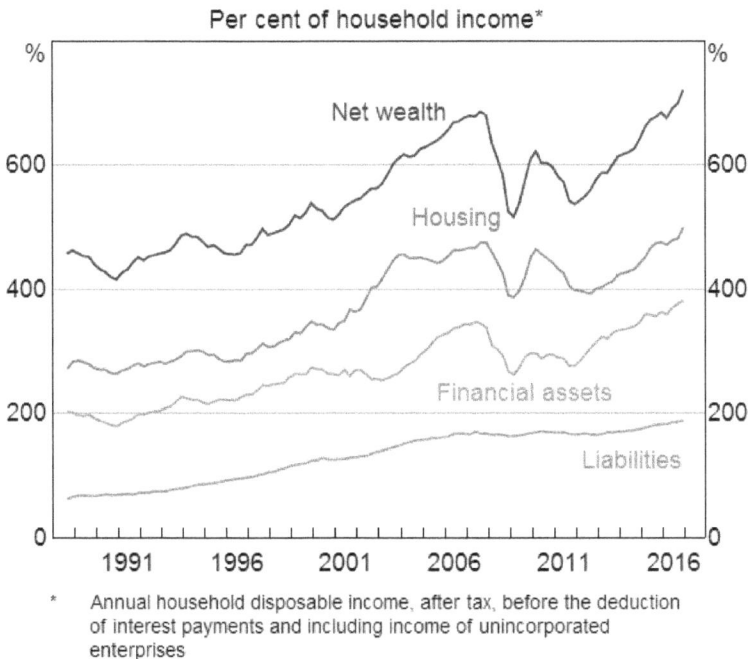

*   Annual household disposable income, after tax, before the deduction
    of interest payments and including income of unincorporated
    enterprises

Figure 4.6 Household assets and liabilities. Source: ABS, RBA.

These three variables are changing, as any quantum of debt has different meanings as these circumstances change. Second, and following this framing, debt has to be seen in the context of household balance sheets and, as we will see, this is exactly how finance and central banks are thinking about the riskiness of debt for households. Debt is different in high income and high wealth households from low income and low wealth households, and in households with considerable savings (superannuation; pre-payment) compared with those without.

But these risks, and hence the viability of debt, are not generally driven by random events (indeed a crisis may be defined as being when random events dominate). Household risks are carefully managed, if not by the households themselves then by those who lend to them and those who regulate the lenders. They are carefully managed, but whether they are successfully managed is a moot point. This is an issue we explore in Chapter 6.

Superannuation

Debt to acquire housing is not the only significant shift in household finance towards investing. Superannuation has become a crucial link in the financialisation process.

Saving for old age was once largely the responsibility of the state and paid for out of tax collections. The 1907 Harvester Judgement, which determined a 'living wage', made no provision for savings for old age. However, in 1908 a national aged pension scheme was introduced, and this was deemed to provide a 'living payment' in retirement. Of course, people on higher wages were able to save and purchase assets to generate additional income in retirement, and they still today receive a range of tax benefits for so doing. But for almost all of the 20th century, old age meant receiving a state pension, with superannuation generally for the professional class, and later for 'permanent' workers in industries with strong unions. Whether these superannuation payments were additional, or an alternative, to state pensions varied over the century (Nielson 2010).

Things changed towards the end of the 20th century, especially with the rise of compulsory superannuation. Australian workers now have (alongside their high debt levels) among the highest savings rates in the world (OECD 2014). At June 2014 Australia's superannuation assets were $1.84 trillion, equivalent to around 116 percent of GDP (Australian Treasury 2015: xix). This level of compulsory savings is, no doubt, part of the reason Australians carry such high debt levels: borrowing can be thought of as a (costly) way of currently (i.e. long before retirement) accessing those compulsory savings.

The basis of any superannuation system is that there exists a pool of funds set aside for investment over the working life, out of which the annual retirement payments would be made. Superannuation therefore always pivots on two inter-related questions:

• Who pays the money into the original pool?
• Who takes on the risk of variable investment returns of the pool?

The current answer to both these questions is that the risks have shifted to workers, drawing them into the role of active investors and risk takers. The emergence of compulsory superannuation in Australia from 1986, and critically from 1992, was a significant policy change, but it wasn't initially framed as an exercise of households speculating in asset markets. It was part of the 1983 and 1986 Prices and Incomes Accords between the ALP (about to assume government) and the unions. In 1986, the government did not want to approve inflation-adjusted wage increases because of fear of further rounds of inflation, so it proposed part of an increase, measured as a 'wage equivalent' in the form of superannuation (AIRC 1986).

That ad hoc rationale created a decisive policy shift in Australia. The initial policy was that superannuation would be additional to the pension, to enhance future living standards (it was 'deferred income') and hence categorically a deduction from wages (not from profits). Although superannuation payments may be transacted by employers, they are not paid for by employers. Superannuation constitutes compulsory saving out of wage income. This has been confirmed in all subsequent reviews of superannuation.

But soon, and especially under a Liberal–National Party government, superannuation became framed as a partial privatisation of the age pension: a direct alternative to reliance on the state's aged pension (Treasury 2004). Intergenerational reports by the Australian Treasury have been developed and used to consistently frame the current ageing population as an unsustainable financial burden on future generations, a proposition that derives from the World Bank's 1994 report *Averting the old age crisis*, which advocated forms of retirement income privatisation. Australia is often held out as a model of partial retirement privatisation success. The argument had become that an ageing population means that states cannot afford to keep paying pensions out of current government income. Individuals will increasingly be required to fund much of their own retirement, in addition to paying taxes during their working lives.

This was, and remains, a peculiar piece of logic, for it turns a calculation on risks into a moral fable about personal self-reliance and responsibility. The substantive issue is actually who will produce all the future goods and (especially) services to supply the consumption needs of an expanding ageing population: an issue of future concern no matter how future spending is funded (it is a future production capacity question before it is a future funding question). With an ageing population there is always the choice whether to meet the growing funding obligation via current taxation or via personal savings. Both provide revenue streams that could be invested rather than consumed. The increased taxation path would mean that higher income and wealthier people would contribute more, while privately funded superannuation means that aged 'pensions' (public and private) are higher for those who save more and that generally means higher income people, and lower for those unable to save during their working life (generally low income people). So the choice to fund the future ageing population via superannuation is not really an issue of distribution between people of different generations (unless you believe that saving money actually creates things), but an issue of distribution between people of different income (and asset) levels.

In terms of who holds the investment risk within the superannuation system, here too there has been a concerted shift. By and large the earlier superannuation schemes were ' defined benefit' (DB) schemes – as with a state pension, a recipient knew exactly what payout (benefit) they would receive on retirement; usually via a formula based on final salary and years of service. So within the scheme, and with the age pension too, the risks of the returns on savings lay with superannuation funds and even with employers,[2] and, in the case of the age pension, with the state.

But there has been a system-wide change from DB to defined contribution (DC) schemes, marketed in the name of choice and extending the scope of coverage to all workers. The argument goes that if people want their superannuation to be safe, they can choose low risk investment profiles, and if they want to chase high, but risky, yields they can. But the shift was also designed more or less explicitly to shift risks of market volatility away from employers and financial institutions and onto workers. With DC schemes the risk of financial performance of

---

2   Unless the employer invested the savings in their own business, in which case workers were carrying a double risk – they could lose their job and their superannuation at the same time.

a fund lies with the superannuant, whose account balance and income in retirement will go up or down according to investment choices of the superannuant and asset market performance. So the person who chooses low risk investment options may have to take low yield, and finish up without sufficient funds for retirement.

The alternative to carrying this risk is to buy an annuity, in which a superannuant passes their superannuation 'pot' of savings to a fund manager in return for a guaranteed annual pay-out. At its best it is like a privately funded version of a government pension. Here, the fund manager carries the risk of market volatility and client longevity (depending on the contract), but for a significant fee. Indeed the gap between the long-run rate of return on a superannuation fund with a balanced portfolio and that same fund converted to an annuity is currently very large, so it is unsurprising that the market is small. Annuities currently make up only 5 percent of market share (Mercer 2014: 2) and fewer than 3 percent of people over 50 years old express any interest in purchasing an annuity (Macrobusiness 2014).

The stated reasons are that people believe they will get ripped off by the fees of annuities, and that the projected retirement income from annuities is too low: people prefer to target higher expected rate of return from market exposure as a means to have a chance of a satisfactory retirement income. So people continue to be exposed to the ups and downs in the stock market; effectively because they have no choice.

In effect, under a DC scheme, compulsory superannuation is compulsion for each person to spend part of their wage taking on risk by financial market speculation, even though it may be much financially wiser and beneficial to use that money to actually de-risk by, for instance, paying off debt on student fees, the family home or credit card. Andrew Haldane, Chief Economist at the Bank of England, noted that there had been:

> a progressively greater share of investment risk being put back to end-investors, with commensurately less being borne by (financial) intermediaries and companies. One clear example is found in the pensions industry, with the structural shift away from Defined Benefit (DB) pensions and toward Defined Contribution (DC) pensions. (2014: 4)

He suggested a key question now was how households will behave in the context of bearing these additional risks.

In the process, superannuation is also a direct subsidy to financial institutions, which enjoy guaranteed funds and commissions coming in fortnightly via compulsory payroll deductions, but no ultimate responsibility for returns on the investment. The finance sector charges superannuation fund members about $23 billion annually in fees, which is about 1.3 percent of GDP and equates to about $2,000 per member, per year. Little wonder investment banker and former Liberal opposition leader John Hewson referred in the 1993 election campaign to the introduction of compulsory superannuation as Paul Keating's great gift to the finance sector, 'which has made consistently super normal profits, in part on the back of ordinary people's savings' (cited in Creighton 2014).

In many ways this change encapsulates much of the broader risk-shift theme (from employers and the state to workers and households): it redefines a critical area of social policy – retirement – as shifting from notions of rights associated with citizenship, to the responsibility of individuals to manage their own risks of retirement provision via participation in financial markets. It feeds into the financialised loop depicted in Figure 4.1.

The forecast future revisions to superannuation accentuate this risk shift, rationalised as an attempt to solve the so-called generation gap. Three proposed reforms stand out.

First, there should be continual increases in the rate of superannuation deductions from wages – from 3 percent in 1992 to 9.5 percent in 2014 and a (currently) projected 12 percent in 2025. The lack of popularity of these increases (for they manifest as lower wage increases or even wage cuts) sees the projected increases continually postponed.

Second, there should be increases in the age at which the age pension can be accessed, lengthening the working life so as to defer when workers might access either their forced superannuation savings or the age pension. Current policy sees the minimum pension age (and hence for most people the age at which they might retire) move from 65 to 67 by 2023,[3] with a proposal to raise it to 70 by 2035 (Coorey 2014).

---

3   See www.humanservices.gov.au/customer/services/centrelink/age-pension.

With a prolonged paid working life comes deferred access not only to superannuation and the pension, but also to the free time of retirement. A third agenda is emerging, which is about who controls those post-retirement savings. The government and superannuation funds prefer that people cannot access those savings as a lump sum, perhaps to pay off debt, but rather require that they have their savings 'managed' under the promise that retiree expenditure from superannuation savings will last as long as possible. Of course it also means that the funds stay generating fees for the fund industry as long as possible.

Conversely, for higher income citizens, the government gives tax concessions to superannuation savings in excess of those compulsorily deducted. These concessions, measured by taxation revenue foregone, increased from $14 billion in 2003–04 to $32 billion in 2012–13 (Cooper 2013: Chapter 2): a figure equivalent to 87 percent of the federal government's 2012–13 direct expenditure on income support for seniors.[4] The tax concessions are one of the fastest growing areas of government 'spending'. An estimated $45 billion in tax revenue will be lost to the budget in 2017. The view is growing amongst opinion makers that taxation concessions to superannuation are too generous to the wealthy (particularly men). The 2016–17 Federal Budget made some amendments in recognition of this fact, but many would say there is still a heavy bias in the system. But there is also a view that political parties are not, at this point, 'brave' enough to take on the political backlash that would be expected to follow the implementation of such reforms.

Paying for a purported intergenerational fiscal gap via private rather than public saving (and indeed via public subsidy to private saving) is therefore a choice to make personal income and wealth the critical determinant of contributions and benefits, and for the private wealth management industry to remain central. Making retirement living standards contingent on labour market income has obvious distributional impacts particularly for lower income earners or those with gaps in labour market participation, especially women. The Australian Human Rights Commission has referred to the gender impact, describing the proposal as women across their life-course not so much acquiring wealth and security but accumulating poverty (AHRC

---

4   Data compiled from Australian Government (2012).

2009). Superannuation is therefore another important component of the financial loop now required of workers and their households.

Securitisation

The process of securitisation is an emerging major site of financial impact on households (see also Appendix 1), and related closely to developments in both superannuation and household debt (and to central bank policy on financial stability).[5]

Securitisation is a process of bundling-up contracts that involve regular payments – loan repayments, insurance payments or payments for services like phone and electricity – and legally separating the ownership of the payments from ownership of the contracts themselves. It involves selling ownership of the payments into financial markets. The seller receives a lump sum; the buyer receives a stream of regular payments. The buyer also takes on the risk that these payments are not regular – that people (or firms) fail to meet their contractual payments.

We raise the issue of securitisation in the context of households, debt and superannuation because most of the securities issued in Australia are backed by household payments, and most of those payments are in the form of debt repayments. By far the largest securitised product is mortgage repayments, giving us residential mortgage-backed securities (RMBSs). In RMBSs the underlying asset is a bundle of mortgages and the buyer of the security is purchasing the monthly interest repayments on those mortgages. But mortgages are not the only household payments to be securitised, as we shall see shortly. Moreover, superannuation funds are among the major purchasers of these securities backed by household payments, and that raises all sorts of interesting issues about risk shifting.

First, we should return to a brief explanation of how securitisation works so its meaning is clear; here in relation to the securitisation of mobile phone payments. Let's say you have a mobile phone contract on which you pay a guaranteed $69 per month over 24 months (perhaps

---

5   For more on the way the financialised household is now also at the centre of financial stability, see Bryan et al. (2009, 2015).

more if you go over limits, but at least $69). The phone company may decide to securitise the compulsory part of your bill, bundled up with thousands of other people's bill payments. The managers of the phone company might wish to access your 24 monthly x $69 payments (a total of $1,656) as soon as possible. Indeed, they may be prepared to sell to someone else ownership of your future payments at a bit of a discount in return for cash upfront. No one will give them $1,656 upfront for payments that will occur up to two years down the track, but perhaps they will pay $1,400 now for the ownership of the 24 monthly payments. That would represent a $1,400 bond (or 14 x $100 bonds) with an annual rate of interest of around 9 percent (that's the conversion of the $256 'gap' into a rate of return). So the phone company gets the cash upfront and an investor now has a bond with a good rate of return. But note that the bondholder now carries the risk of people defaulting on their phone contracts. That risk was an explicit part of the sale, built into the discount on the total paid.

It will be immediately apparent that what is true of mobile phone contracts applies no less to a raft of other household payments. Mortgage, rent and car loan payments, health, home and car insurance payments, payments for electricity, gas and water utilities, credit card and student debt repayments and toll road payments are all being actually or potentially securitised (especially in the United States and increasingly in Australia).

What scale of securities issuance are we looking at? Conventionally, analysis distinguishes between securities backed by house mortgages (RMBSs) and securities backed by other household contract payments – asset-backed securities (ABSs). Around the world, RMBSs are the largest asset class.

The US experience during the GFC of poorly rated risks on bundles of mortgage payments and subprime mortgage defaults trashed the market reputation of RMBSs globally. Figure 4.7 shows that, in Australia, issuance of new RMBSs fell from almost $60 billion in 2007 to less than $8 billion in 2008.

Surprisingly, the RMBSs market started to rebuild by 2009. In the USA, this happened via the central bank buying RMBSs as part of its Quantitative Easing program. In Australia the state has played no such role. But Figure 4.7 also shows that the market in Australia is in any case

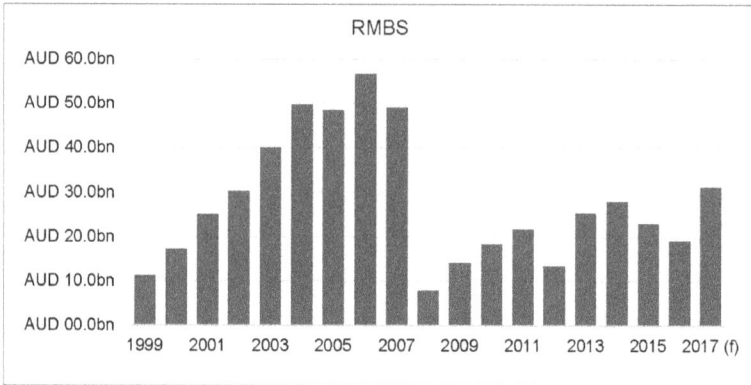

Figure 4.7 Australian RMBSs issuance 1999–2017. Source: Macquarie Bank; Australian Securitisation Forum (www.securitisation.com.au/marketsnapshot).

returning, now involving more than $20 billion of issuance per year – by international standards a rapid return to growth. Today in Australia the risk assessment on these bundles of mortgages is much more careful: every mortgage in a securitisation is individually valued and insured for its default risk (Standard & Poor's 2015: 31).[6] Increasingly, it is the non-bank mortgage originators like ME Bank, Aussie, RAMS and Real that are issuing Australia's RMBSs (Aylmer 2016).

It is notable that the recovery is via local (Australian) demand for Australian RMBSs, with the international market, which dominated before the GFC, virtually disappearing. This reiterates the importance of local investment institutions (including superannuation funds) in the purchase of Australian RMBSs. With less than 8 percent of the value of mortgages in Australia being securitised (Standard & Poor's 2015: 24), there is still plenty of scope for growth.

---

6   'For RMBS, these data include: 62 fields related specifically to the loan, such as loan balances, interest rates and arrears measures; 18 fields related to the borrower, such as borrower income and employment type; and 13 fields that detail the collateral underpinning the mortgage, including the postcode and property valuation' (Aylmer 2016).

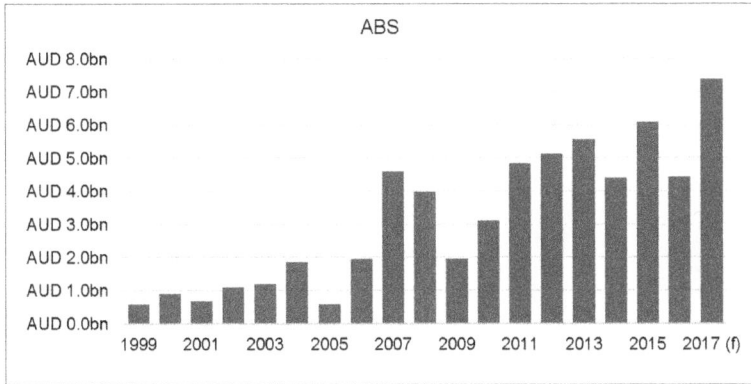

Figure 4.8 Australian ABSs issuance 1999–2017. Source: Macquarie Bank; Australian Securitisation Forum www.securitisation.com.au/marketsnapshot.

Securities backed by mortgages are not the only emerging form of securitisation of household payments. They remain the standard bearer of the securitisation market, but those not backed specifically by mortgages are called asset-backed securities (ABSs), and they too are growing again. In the US, ABSs backed by car loans, student-loans, rental receipts and credit card receivables are starting to grow significantly. In Australia ABSs are also growing, but the overall market still remains small, not exceeding $6 billion per year, as seen in Figure 4.8.

It is interesting to see that, while this market grew more slowly than the RMBSs market pre-2007, it has recovered more rapidly, and with a significant foreign market in US dollars and Euros.

Figure 4.9 shows the largest components of ABSs issuance in Australia, with motor vehicle loans the dominant underlying asset.

Securities backed by other forms of household contractual payment are only now starting to emerge and there is vast potential for growth. As explained by the Australian Securitisation Forum (2014: 7):

Securitisation will be an important part of Australia's financial landscape in the future … :

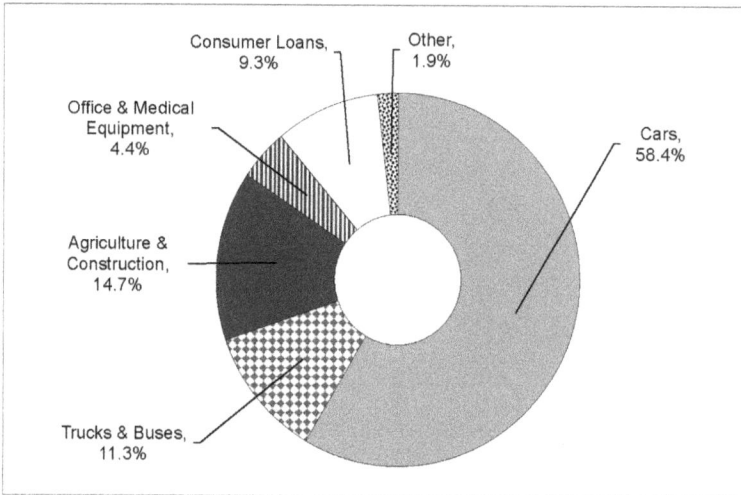

Figure 4.9 ABSs asset class breakdown, 2013. Source: Australian Securitisation Forum (2014: 12).

1. Securitisation technology is an important tool for transforming pools of relatively illiquid assets into more liquid investible securities, including residential mortgages and infrastructure assets;
2. Securitisation forms an essential funding source for smaller lenders, particularly non-ADI lenders [Australian deposit-taking institutions are, in simple terms, banks], and therefore is important for competition; and
3. Securitisation efficiently generates high quality and *safe* securities, providing a key source of fixed income investment products suitable for superannuation and retirement income sectors. [our emphasis]

Four points need to be emphasised about the process of securitisation. The first is that securities backed by household payments mark a significant development in the financial role of households. From the perspective of financial markets, this development involves converting previously illiquid assets like mortgages into liquid, globally traded financial products. It opens up to financial markets potential access to an enormous site of wealth – the household and lots of its fixed spending commitments – conventionally thought disconnected and remote from global finance. So while householders may believe they are just repaying a mortgage or car loan to the National Australia Bank, or paying an electricity bill to Origin Energy, they are, potentially at least, also providing an input into a globally traded security.

In this way, households can be seen as linked to the *production* of a financial asset or service no less than someone working on a factory production line. Many people have rightly emphasised the distributional dimension to risk shifting through finance. We want to push beyond the distributional dimension and suggest that the process of risk management by households that enables these household payments to be made reliable is also an act of production or at least the provision of a (valuable) financial service. Davis (2010: 78) draws the parallel instead with corporations, referring to households as de facto 'issuers' of asset-backed securities. In either framing, the point is that households are involved in the production/issuance of financial assets in new ways, giving households a financial market involvement and power they do not realise they have.

Second, the key to building these new securities based on household payments is to increase the proportion of household payments made by means of time-based contracts rather than cash or un-contracted purchases. We can call it the 'contractualisation' of households. Contractualisation clearly applies to loans for housing, cars, retirement homes and education but things like rental payments, electricity, solar panels, water, phone, internet and television are now all provided under one and two year contracts to households. This contractual form makes those payments potentially securitisable. This trend we will take up in Chapter 6 as an issue behind household financial management.

In the current context, we simply note that these fixed long-term commitments made to utility and other service providers now appear to the household like debts (mortgage, car loan, credit card, etc.), in the sense that they are all contracts that create fixed obligations for regular monthly payments. Indeed, utility service providers and others are starting to use the same credit reference checks as credit card and other credit providers to establish whether a household is likely to meet their contractual terms of service. From the point of view of a household, why would we distinguish between a contract for a car loan repayment and a contract for purchase of mobile phone or internet use? What is a 'debt' and what is a 'purchase' on instalment plan? The distinctions start to blur. Perhaps, then, the financial challenges to households are not debts per se, but the full range of contractual (fixed) payments and the. associated risks they face. We explore some of the implications of this observation in Chapter 7.

Third, in the process of securitisation, the risk of default gets traded along with the income streams. It is therefore critical to the securities market that individual and household default risk can be and is measured accurately, for it will determine how risky a security is and hence its value in the market. One of the central causes of the GFC was that in the USA mortgage-backed securities with shonky subprime loans included in them were being rated AAA: people thought the securities they were buying were safe from default, but they clearly weren't. That's when panic hit the markets, for everyone suddenly understood there was default risk but no one could reliably say how much and where that risk was, and so wanted to sell them off. For finance and state agencies concerned with financial stability, the trading of financial instruments with exposure to household default risk also means that households need to be monitored closely, to determine their likelihood of defaulting on any of their securitisable contracts, and potentially 'managed' more closely to make sure they keep paying their bills. The RBA reports that it maintains a dataset covering a quarter of all loans, which goes down to the level of individual (anonymised) loans, on whether people are ahead in their repayments (see Figure 4.3) in order to monitor their exposure to asset-backed securities (Lowe 2017b, n. 4).

Fourth, securitisation impacts on the price of the underlying asset. Securitised household payments are competing in global markets of risk/return calculation. RMBSs must offer a yield (rate of return) proportionate to their risk. This means that the interest rate on the mortgage must be sufficient to generate the appropriate rate of return on the securitised mortgage payment. It means also that the price of electricity must be sufficient to generate a competitive (i.e. risk adjusted) yield on securitised electricity payments. This overriding financial requirement, as much as the labour and other input costs of actual production of electricity, will drive the retail price of electricity. The higher the risk that households will default on their electricity bills, the more risky the security, and that means that for someone to purchase it they will want a higher expected yield than if the risks were low. A vicious circle potentially arises: electricity prices are pushed up to increase the yield on securities, but then the risk of default grows, so the price of electricity must go even higher to secure a competitive yield. There forms a potential spiral of increasing prices and increasing risk. The Australian Energy Regulator (AER), which approves changes in the retail price of electricity in Australia, includes an explicit rate of return guideline which allows for the cost of funds and a competitive yield on investment to be built into utility pricing.[7] As securitisation of electricity bills expands, the yield on securities logically enters into AER electricity price calculations. This yield dimension of securitisation gets left out of the debates about rapidly increasing energy pricing in Australia, because no one is (yet) explicitly framing household electricity bill payments as (primarily) a financial asset.

The household financial loop

In Figure 4.1 we identified debt, superannuation and securitisation combining in a loop to elevate ordinary people and their work, consumption, saving and borrowing patterns to the core of global finance. It is a confronting trajectory but also one, we hope later to show, that opens up political potential. We can summarise the loop on the basis of the information revealed in this chapter.

Superannuation creates a problem. Every week, more than $1 billion comes out of Australian pay packets as compulsory super contributions (and a further $2 billion comes out in the form of tax concessional voluntary contributions) and lands with financial institutions for investing. About 25 percent goes internationally into equities and bonds; most of it stays in Australia (and offshore funds are

---

7   See AER Rate of Return Guideline at www.aer.gov.au/node/18859.

diversifying into Australia too). Approximately 25 percent of the funds that stay in Australia go into the stock market, 20 percent goes into cash and Australian government bonds, 10 percent into property, and 12 percent goes into more risky, alternative investments such as in private equity buyouts and hedge funds.[8] Still only a small amount currently goes into the purchase of securities backed by household payments, but we anticipate it will grow over time.

Why do we expect it to grow? It is because the Australian financial market is perpetually short of safe assets with good yields. In this context that the then Reserve Bank Governor Glenn Stevens (2015) critically observed:

> The key question is: how will an adequate flow of income be generated for the retired community in the future, in a world in which long-term nominal returns on low-risk assets are so low?

A difficult agenda for financial institutions is to find higher-yielding, 'safe', AAA-rated assets: assets that will give a good yield for household superannuation payments but hold their value even when markets are volatile. Andrew Haldane (2014), Chief Economist at the Bank of England, has noted that, with asset managers getting out of investment in equities ('de-equitization' he calls it) because of their volatility, there is an increasing appeal of securitisation and 'the creation of a new class of securitisations which clearly differentiate themselves from the mistakes of the past. A "high-quality" securitisation product might comprise much simpler structuring of payoffs and high and transparent underwriting standards'.

In financial market terms, lower risk is also seen to be about matching the time horizons of assets and liabilities. Superannuation is a long-term savings vehicle, and financial institutions would like long-term assets to match that. Traditionally this meant treasury bonds, but with official interest rates around the world so low (and even negative in

---

8   We are grateful to Alex Dunnin, from leading financial services information and research company the Rainmaker Group, for the superannuation contribution and asset allocation data, as well as for discussions about superannuation more generally.

some countries), large-scale investors are seeing the yield on treasuries as too low to treat as a significant store of wealth. Securitised household payments promise to fill this gap.

It is of course a delicate balance. Capital wants households to continue to take on debt and time-based contractualised commitments, for this sustains economic growth, and they want to securitise the debt and other contract payments to create financial assets. But they also need to be sure that too many people won't default on their loans or other contracts. To return to our 20th- and 21st-century comparison, it is the financialised version of Henry Ford's desire to pay wages consistent with workers being able to purchase the cars they produced, only now it is about ensuring that workers can afford to repay on the contracts that support the securities backed by household payments.

We will look in Chapters 5 and 6 at the way in which households are being increasingly financially 'overseen' and 'managed' in a way analogous to workers in a mass-production factory being 'overseen' and 'managed'.

But there is a significant and broader social/cultural shift here that should not pass unrecognised. The developments described above involve a re-tooling of individuals and households as 'financialised subjects' who will play out their role as workers, consumers, investors and reliable producers of the payments that feed into RMBSs and ABSs.

Through education and moral persuasion (financial literacy), reform of the financial planning industry, changing bank lending practices and bankruptcy laws, and encouraging households to take out more insurance, there is a concerted attempt to build the reliability of household payments and hence secure the value of assets backed by household payments. Further developments in this direction may involve proposals to permit people to access superannuation to stave off financial insolvency and proposals for guaranteed minimum incomes (especially if a garnishee order ensures contract payments have first call on that income). In Chapter 6 we will return to this theme, to frame households as playing a future role as the key buttress against financial instability.

To manage these risks, households are expected to become financially literate, or to employ a financial adviser in order to know which superannuation scheme is successful, to know their own preferred risk profile, and, bizarrely, even to know their date of death or to insure against living too long.

The implicit state policy logic here is that while there is an expectation of financial self-management, there are many areas where people can't be relied on to behave 'rationally' and so must be compelled (or 'nudged') to behave in financially responsible ways. At this stage of reading you probably won't be surprised to learn that this vision of household financial 'responsibility' is generally about increasing rather than decreasing household exposure to financial markets.

The financial planning industry, which came into existence prior to superannuation to sell life insurance policies, is now being asked to play a state-like role and guide people in their superannuation choices and general financial management. However, this industry has a chequered history with many cases of incompetence, pursuit of commissions over client needs and outright fraud. Regulator investigation of the industry regularly reveals large-scale experiences of deception and incompetence.

The Australian Securities and Investment Commission (ASIC) is the regulator responsible for community protection. In a speech on financial institution conduct, ASIC Commissioner Greg Tanzer (2015: 4) offered the following summary:

> When I talk about poor outcomes for customers, this is a genteel way of saying people got fleeced. And, sadly, those who get fleeced are usually everyday Australians, not wealthy people who can make a major loss and not blink. That is, those affected by poor culture are usually those who can least afford it.
>
> Several large Australian banks have already admitted to misconduct in their financial planning and other services, including forged client signatures, file reconstructions, and poor advice. There remains ongoing pressure on the federal government to call a Royal Commission into bank misconduct.

So in many ways, financial planners – the sources of advice on financial risk management – have often escalated household financial risk, not mitigated it.

Conclusion

In survey after survey, individuals and households report feeling more financially stressed and anxious. We also know that more and more people are finding themselves foregoing necessary expenditures to meet their fixed commitments. This is no accident. It's not just that some households are getting a bigger slice of the economic pie at the expense of others, though that is also happening. More and more life-course risks have been shifted to households and increasingly this means greater exposure for them to financial markets and financial risks. While some live more financially stressed and precarious lives than others, we all live on a risk continuum, whereby exposure to the financial consequences of life-course events can trip us up. We are all subject to a range of financial risks, and this makes us risky subjects.

But this is not just a distributional story. Out of the regular income and payment streams of households, financial institutions are developing a range of new financial products. These products are seducing households to absorb more risk via the contracts they sign and requiring them to find new ways to stabilise their budgets to ensure that the risks of payment default are minimised. In producing that stability, households are also producing a range of reliable income and payment streams that financial institutions are packaging up (securitising) and selling in financial markets. In these ways households have now moved to centre stage of the economy in the novel role of suppliers of the ingredients of securitised financial assets. This shift is both transforming our understanding of how class relations work and how value is created in the economy.

This requirement of household stability in contractual terms is not spontaneous, just as making us reliable workers in a factory was not, and is not, spontaneous, despite the way 'the market' is depicted as if it were. Both have involved close supervision, facilitating state legislation and cultural change. Just as a surplus could be extracted from workers in production, so close supervision of finance enables a surplus to be extracted from households. It is a surplus conceived in financial risk transfer: that the risks going into households (especially through precarious and volatile income) are less than the risks coming out (the risk of household defaults). Households are systematically absorbing risk on behalf of financial markets.

Alongside workers generating a 'production' surplus derived from them producing more output than they receive in wages, we now have households generating a 'risk' surplus. This surplus derives from households making contract payments that show less risk than those households experience in financialised daily life.

To build this argument we must explore the household as an emerging financial unit, in terms of both the financial responsibilities expected of households and the rapidly growing financial monitoring (and management) of households by financial institutions and governments. This theme is taken up in the next chapter.

5

A hedge fund of your own life: households in financial markets

Financial matters occurring inside and outside the home have traditionally been thought of as quite different. The social arrangement was broadly that households acquired income via work in the labour market (or by welfare and pensions) but once the pay arrived inside the home, it became the household's own business. Indeed, a range of government regulatory policies sought to keep household financial matters fairly simple, especially by regulating banks to ensure the household didn't take on too much debt or make too many financial commitments. The RBA's Guy Debelle (2010a: 1) noted that, in the 1960s and 1970s, the financial system was heavily regulated including 'directives on the overall quantity of loans banks could make, as well as moral suasion on who they should lend to'. The point here is that even the regulation of household thrift and stability was undertaken from outside the household – mainly by ensuring the provision of affordable housing (along with regulating labour markets for a living wage) and preventing financial institutions from over-lending to households.

These days the pay is no longer the household's business, with striking ramifications. Just as there is now a growing calculation of labour market risks, which sees those risks systematically transferred to workers (see Chapter 3), so too there is a growing calculation of household life-course risks, which sees many of these risks (formerly managed by governments) systematically transferred to households and now increasingly transacted through financial or financialised service markets. Our objective in this chapter is to identify what is systematic about this risk shift to households via financial markets.

The reason for giving detailed attention to this issue is straightforward. Financial institutions have (re)discovered that household wealth and risk management represent a fabulous terrain for business and profitability. This terrain had been poorly managed (as graphically illustrated in US subprime lending) in the lead-up to the GFC, but if household financial management can be rectified and stabilised, and if households can be made responsible repayers of their contracts, then enormous new business opportunities will emerge.

Central here are loans to households, but there is a further dimension too: our proposition from Chapter 4 about an increasing issuance (and likelihood of issuance) of financial securities backed by regular household (re)payments. These securities typically involve on-selling of the regular (monthly) repayments on contracts that include credit repayments but also a range of household payments on contract like rent, insurance and utilities. These are at the base of new financial interest in households, to among other things:

- lend to households to buy assets,
- sell insurance products to households so they can hedge a range of household risks,
- bundle the associated loan repayments into pools of securities (or corporate forms – like telephone and bandwidth resellers that are based on them), and
- securitise not only loan repayments but repayments of a range of contracted services, from utilities like energy and water to insurance payments.

Potentially, these securitised household payments can be both safe (in the sense of complying with their estimated default risk) and profitable, filling a vital space at the 'secure', low risk end of financial institutions' investment portfolios. But, and this is the critical link in our argument, in the process of this (re)discovery, finance turns each household into parts of a virtual factory of financial asset production and risk management. So the question comes down to what is distinctive about household risks that make households an easy target for risk shifting.

In this chapter, we explain this process and how, in the world of finance, households are being thought of as businesses with assets and liabilities – that is, as 'balance sheets'. Indeed, we are increasingly being expected to think of ourselves in the same terms! To do this requires looking at quite a bit of data, for our novel proposition needs to be supported by clear evidence. It also requires the reader to think a bit like an accountant. It may be uncomfortable, but it's not that difficult!

Household accounts

We begin our conception of the financialised household via an exploration of accounts of a household as if it were a business. Any business accounting framework is made up of two basic accounts:

1. the profit and loss statement (income and expenditure account) – dealing with the inflows and outflows of money over time, and
2. the balance sheet (assets and liabilities account), looking at the level of net wealth at a point in time.

In each account, we segment the population of Australian households into five groups or 'quintiles' based on ranking the population's households by either income or wealth (income is relevant to the income and expenditure account; wealth to the assets and liabilities account):

- the lowest 20 percent of income earners or wealth holders are called the first quintile,
- the middle three quintiles (which we call middle Australia), and
- the highest 20 percent of income earners/wealth holders, called the fifth quintile.

We have bunched the middle three quintiles together, for although these populations differ in income and wealth, they have broadly the same balance sheet and income–expenditure profiles (see Appendix 2 for an explanation).

We will examine each account in turn.

Income and expenditure account

Table 5.1 shows the main categories that make up the household income and expenditure account, based broadly on Australian Bureau of Statistics classifications.

The first thing apparent in Table 5.1 is how few are the ways households acquire income compared with the diverse forms of expenditure. Mostly income is from work (wages and salaries, or sole trading) or from government pensions or allowances (with what used to be called the social wage). This narrow range makes households vulnerable to income shocks. It is only in the top quintile that other income (profit, interest and rent) are significant sources of income.

We now turn to some numbers. Looking first at income, it is apparent from Figure 5.1 that income is growing in all quintiles, but so too is income inequality, shown in the widening absolute gap between quintiles. If we were to look 'inside' the first and fifth quintiles, we would see extreme poverty at one end and a class of 'super-rich' at the other. We would also see growing volatility of individual incomes, for reasons addressed in Chapters 3 and 4.

Turning to expenditure, this too has kept rising, partly funded by income and partly via debt (see Chapter 4). Not surprisingly, higher income quintiles spend more than lower income ones, but of particular significance are household loan payments as a form of expenditure. (We will see in Chapter 6 how the monitoring of this expenditure has changed over time.)

This evidence is not easy to show in an aggregated way, for within any quintile some households carry very high levels of debt and hence high repayments, and some carry very low debt and hence low repayments. For the same level of income, people entering the housing market will generally have much higher debt repayments than someone who has had their loan significantly paid off. And of course those who are renting will show lower housing debt but the fixed commitments of rent constitute a similar expenditure burden.

So averages can be deceptive, but we must start there. The initial focus is on households with a mortgage. Figure 5.2 identifies those within each income quintile who hold some mortgage debt, and looks at their total loan repayments (for all forms of credit) as a percentage of income. We might expect the lowest income households to spend the

Income	Expenditure
Wages and salaries	Current housing costs
Own unincorporated business income	• Rent payments • Mortgage repayments – interest component
Government pensions and allowances	Mortgage repayments – principal component (selected dwelling)
Other income	• Other • Other loan repayments
	Domestic fuel and power (selected dwelling)
	Food and non-alcoholic beverages
	Clothing & footwear
	Household furnishings & equipment
	Household services & operation
	• Childcare services • Telephone accounts
	Medical care and health expenses
	Transport
	Communication*
	Education*
	Personal care
	Recreation
	Superannuation & life insurance
	Income tax

Table 5.1 Income and expenditure account: key categories. *Communication and Education were two new categories included in the classification framework in 2015-16, in recognition of the growth in this type of expenditure by Australian households.

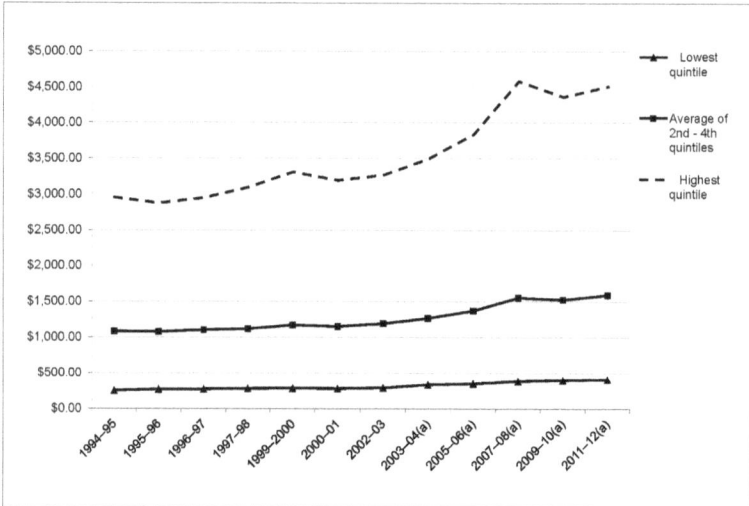

Figure 5.1 Gross household weekly income by quintile, 1994–95 to 2015–16 (consumer price index [CPI] adjusted to 2016 values). Source: ABS, 6523.0 Household Income and Income Distribution Australia - Detailed Tables, 2011–12. Estimates presented are for 2007–8 onwards are not directly comparable with estimates for previous cycles due to the improvements made to measuring income introduced in the 2007–8 cycle. Estimates for 2003–4 and 2005–6 have been recompiled to reflect the new measures of income, however not all components introduced in 2007–8 are available for earlier cycles.

highest percentage of income on loan repayments, and the opposite for the top quintile. Is that the case? It is, but the end of the GFC (2009 in the data) represents a critical turning point.

Within the lowest quintile, most households are renters, and so are not included in data related to mortgages. Their difficulty is the growing share of rent in their expenditure. Those with a mortgage spent an increasing percentage of income on repayments up to 2009, after which the percentage fell significantly, while still remaining high compared with other quintiles.

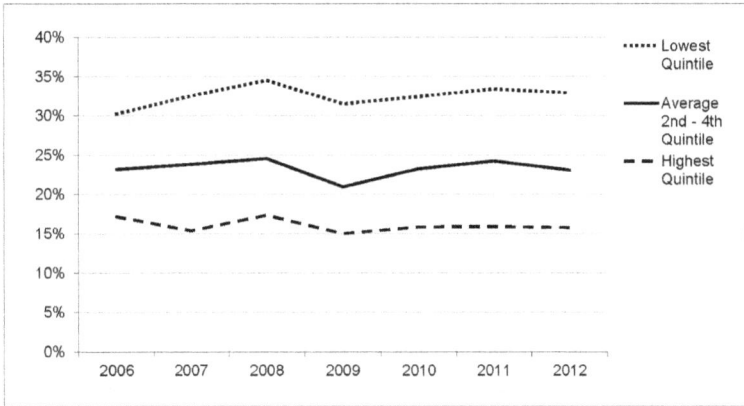

Figure 5.2 Interest payments as percentage of gross household income by quintile, 2006–12 (for households with some mortgage).

In the middle quintiles, conversely, loan repayments as a percentage of income are significantly below those in the lowest quintile, but a much higher proportion of people in this quintile carry a mortgage. With the conventionally defined 'safe' level interest payment of 30 percent of income (above which people are considered to be suffering mortgage stress, see Chapter 6) we see that the average of this cohort is approaching this figure: those who cross the 30 percent threshold are far from outliers. The highest quintile, with lots of cash flow, is well within safe limits and has been stable.

Another, related concern is to look at household expenditure as a basis for securitisation: an issue which includes debt repayments, but other household contract payments too. Hence we want to see which household expenditures are currently securitised, but also, as we think about evolving financial agendas, the sorts of household payments that are potentially 'securitisable'.

The simplest, essential condition of 'securitisability' is that expenditures are made through multi-year contracts. This makes payments both regular and predictable, and that's what buyers of securities want. We define an expenditure as securitisable if there is evidence that somewhere (it will be primarily in the United States) this type of expenditure has already been securitised. (See Appendix 2 for explanation of our classifications.)

We would expect that many contractual payments will be for services or things that households need, so we will get to issues of 'securitisable' household payments in two stages. First, we identify a division of household payments into discretionary and fixed (or non-discretionary) expenditure: how much of household income is committed (fixed) in meeting costs of daily living, like housing, food and utilities, and how much could be called discretionary, both in the sense of being avoidable and that households can choose which categories to spend in. Note that 'fixed' is not to be read here simply as 'subsistence' in the poverty sense; rather, it is used here in a financial (and usually contractual) sense of being financially locked-in. Hence, repaying a loan on a $5 million house is classified here as non-discretionary in the sense that it is contractually committed, even though it is paying for housing services that are almost certainly not what we would conventionally think of as a necessity. Appendix 2 provides a summary of how we divide expenditure into discretionary and non-discretionary.

Why is this distinction between fixed and discretionary expenditure important? There are two reasons. One often used reason is that this distinction tells us something critical about standards of living: whether people earn enough to spend something on luxuries rather than necessities. It is an important question, but in the context of addressing risk and finance it is one we are interested in for a different reason. We are interested in the non-discretionary share of spending because financial institutions know that those household expenditures are necessary for households to function and therefore more easily legally contracted.

The second, related, reason the fixed-discretionary income distinction is important to financial markets is its centrality to securitisation. Many fixed expenditures are (or could be) made into contracts for payment over at least a year, and hence those payments become securitisable.

Although it is important not to confuse fixed expenditure with the purchase of necessities – necessities may be fixed expenditures. Many of these are paid under contracts (rents, mortgages, many consumer durables, utilities). They are immediate targets for securitisation, households have a large incentive to not default on contracts for necessities – for then they lose their home or car or electricity and gas.

But not all fixed expenditures are for necessities. There is also a clear trend to turn non-necessary consumption expenditures into contracts. Think of things like gym membership, donations to charities, university fees or indeed childcare. Childcare may be surprising here. We have included childcare because it is readily securitisable and there are cases in the USA of securitised childcare payments. These expenses were once more or less discretionary and spot payments, but are now, as with childcare as a necessary expense for earning a second income for many households, necessary and increasingly locked in as contracts. For the duration of the contract they become fixed, and hence securitisable.

So we look first at the evidence of the division between fixed and discretionary expenditure as a way of moving the analysis to the related financial division between securitisable and non-securitisable expenditure.

Figure 5.3 shows the division between fixed and discretionary expenditure as overall income has grown since the mid-1980s. (At this point we are addressing overall national averages: differences between quintiles will be added shortly.) Despite households undertaking more and more hours of work (see Chapter 3), the evidence shows that there has been little change in the proportion of household income that is discretionary.

In the United States, this phenomenon is referred to as the 'two-income trap', following a famous study by former Harvard law professor and now US Senator Elizabeth Warren and Amelia Tyagi (2003). Despite a significant increase in household participation in paid labour markets between the mid-1980s and mid-2000s, households in their study had a smaller proportion of discretionary spending capacity out of their total household income. Instead the extra household working hours gave rise to the costs of childcare, after school care, the requirement to have a second car and pay for other time-saving expenditures, leaving little discretionary funds from the extra labour income. In Australia, the shift is not as dramatic as in the USA, but it is still clear that, for most households, growing incomes are not generating significant increases in discretionary expenditure.

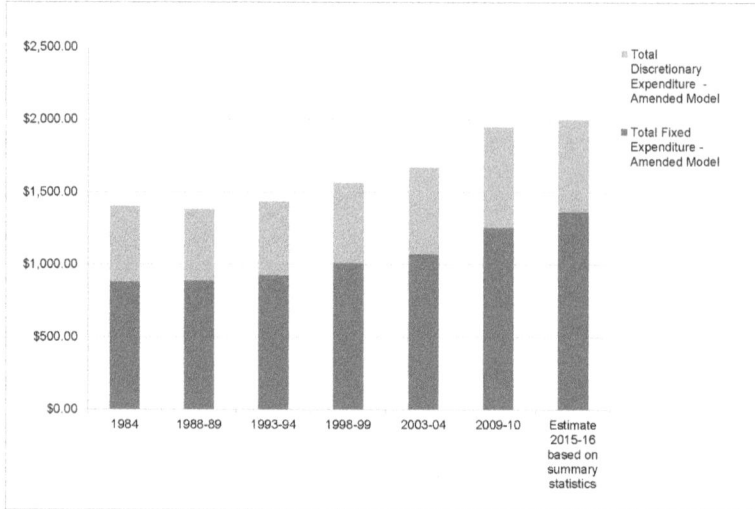

Figure 5.3 Growth in weekly fixed and discretionary expenditure – average all households, 1984 to 2015–16 (CPI adjusted to 2016 values). Source: ABS 6530.0 Household Expenditure Survey, Australia: Detailed Expenditure Items, 1984 to 2009–10.

Figure 5.4 breaks these data down and shows these changes by household income quintiles so we can get a sense as to whether this situation is different for high and low income households. Since 1984 the lowest quintile's share of fixed and discretionary expenditure has not varied significantly; the middle quintiles have increased by 3 percent. In effect, most of the growth in household income has been allocated to meeting current and new fixed expenditures. This gives some statistical backing to anecdotal and survey evidence that people feel they are doing more just to stand still. The fifth quintile's proportion of fixed expenditure increased by 6 percent (its proportion of discretionary expenditure fell 6 percent). This may be surprising, but it is a sign of its increasing expenditure locked in to contractual payments. It may look anomalous that, with growing incomes, the wealthiest people's expenditures become increasingly dominated by

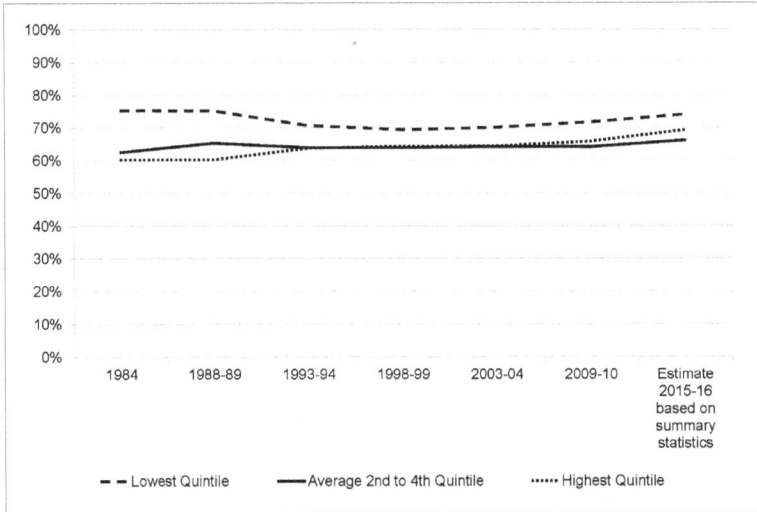

Figure 5.4 Growth in fixed expenditure as a share of total expenditure by quintile, 1984 to 2015–16. Source: ABS 6530.0 Household Expenditure Survey, Australia: Detailed Expenditure Items, 1984 to 2009–10.

fixed expenditures, but note that we are not including savings, and that the way we have defined 'fixed' expenditure includes interest payments on investment assets. High income households may simply be 'locking in' expenditures on the purchase of assets, like second houses and shares. So this figure needs to be interpreted in the context of overall dynamics of household balance sheets.

Why has growing income not led to freeing up a larger portion of income for discretionary expenditure? There are five reasons for growing non-discretionary (fixed) expenditures:

1. Housing costs – mortgage repayments but also rent. People are allocating more and more of their disposable income to funding housing. This issue was addressed in Chapter 3, and will be considered further shortly. As there are many retired people in the lowest quintile, they tend to not have high mortgage and education/childcare costs. This is central to the fixed share of

115

income falling. The average increase (i.e. including also people with no housing costs) was from 11 percent of household expenditure in 1984 to 21 percent in 2016.

2. Childcare, school and university fees. Not all households face these costs, but for those who do, they have been growing rapidly.

3. Utilities (gas, electricity, phone, etc.). Expenditures on these have grown faster than inflation and average incomes. For example, in the ten years to March 2017, electricity costs increased by 124 percent, health costs 60 percent, and property rates and charges by 83 percent, compared with a CPI (inflation) increase of 29 percent (Association of Superannuation Funds of Australia 2017). In June 2017 Energy Australia announced electricity price increases of 19 percent and gas price increases of almost 7 percent (see Cormack 2017).

4. Compulsory superannuation deductions from take-home pay (see Chapter 4). These increased from zero in 1984, starting at 3 percent in 1992 and growing to 8 percent in 2000 and are currently 9.25 percent. The increase to 9.25 percent occurred after the survey period.

5. Insurance. Some households are spending more of their income on a range of different insurance policies as a way of dealing with life's uncertainties. The average increase was from 7 percent of household expenditure in 1984 to 11 percent in 2016. See also Figure 5.8.

So in Figure 5.5 we isolate these five reasons, and see how much they have contributed to the growth of household expenditure since the mid-1980s. It is apparent for households on average that these five factors increased from 25 percent to 41 percent of total expenditure. Of course for some households, especially those with high mortgages or rental payments, the figure is much higher than 41 percent (even in 2016). But as a general national trend, this growth is significant, for within it is the expenditures most readily securitised. It signals that financial markets are being provided with a constantly growing pool of actual and potentially securitisable household payments.

How does the fixed/discretionary division translate to a difference between 'securitisable' and 'non-securitisable' household expenditures? While not all fixed expenditures are securitisable, most securitisable expenditures are fixed. In Figure 5.6 we show the relationship between

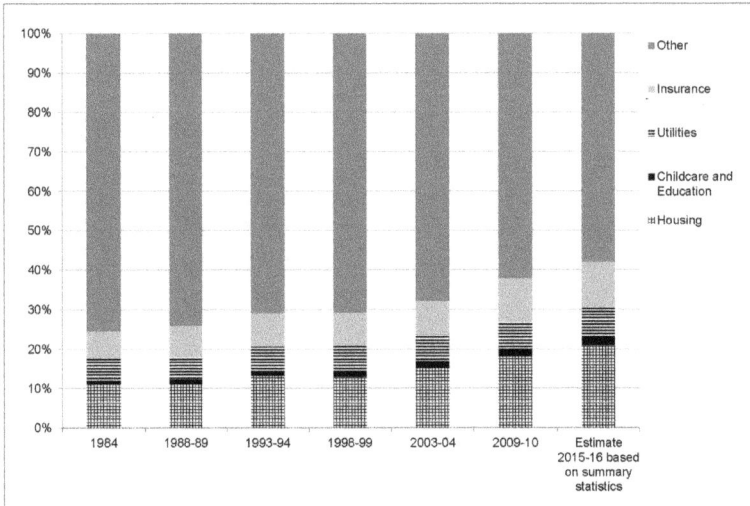

Figure 5.5 Change in net share by expenditure type, 1984 to 2015–16. Source: ABS 6530.0 Household Expenditure Survey, Australia: Detailed Expenditure Items, 1984 to 2009-10. NB: Insurance category includes superannuation and life insurance, as the ABS data does not provide separate figures .

all household expenditure and securitisable expenditures by quintiles in 2010 – the most recently available data. So while Figure 5.5 showed the pool of potentially securitisable expenditures is getting bigger, Figure 5.6 shows which households are feeding expenditures into the pool.

This figure reveals some critical information. Most obviously, the heights of the bars tell us that the lowest-income quintile spends on average less than $700 per week, while the highest-income quintile spends over $4,200 per week. Further, the securitisable expenditures of the first quintile households is a larger percentage of household expenditures than in other quintiles, though this is hardly surprising because expenditure on housing, utilities insurance and education make up a larger percentage of all low income household expenditure.

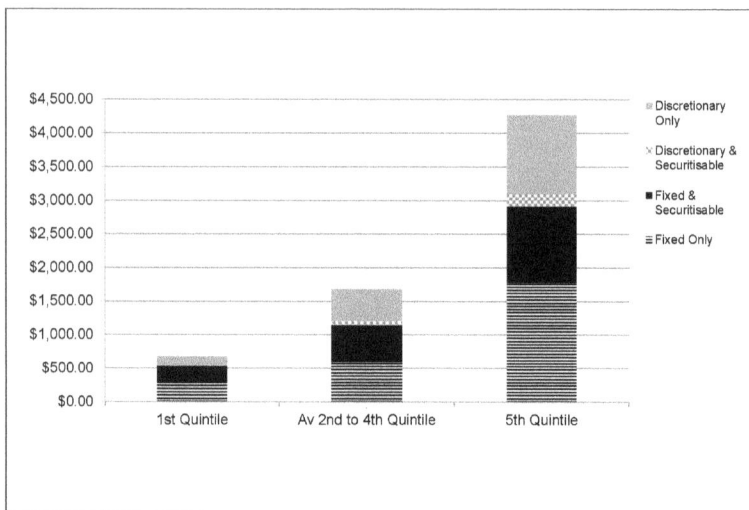

Figure 5.6 Gross household expenditure – fixed, discretionary and securitisable, by gross income quintile, 2015–16 (CPI adjusted to 2016 values). Source: ABS 6530.0 Household Expenditure Survey, Australia: Detailed Expenditure Items, 1984 to 2009-10.

As we noted earlier, however, the question for finance is not so much about these distributional percentages or even the affordability of modern living, but the value of the securities that could be issued from households' contractual payments, and the riskiness of those payments. Here we see that $1,317 per week from the highest quintile of households is credibly available to be securitised; most, but not all of it, from fixed expenditures. For the middle quintiles, it is $606 per week, including some discretionary expenditures. For the lowest quintile, the figure is just $262 per week; all of it fixed expenditure.

For the financial securitisers, as we will see shortly and especially in Chapter 6, an agenda opens up from this evidence. Broadly, the expenditures of the highest quintile look desirable for securitisation, but if that process is going to achieve significant volumes, it has to reach well into the household payments of middle Australia. Just like

Henry Ford and his cars, finance wants mass production of financial securities. It is, therefore, the middle quintiles that warrant closest attention: financial institutions want to make sure that these middle-income households can help produce large volumes of financialised payments, but they also want to ensure they are not at significant risk of non-payment or default. More technically, the proposition is that securitisers want household payments where the rate of default is highly predictable, and individual households do not exceed their predicted rate, but this sharper proposition will be developed in Chapter 6. (First quintile households are therefore less the objects of securitisation, both for value and risk reasons.)

Some critical questions arise in this framework. How many (and what sort of) financial contracts can households with different income and expenditure characteristics safely carry? What is the default risk for different levels of income and household type? What is the impact of growing volatility of income flows (associated with more precarious work and retirement incomes driven by financial market performances) and of expenditures on the capacity of households to stay on contract? Calculating these household default risks is becoming a vital issue for financial markets, and they now invest heavily to get to the answers. The exploration of this specific issue must wait till Chapter 6.

The viability (and default risk) of households depends not just on their income and expenditure patterns, but on their wealth holdings too. We therefore first need to follow financial market analysis into an investigation of household assets and liabilities – into their 'balance sheets'.

Assets and liabilities account

Income and expenditure data are only one 'take' on households as pseudo-businesses. The other 'take' concerns the acquisition of assets and wealth. The assets and liabilities (balance sheet) account looks at household wealth and debt obligations (net wealth). Table 5.2 shows the main categories that make up the assets and liabilities account.

Looking first at assets, it can be noted that the skills and capacity to work of household members is central but is not (yet) presented in data sources and valued as an asset (either in terms of the workers' value in paid employment or the value of household services produced inside the

Assets	Liabilities
Skills/labour power*	Property debt
Property • Home • Other property	• Home – primary residence • Other property
Home contents	Personal debt
Bank accounts	• Car loans • Investment loans • Personal loans
Superannuation	• Hire purchase • Credit card debt
Equity investments	• HECS debt • Business debt
Business assets	
Vehicles	Overdue household bills
Other assets • Cash investments • Trust funds • Life insurance • Collectibles	

Table 5.2 Assets and liabilities account: key categories; *no data collection agencies include a measure or value of skills; but they should.

home). This may seem a surprising omission, both because economists are fond of calling skills 'human capital' and because the income derived from human capital, shown in the income account (wages and salaries), is the major source of income for most households. Moreover, as education fees climb, leading to a build-up of student debt, education comes to be framed more as an investment in skill, leading to the (reasonable) calculation of whether expected future income makes it worth taking on the repayments of student debt. These issues all point to skills being framed in the language of a capital asset. But currently it isn't. The reason for this exclusion is probably associated with the desire to keep the rights of non-labour assets and skill assets embedded in labour treated differently for property and other reasons of legal obligation. Specifically, skills cannot be traded: you cannot sell ownership of your human capital, for that would be slavery.[1] So they don't fit the standard financial model of an 'asset'. This is yet another dimension in which finance has trouble dealing analytically with labour.

Because of this exclusion of skills/human capital from official data, we cannot give this asset a measure, even though, for many households, it is no doubt one of their most valuable 'assets'. If skills/human capital were to be added to this account (notionally the value of future income-earning capacity), the differences in wealth between quintiles would generally be amplified, although with qualifications. For retired people, their labour market skills no longer have financial value, and retired people are in all quintiles. A similar problem exists for valuing the unpaid labour undertaken in households. But, age and domestic labour aside, wages are some proxy for the current financial value of human capital, and wages are generally higher in high wealth households than in low ones.[2] Nonetheless, it is also likely that the skills/human capital would make up a larger percentage of household assets of lower wealth households than of higher wealth households.

Liabilities, conversely, are really the various forms of debt a household acquires, most of it for the purchase of an asset (houses, cars, consumer durables, and education). Some debt, especially personal debt and credit card debt, may also be used to fund current consumption, to balance out irregular income flows, or for large one-off or unforeseen expenses (like medical bills, or repairing a car).

The evidence shows that average real household net worth (assets less liabilities) was relatively unchanged from the late 1980s to late 1990s but grew steadily over the 2000s to a peak in 2007, when it fell in the GFC. It has now come some way back to 2007 levels. Data from the Reserve Bank of Australia show that net household wealth has been

---

1   However, in the United States some universities are offering to replace student loans with a share of post-college/university income, so the option of selling some of your human capital 'by degrees' is now appearing.

2   See Finlay (2012) for a consideration of retired people and the difference between their positions in wealth and income quintiles.

recovering since 2010, although by 2013 the figure was still 6.5 percent below that 2007 peak (Finlay 2012: 20; RBA 2013: 46).

But averages belie different outcomes and, importantly for our analysis, diverging risks across wealth quintiles. The most recent quintile data, presented in Table 5.3, warrant investigation.

This snapshot shows wide diversity in the net wealth of households across quintiles: from just $3,877 for the first quintile to nearly $2.3 million for the fifth quintile. It is in some ways a more dramatic statement of modern inequality than income inequality. To make matters even more stark, within each quintile there is also diversity: at the top of the fifth quintile net wealth is measured in hundreds of millions, and for some in the billions. By contrast, at the bottom of the first quintile wealth is negative. However, it is the patterns of asset and liability holding in each quintile that is most revealing.

For the majority of the first quintile, the home is the largest single asset category, making up one-quarter of their total assets. (Many households in this quintile are in rental accommodation and so have no housing equity: home contents is often their largest asset.)[3]

Generally without mortgages, these households also have a significantly higher proportion of their wealth held as bank savings than do more wealthy households. This is consistent with RBA data on savings trends presented in Lowe (2011).

For the middle quintiles, the family home is clearly the largest asset (55 percent of all assets). Superannuation (mainly compulsory), investment property equity and motor vehicles round out the main assets of middle Australians.

For the fifth quintile, while the family home is the highest single asset, thereafter assets are diversified across a range of classes – superannuation, shares, trusts, businesses and investment properties.

In summary, we can say that for people of working age, there are marked differences between quintiles. If we take into consideration work skills and the ability to work, we can make the following generalisation about the key differences between quintile asset holdings:

---

3   This is not apparent from Table 5.3, but discernible from the equivalent ABS data, found at ABS Cat. 6554.0.

Selected household net worth quintiles for 2014 (these figures have been adjusted for inflation to 2016 values[a])			
	Lowest quintile	Average of the 2nd to 4th quintile	Highest quintile
Assets[b]	**47 285**	**563 682**	**2 536 265**
Bank accounts	4 212	31 573	144 448
Superannuation	10 083	102 144	600 378
Cash investments	0	754	5 493
Equity investments	358	10 787	176 657
Trust funds	474	3 040	57 504
Life insurance	302	6 663	49 517
Property assets[b]	17 472	373 861	1 301 674
Own home	*11 270*	*307 838*	*861 839*
Other property	*6 202*	*66 023*	*439 835*
Business assets	6 460	8 668	143 317
Collectibles	575	2 562	11 622
Vehicles	7 349	23 630	45 655
Liabilities[b]	**43 408**	**159 854**	**264 800**
Credit card debt	1 074	1 624	1 192
Property debt[b]	20 621	141 102	213 274
Own home	*12 047*	*111 109*	*118 124*
Other property	*8 574*	*29 993*	*95 150*
HECS debt	7 398	3 143	2 300
Other personal debt	9 020	11 603	22 300
Business debt	5 021	2 282	28 016
Overdue household bills	254	100	18
Net Worth[b]	**3 877**	**403 828**	**2 271 465**

Table 5.3 Average value of the components of household wealth for selected household net worth quintiles – 2014. Source: HILDA Survey 2015. NB: Figures based on aggregate for each quintile.[a] While the figures presented have been adjusted for inflation, they clearly understate current asset values, particularly for property. The objective here is to provide a broad balance sheet picture, not to provide a full valuation per se.[b] These figures are the totals of the amounts presented on this balance sheet and differ from the aggregate totals for each quintile.

- First quintile: skills.
- Middle quintiles: skills and the family home. The essential reason we cluster the three middle quintiles together is that they all share this profile.
- Fifth quintile: financial investment, assets and property.

When we turn to household liabilities, we already know from Chapter 4 that wealthy households also have the highest level of liabilities (the fifth quintile holds about half of all household debt), but they also have the lowest liabilities to asset ratio. In financial terms, wealthy households have low financial leverage (i.e. compared to their assets their debt levels are quite low), showing they are in the best position to service their debts. Only 44 percent of their debt relates to their home mortgage.

The middle quintiles are generally carrying much heavier levels of debt on their own home, and on average 70 percent of debt is tied to their home mortgage. They generally have little personal debt or business debt, but the highest credit card debt: some sign that cash flow can be a problem in these heavily mortgaged households.

Poorer households of the first quintile have the opposite asset and liability structure. Mainstream banks see their lack of assets as making them too risky, and thus banks are reluctant to lend them money over longer periods, to purchase homes or cars. So a whole suite of other (generally high cost, and often predatory) financial institutions have grown up to service the financial needs of these asset poor households: such as payday lenders and hockshops.

Household hedge funds?

On the basis of this descriptive evidence of income and expenditure accounts and asset and liability accounts, what sense do we make of households being invoked to think, calculate and act like finance – to become 'financialised'? Here we use the analogy of the household as a hedge fund.

The analogy is used in part ironically and in part also provocatively – for hedge funds proper are traditionally the investment vehicles of the very rich with large amounts of surplus cash, not ordinary people. Further, 'real' hedge funds go looking for risk to trade, whereas households find that risks are coming at them and they have no choice but to manage them. It is also the case that poorer households are not part of the analogy, and certainly not the 18 percent of adult Australians that are 'severely' excluded from financial services (Connolly 2013). These people are probably not living as a hedge fund (although they may exist in households that are), but they are still carrying significant (indeed often unmanageable) financial risks. Moreover, we must note that we are invoking the conception of what hedge funds did from the 1950s till the 1980s, for today hedge funds operate on a wide range of different principles. We should also note that the long/short positions of early hedge funds are now far more complex, and generally driven by less cautious practices.

To open up the analogy, we must first explain a little about the nature of hedge funds. Essentially, the original hedge funds (for their organisation has evolved) had two elements: leverage and long–short positions.

Leverage

As the term implies, leverage is about taking financial positions to multiply possible gains and losses. In its day-to-day meaning, leverage refers to using money you don't own (usually by borrowing it) to increase your exposure to a particular asset or event. Using borrowed money to buy assets means you often have little equity in the asset, and so investment risks are higher. Think of holding $10 of equity and borrowing $90 to buy an asset for $100. If the asset price rises to $120, you have made a 200 percent profit on your $10 investment (less interest payments). If the asset price falls below $90, your investment is now insolvent, and you are unable to repay your creditors.

We will come to how leverage applies in households, but think about buying a house with an initially small deposit (or, at the extreme, using interest-only loans) or accumulating student debt to fund going to TAFE or university and you can start to see the analogy.

Long–short positions

The terms long and short refer to the way an investor looks to profit from (or insure against) an asset by taking positions on the expectation of movements in the future price, either upwards or downwards. To 'go long' is to invest in an asset that is expected to go up in price. You buy and hold. To 'short' an asset is to take a position that will profit (or protect you) from a possible future fall in the price of an asset. To take a short position you lock in a price now for delivery in the future, in the expectation that when the future comes the price will be lower. In our daily life this is about insurance, and so you might pay to insure against a future adverse event. In financial markets, this is where the futures and options (derivative) contracts we introduced in Chapter 2 were originally used.

With the risks of high leverage, the original hedge fund managers were somewhat careful about their investing. They wanted to back what they thought were winning investments (going 'long'), but also to cover (or insure) their bets by 'hedging' (hence the fund's name) and so they also took related short positions to protect them if the long position did not turn out as expected. In effect, they very consciously calculated the risks of the future and strategised around those risks.

The classic long–short investment strategy might involve a long position on General Motors, in the belief their shares will go up over time. But there could be a fear that unforeseen things beyond the control of GM could get worse, dragging GM shares lower. So the hedge fund would place a secondary bet (a short position) on competitor shares (like Ford or Toyota) going down, or the overall stock market going down, or interest rates going up, etc. These alternative (short) positions are a form of insurance on the (long) GM bet. Hedge funds also used their leverage to profit from small differences in the price of the same assets in different markets (known as arbitrage).

How does this combination of leverage plus long/short positions help as a description of Australian households?

Household leverage in Australia

Leverage most obviously relates to house purchases and other forms of debt. In Chapter 4 we identified household leverage in the growing level of debt, especially for the purchase of houses. There are two relevant measure of leverage.

The first is a flow measures of leverage and can be seen in the income and expenditure account. The measure of leverage here is the amount of interest payments relative to income (the means by which debt will be repaid). Between 1983 and 2014 interest payments as a percentage of all household income doubled to 13 percent. With interest rate cuts since 2010 it has stabilised at around 8.5–9 percent. The most recent financial system inquiry (Murray 2014b: 82) reported the following about household leverage:

> Since 1997, household leverage has increased from debt equivalent (the ratio of debt to annualized household disposable income) of around 0.8 years of gross disposable income to around 1.5 years of income in 2008 – household leverage has since stabilized at around this level.

The second is a stock measure of leverage, and can be seen as the balance sheet perspective. The measure of leverage here is the amount of debt relative to asset values (whether the value of purchased assets has grown faster than the debt). Between 1983 and 2014 the value of debt as a proportion of all household assets increased from 7.2 percent in the late 1980s peaking at 18 percent in 2012, before falling slightly to 16.6 percent in 2014. It would have been a much bigger increase except that house prices grew steadily in the post-2010 period.

Overall, *whether measured by the income and expenditure account or the balance sheet, by historical standards, Australian households are highly leveraged.* This higher leverage leaves them with a greater exposure to changes in asset prices (especially housing but also, via superannuation, the stock market) *and* to any loss of capacity to service debt (especially via sickness and unemployment).

These averages hide wide disparities across income/wealth quintiles and age groups, with debt to asset ratios much higher in poorer and younger households, especially if those households are attempting to purchase a house and/or have an adult out of paid work, say for child rearing. For instance, in terms of age, households where the age of the reference person (the survey term for the principal earner) is between 25 and 34 have on average a ratio of debt to total assets of 36 percent (up from 28 percent in 2002), compared to households where the age of the reference person is 45–54 of 21 percent, 55–64 of 9 percent and 65–74 of 1 percent. This is despite the fact that younger households are now much less likely to be purchasing homes than in the past. Also in terms of wealth, those households with low net worth tend have very high debt to assets (99 percent for those households in the lowest net worth quintile), while those with a high net worth had low debt to assets ratio (11 percent for those in the highest net worth quintile).

Figure 5.7 shows household leverage in Australia by quintiles of income and of wealth. The difference between wealth and income is important because neither alone captures the leverage issue in isolation in terms of the risk exposure to finance or financial volatility. A household may be on a relatively low income but in terms of net assets be quite wealthy (e.g. retirees). On the other hand, a household might have a high income but relatively low wealth (e.g. young professionals). For finance this is important in terms of their thinking about the risks of each household type, so the evidence is significant.

When we look at income quintiles, it is apparent that for all quintiles debt ratios, however measured, are increasing. But whether we measure by income and expenditure or by assets and liabilities makes a difference between quintiles. The lowest quintile is lowest in debt-to-income measures because its capacity to borrow is very low and it has the highest on debt-to-assets ratio because it has so few assets to offset its debts. For the other four quintiles (where the borrowing is more quantitatively significant), we might generally expect the middle to situate between the top and the bottom. But on the figure debt-to-income, where quintiles are measured by net worth, and in the figure of debt-to-assets, where quintiles are measured by income, the middle is higher than both the bottom and the top. In other words, the middle quintiles are the most exposed to debt and the risk of default. The middle quintiles have to pay relatively more income as interest than the rich to sustain their position in asset acquisition. It is therefore the leverage of middle-income households that is the most important in risk terms. This leverage can be understood in terms of the household loop explained in Chapter 4.

This raises the question of how households, especially the middle, are managing that exposure, taking particular note of the vulnerable

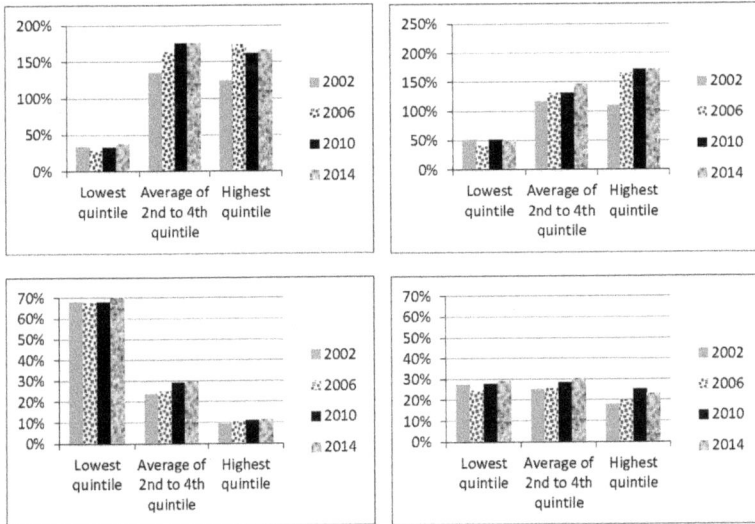

Figure 5.7 Household leverage indebted households, median debt to income, 2002–2014. Clockwise from top-right: median debt to income - quintiles by net worth; median debt to income - quintiles by net income; median debt to assets - quintiles by net worth; median debt to asset - quintiles by net income. Source: HILDA Survey 2015. NB: calculations are based per household, not aggregated. See Appendix 2 for further details.

position of the middle. In hedge fund terms, this takes us to their long (speculative) and short (hedged) positions.

Household 'long' positions

One way that financial institutions like hedge funds manage risks is to spread their investments across different types of assets (known as asset classes). The idea here is that the prices of different asset classes move in different ways at different times, so by spreading investments (diversifying in financial jargon) across those markets there is protection against declines in any one asset market.

The household asset categories shown in Table 5.2 might be thought of as a version of the portfolio of a hedge fund: it is diversified between cash, equities, bonds, trusts, property, and so on. From Table 5.3 we have already made some general observations of the long positions of different quintiles.

To reiterate, wealthy households tend to be diversified across all asset categories; middle-income households are very heavily concentrated in housing (they are undiversified); and poorer households, while still concentrated in their asset classes, are more diversified than the middle, and hold a higher proportion of their assets in bank savings accounts.

State policies have played a central role in this profile of long positions. The undiversified asset structure of the middle quintiles is significantly driven by laws that draw investment into the 'family home' by making the home free from capital gains tax and various concessions for first home buyers. For high wealth households the state has facilitated asset diversification not just by policies that facilitate their growing wealth, but by laws on family income sharing via trusts, negative gearing, capital gains, superannuation tax concessions, as well as laws that permit capital losses to be written off against capital gains.

We can make the following generalisation about household long positions:

- Lowest quintile: low leveraged and relatively diversified in their assets.
- Middle quintiles: very highly leveraged (related to housing) and undiversified in their asset holdings (predominantly property).
- Fifth quintile: moderately leveraged and widely diversified in their asset classes.

We now reach a critical conclusion. While *lower-income households are most exposed to poverty (the inability to meet basic needs), middle Australia is the most exposed to financial risk and* stress. Framed slightly differently, low-income households are the biggest losers on income distribution, but middle-income households are the biggest potential losers on risk distribution. They are highly exposed to financial risk.

While financial institutions are agnostic with respect to issues of income inequality, they are very concerned with riskiness. This is an issue we return to in Chapter 6.

Household 'short' positions

Taking short positions in financial markets (insurance) supposedly offers a solution to the growing levels of household risk. A 'short' position might be thought of as way of minimising (or laying-off) risk – a sort of insurance policy (or hedge) against the potential for an asset price going down, or for an event to occur that means people can't meet one of the payments on their long (fixed) positions. The range of possible household 'short' positions is summarised in Table 5.4, which presents the five primary assets of all households and the corresponding available hedging instruments.

Possible hedging instruments are predominantly insurance contracts, or additional forms of labour (either directly increasing paid work or reducing purchases and doing more work 'in-house'). In financial language these insurance contracts are options – you purchase the right to a payout only if certain contingencies occur.

With households holding increasing assets and with increasing leverage, one might expect to see an increase in the holding of short positions to offset the growing risks of long positions, in the style of the original, risk conscious hedge funds.

Yet survey data show that many people hold little or no hedges against the value of their assets. A 2012 survey of 50,000 Australians by the UNSW Centre for Social Impact for National Australia Bank (Connolly 2013: 13) revealed that 19.5 percent of people have no house, home contents or comprehensive motor vehicle insurance (the only three forms of insurance surveyed), leaving them highly financially exposed if an adverse event were to occur.

This may not simply be risk choice. It is also about affordability. For those who do insure, the cost is growing rapidly. Insurance Council of Australia data show that, since 2001, the average premium on house insurance has grown seven times the rate of inflation and home contents insurance has grown at twice the rate of inflation.[4] Part of this relative growth may be attributed to a growth in the value of houses and assets to be insured, but Connolly (2013: 15) reports an

---

4   See Insurance Statistics Australia: www.insurancecouncil.com.au/industry-statistics-data/gi-statistics/contents.

Asset	Hedge
Residential property / Investment property	House insurance
	Income/mortgage insurance
	Mortgage prepayments*
	Case-Shiller house price options**
	Workplace leave (for people in permanent work) protects income for loan repayment
	Regular maintenance/renovation
	Making additional loan repayments
Home contents	Home contents insurance
	Product warranties
	Income insurance
	Workplace leave (for people in permanent work) protects income for loan repayment
Superannuation	Low risk investment options
	Purchase of an endowment
	Access to age pension
	Self-managed funds for high net worth households and access to tax concessions
Motor vehicle	Third party insurance (compulsory)

Asset	Hedge
	Comprehensive (with varying no claim bonus etc.) insurance
	Regular car maintenance
	Income insurance
	Workplace leave (for people in permanent work) protects income for loan repayment.
Employment skill / Human capital	Health insurance
	Health checks Investment in ongoing skill acquisition
	Income and redundancy insurance
	Increase paid working hours (adding more household members into paid workforce, moving from part-time to full-time; overtime)

Table 5.4 Household asset hedges; * In Australia in 2013, in aggregate households are 'ahead' to the equivalent of about 20 months of repayments of interest plus principal. This permits an average of 20 months of non-mortgage payments without being in mortgage stress. But should interest rates increase, this figure will drop rapidly (RBA 2013: 45). **See Chapter 2 for a discussion of these. They are not yet available in Australia.

8.9 percent increase in price of home contents insurance from 2011 to 2012. Not surprisingly, therefore, the take-up of home insurance is low among lower wealth households. The Centre for Social Impact survey (Connolly 2013: 22–7) revealed that 40 percent of people have no home contents insurance, and that more than 50 percent of the population perceive their contents to be under-insured.

Of those households that do some insuring, the lowest income quintile households have always spent more on insurance as a proportion of income than the rest of the population. This may be surprising, but many insurance costs, like medical, home and vehicle are not, or only partially, related to income levels, and some are compulsory.

Figure 5.8 shows evidence for households who do undertake some form of insurance.[5] It reveals that only households in this lowest quintile have increased their insurance commitments in the past decade and they have done so significantly. They now spend 16 percent of their disposable income on insurance. The growth since 2011 is mainly associated with changes in health insurance, but even for home, contents and vehicle insurance, the lowest quintile is spending a far higher percentage of income than are the other four quintiles. This increase is explained mostly by changes to the private health insurance rebates in the taxation system. In the 2011–12 financial year the government made changes to the Medicare levy surcharge. It was designed to give tax penalties to people who did not undertake private health insurance. While not directed specifically at low-income earners, the data show a massive growth in the rate at which low-income people took up private health insurance. The percentage of first quintile people taking out health insurance increased from 30 percent in 2011 to 75 percent in 2012. From 2006 to 2011 the bottom quintile spent around four times as much as the other quintiles. In 2012 it spent eight times as much.

The middle quintiles, which have had the highest growth in leverage (borrowing), and the least liquid asset portfolios, have had no growth in financial hedging through insurance, leaving them more highly exposed to asset price falls or loss of income to meet repayments. Middle- and high-income households did nonetheless respond to the Medicare surcharge, but less dramatically than for low-income households. On the other hand, for the top quintile the rate of health insurance went from above 80 percent to almost 100 percent.

Why then is middle Australia in this risky position, as undiversified, illiquid and under-insured? A simple answer is that there is a lack of discretionary income to convert into insurance payments and other

---

5   According to research by Banks and Bowman (2017) at the Brotherhood of St Laurence, some people on low incomes put insurance cover first – even if it means doing without basic goods.

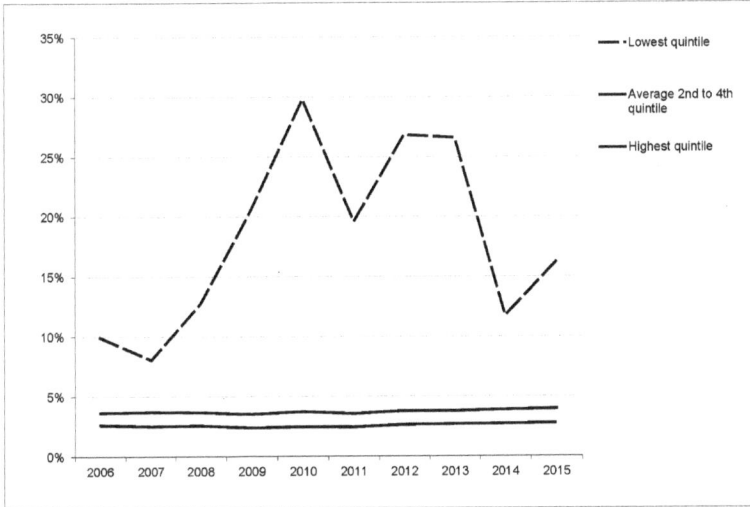

Figure 5.8 Income spent on insurance products as a proportion of net income, by income quintile, 2006–15(insured households only. Per household data, respondents with zero incomes but with insurance, excluded (while these cases were excluded their exclusion had no impact on ratios (less than 0.05%). Source: HILDA Survey, 2015.

hedges, and that, after two decades of growing household labour market participation, there is little or no significant scope to increase labour market participation to generate more household income. Little wonder then that the finance sector describes many Australians not only as under-banked, but also under-insured against many risks. We have seen insurance companies responding by offering basic insurance policies with a range of add-on features – you can choose a higher excess to bring the premium down, or you can nominate a health insurance policy that does not cover a range of treatments (with these now being optional extras) so as to reduce your base premium. We can anticipate a rapidly expanding range of insurance products being offered to lower- and middle-income households.

Households as risk absorbers

Our second proposition in this chapter is that, in their combination of leverage and long/short positions, households are systematic financial risk absorbers. We have already presented the evidence required to support this proposition. We therefore just seek to reiterate and elaborate on two points.

First, in their asset holdings, households generally, but especially middle-income households, are highly undiversified. The asset classes they hold are essential to daily life – a home and its contents, some labour market skills and perhaps a car. High-income households are more diversified via a range of financial assets, and low-income households are more diversified because their modest wealth is not concentrated in residential housing.

Second, the core asset holdings of households – especially middle- and lower-income households – are not only undiversified; they are also highly illiquid or 'locked in' (especially skills, houses and home contents). These asset classes are locked in because they are predominantly related to meeting subsistence needs. Liquidity is the capacity to sell quickly, without high costs and without the need to offer heavy discounts to offload an asset. Holders of liquid assets can sell quickly and easily as asset prices move, and so sell (or take on, if they choose) various risks in an intentional and calculative way. Illiquidity means that asset holders cannot rapidly trade their positions and are stuck holding assets even though their prices may be changing.

The liquidity of different household asset classes is summarised in Table 5.5.

This is where the comparison of households with companies and financial institutions starts to fall away. Households, like businesses, may have become more leveraged and more exposed to market-linked assets. And there has been much cultural and ideological mileage in depicting households as having the attributes of businesses. But the critical difference is that, below the fifth quintile, households are illiquid. Their 'business' is meeting subsistence needs, not chasing yield between asset classes.

But it is precisely where the analogy falls away that that the critical strategic policy issues for the immediate future are to be found. In

Asset	Liquidity
Residential property / Investment property	**Low liquidity.** While people move houses, and can choose to sell and rent, selling takes time and is costly. Products providing equity redraw exist (e.g. reverse mortgages). They provide liquidity, but there are extensive warnings about purchasing such products (See the Australian Securities and Investments Commission warnings at https://tinyurl.com/7bcaxek).
Home contents	**Low liquidity.** Can be traded, but on places like eBay, second-hand dealers etc. the markdown from original purchase price is considerable.
Superannuation	**Variable liquidity.** Illiquid from one perspective, for it is a compulsory asset class. Within superannuation, highly liquid if 'growth' options chosen; low liquidity if self-managed funds invested in real estate.
Motor vehicle	**Low liquidity.** Cars are sold at considerable markdown, especially for a quick sale.
Employment skill / Human capital	**Very low liquidity.** A skill is embedded in a person. The skill is only 'tradeable' via retraining, which is expensive and takes years. Multiple members of a household working adds some degree of liquidity to the household's skill portfolio.

Table 5.5 Household asset liquidity.

essence, the illiquidity of households is what makes them ideal targets of risk shifting. Financial markets 'get' the failure of the analogy and they trade on it!

Should households therefore try to de-risk (take more short positions to hedge their market positions) and attempt to become more liquid (have less exposure to the big price volatilities of asset markets)? The leading exponent of this view is Professor Robert Shiller of Yale University, and winner of the Nobel Prize in Economic Science in 2013. He calls for the introduction of a raft of new financial products (framed as hedging and insurance instruments) into the financial loop we depicted in Chapter 4. Shiller (2012) contends that financial innovation in this domain is the key to the 'good society' and that the products he advocates are 'democratizing' finance by bringing the benefits of Wall Street to the customers of Walmart (2003). For more than a decade he has been advocating things like:

> livelihood insurance, to protect against anything from loss of income due to illness to finding the skills you possess having diminished value in the labour market; and suburb and postcode house price futures, so that you can hedge your exposure to house price changes (Shiller 2003: 4–5).

The trouble is, of course, that the more a household buys these hedging products, the less discretionary income they will hold. For lower-income households, there is simply no choice but to carry more and more risks. For those up the income scale they are being asked to make a choice: are you prepared to give up all your upside risk (income growth, house price growth, etc.) in order to reduce downside risk?

In social terms, it is a toxic choice. But it is not just the pro-market economists like Shiller advocating this position. The European transitional labour market (TLM) agenda we raised in Chapter 3 is part of a 'left' social democratic agenda, but is similarly inclined to use insurance contracts to replace the (implicit) insurance role the state and employers played in the postwar period.The TLM literature advocates the use of a range of measures such as the transformation of statutory or company-specific job protection measures with forms of compulsory mobility insurance, from workers' wages, which a worker can draw on in the case of redundancy. Another example is wage insurance so that a redundant worker can take a lower paying job but 'top-up' their salary for a specific period of time. These and other 'active' insurances and securities are said to encourage workers to manage risky events and decisions around employment and incomes (Schmid 2006).

De-risking, 'short' options for households are developing not only via insurance products. The growth of 'equity redraw' products (including the retirement products sometimes called 'reverse mortgages') offered by banks another market-based alternative path to liquidity in the hitherto illiquid asset of the family home. In essence, equity redraw enables people to convert to cash some of the equity they hold in their home, and thus realise in the present the benefits of house price appreciation as income, without having to sell their house. (In Chapter 4 equity redraw products are discussed briefly in relation to access to state pensions, and the potential requirement that people draw down equity before being entitled to pension payments.) Equity redraw looks appealing, for it in effect converts your home into a personal bank, where you build up equity and later draw it down. But it comes with major cautions. The financial regulator ASIC offers the following warning that some of these 'products', especially those being sold to retirees are expensive and risky:

- Interest rates are generally higher than average home loans.
- The debt can rise quickly as the interest compounds over the term of the loan – this is the effect of compound interest and is something you need to be aware of before making any decisions.

Important
You may come across companies that offer you an income stream in return for the capital growth on your home (a property option). While the cashflow may look attractive now, the income you receive will probably be much lower than the capital appreciation of your home that you are forgoing. These types of offers are unlikely to be covered by credit or financial services laws, meaning you will not have access to important consumer protections. (See https://tinyurl.com/y78g2c8z)

In combination, these market agendas seek to make the illiquid attributes of households more liquid, yet require people to trade away more and more of the upside of increasing living standards so as insure against the possible downsides of instability and illiquidity.

Riding the risks

Carrying high risk need not always be a bad position – it depends on how markets move – but it is an uncertain and sometimes precarious one. Illiquidity is one of the key problems: that when prices move the 'wrong' way, there is no real alternative but wear the costs.

To date, the risks that come with illiquidity of low income and middle Australia have generally been mixed, but that has come about by a combination of enormous state stimulus domestically, ongoing Chinese industrialisation and what amounts to good luck. None of these could have been predicted then and can't be relied upon in the future.

Employment has been a mixed experience, with all workers taking on more risk. Not surprisingly, that has been a good risk for some, whose incomes have grown rapidly, and a bad risk for many who have faced under-employment, unemployment, lengthening hours and/or job intensity or stagnant/volatile wages.

Housing has generally been a good investment to date, especially the earlier that exposure was secured, except in regions where industries have closed and people have left. RBA data (2013: 46) show that between 1995 and 2013 dwelling prices have grown by around 350 percent, while over the same period share prices (a liquid asset) grew by 250 percent, and have been significantly more volatile.[6]

But the risks of housing remain. There is constant conjecture, from reputable (and some less reputable) commentators that Australian house prices are significantly overvalued. In 2008, the International Monetary Fund identified Australia as the fourth most vulnerable in the world to a housing market price correction, with prices around 25 percent overvalued. Of the three more vulnerable than Australia, each underwent substantial correction, especially Ireland (IMF 2008: 11–14). Similarly, in 2013 the British business magazine *The Economist* (2013) nominated Australian housing as still being 24 percent overvalued. In 2015 credit ratings agency Moody's stated that 'Australia's housing market risks are skewed towards the downside'. The Reserve Bank of Australia has historically given assurances that price growth is not the expression of a bubble, although as time passes the RBA's position becomes more concerned about the risks of house price falls. For example, in mid-2015 RBA Governor Glenn Stevens

---

6   Haneward and Sherris (2011: 31) point to the variability within the long-term trend in house prices. In a study of Sydney house prices by postcode, they observe that 'House price growth exhibits very large variations over short time horizons with standard deviations of up to 150% of average growth rates', although these variations reduce for longer time horizons.

described pockets of the Sydney and Melbourne property market as 'crazy' (Mulligan and Atfield 2015). In 2017, the new Governor, Philip Lowe, reported somewhat more cautiously that his 'overall assessment is that the recent increase in household debt relative to our incomes has made the economy less resilient to future shocks' (Lowe 2017b). The future of Australian house prices, and hence the financial fortunes of most Australian households, remains an issue of ongoing conjecture.[7]

After property, the largest listed household financial asset is superannuation, to which we can add the direct share portfolios of the top quintile for, in general, the risks of superannuation are closely related to those of the stock market (Rainmaker 2010: 8). An international survey by HSBC (2013) reports that since the GFC Australian superannuants had the biggest drop in superannuation income among the 15 countries surveyed and that one-in-six people who are not already fully retired said they expected they will never be able to afford to fully retire from paid employment (See also Collett 2013).

Overall, there is clear evidence that household net worth (the structure of assets and liabilities in the household balance sheet) may have grown but it has also become more financially volatile. This trend predates the GFC by almost a decade, and has continued at an increasing rate since.

This growing volatility is now recognised in economic policy circles. The RBA and private credit reporting agencies do regular stress tests of the Australian economy, where they estimate the likely effects of adverse economic or financial events (such as a growth in unemployment, rising interest rates, a recession or property price crash). What they are trying to work out is whether and how many households and businesses will crack in a downturn. We explore this household research in Chapter 6.

---

7   For a simple contrast of views, see https://tinyurl.com/y9k76tlb.

Conclusion

We now have a much clearer picture of what is systematic about risk shifting to ordinary people, and how it is being built into the very structure of financialised capitalist economies like Australia.

Households are now being required to self-manage many more life-course risks, and we can see this in rising debt, compulsory superannuation and many more contractualised payments for services. Middle-income and poorer Australian households – especially the former – are holding leveraged and illiquid financial positions, where many are insufficiently hedged because they cannot afford to do so, and the costs of hedging are growing faster than incomes. Moreover, for financial institutions this transformation of household finance, and especially of middle-income households, is not just an end in itself. It is the means by which these households' payments become the inputs to the process of securitisation.

This is not a story of a lack of financial literacy (although nor is it a refutation of the benefits of financial competence). It is about the role of ordinary people as workers who need places to live, education, health care and savings for old age. To frame the meeting of these basic needs in terms of the acquisition of financial assets is the sign of a deep cultural shift in economic thinking that sees the social world through the lens of business and financial risk.

But once that jump in thinking happens, we immediately see that households are sitting ducks in the market for risk. They hold assets they need for basic living and are emotionally attached to – they don't and can't trade simply in response to current and expected price movements. So they hold more and more risks they cannot offload.

In the context of the 'big league' of finance, these illiquid households are good news. Households can be sold large loans, expensive insurance and multi-year utility contracts. They can be counted on to try to keep meeting the contractual payments even when they are insolvent, for to fail to do so means the loss of access to gas, water and electricity and the repossession of the car or furniture or even the home itself.

Moreover, on the backs of these regular payments for a home, car, utilities, education and insurance are being built a range of asset- and mortgage-backed securities for sale in global markets (see Chapter 4). These securities are highly liquid – buyers now trust their quality and trade them actively. (In Chapter 6 we will see how households are being monitored so as to ensure their payments are trustworthy.)

So the asset illiquidity of households, which is a financial cost to those households, appears as a virtue for financial markets. Illiquidity means people will keep paying if they possibly can, so the income streams that have been securitised keep flowing. Household 'stuckness' is the foundation on which the reputations of household-backed securities are built.

Therein lies a systemic transfer of risk to households: households absorb the precariousness of their illiquid balance sheets, and on that basis liquid securities far less risky than the households underlying them are produced and traded. In effect, there is a 'liquidity risk spread' and a 'risk surplus' being extracted from households. It is comparable with the surplus extracted in the world of paid work.

To date, however, this risk has had an upside for many households in Australia. Increasing house prices have been the saviour of many illiquid households, and even if house prices were to fall moderately, many households (excluding the recent entrants to the housing market and those who might become unemployed) would still be ahead on their balance sheets.

Yet this upside, manifesting as increasing wealth for many lower- and middle-income households, now becomes a target of the state. In current economic policy, there is increasing discussion about the state pulling back those upside gains from housing, by a policy regime known as 'asset-based welfare'. Central here is the question of whether 'the family home', now conceived as a financial asset, should enter into calculations of people's eligibility for welfare payments, especially currently the age pension. Increasing economic opinion is that the home should come into such calculations, even if initially at the top of the wealth spectrum. Notable advocates of such change are the Productivity Commission (2011, 2013); the National Commission of Audit; David Murray, former head of the Commonwealth Bank and the Future Fund; and former RBA Board member Professor Warwick McKibbon (See Khadem 2015). The emerging proposition of asset-based welfare, however, is that people should not presume rights to government welfare in times of income hardship, and be required to draw down some or all of the equity from their home before gaining eligibility for welfare and an age pension.

By invoking asset-based welfare, the state is effectively seeking to take back the upside gains of housing investment, but of course only from those who seek to claim welfare benefits. Wealthier households (many of whom have benefited from significant tax concessions from negative gearing and superannuation tax concessions) retire with enough money and assets not to qualify for the age pension, and hence do not have to release back to the state those gains from asset appreciation.

That's the longer-term distributional projection, with quite frightening implications.

But notice there is a significant political framing that follows from our analysis. It makes clear that most of the exposure to financial illiquidity is being borne in middle Australia. If we shift our analysis from *income* distribution (and the widening disparities between rich and poor) to *risk* distribution (where financial risks are held in Australian society) it is clear that it is the middle that is most exposed. Indeed, we would argue that this distribution of risk has wider consequences, because in absorbing those risks through what we have in Chapter 4 called an expanding financial loop, (especially) middle-income households are, in a more or less direct way, 'producing' additional financial products and profits for capital. Any policy and wider political agenda to challenge how capitalism is being experienced in Australia needs to be taking this risk issue into account.

6
Making households profitable for finance

Where is most of Australia's wealth found? The answer is clear (Claes 2016): 60 percent of it is in housing. At the end of 2016, these were the figures:

- Residential real estate $6.7 trillion
- Australian superannuation $2.1 trillion
- Companies on the stock exchange $1.7 trillion
- Commercial real estate $0.88 trillion. (Claes 2016)

Connected to residential real estate wealth is $1.6 trillion in outstanding mortgage debt that regularly draws down repayments out of household income.

Nobel Prize-winning economist Robert Shiller (2003: 9) reminds us that:

> Far more important to the world's economies than the stock markets are wage and salary incomes and other non-financial sources of livelihood such as the economic value of our homes and apartments. That is where the bulk of our wealth is found.

The US Federal Reserve has estimated that if we thought of all households as paying a rent for the house they occupy (a rough measure of the financial value of the shelter services provided by housing), then these 'rental' payments alone would, in effect, make up more than 8 percent of GDP (Rappaport 2010: 35).

It is hardly surprising, therefore, that financial markets demand more and more exposure to assets backed by housing and household payments (mortgage-backed, and other asset and household payment backed securities (MBSs and ABSs)). Finance goes where the money is and it has found ways to unlock household wealth and access the money that comes into and out of households on a giant scale.

Yet in Chapter 5 we showed that, in the process of financial institutions accessing household assets and income, financial risks and costs are being systematically transferred to households. The expectation that households will manage their financial balance sheets like personal hedge funds implies a fraught and uncertain balance. Because most households are illiquid (unable to change their financial circumstance very quickly or cheaply), their financial positions are more volatile. It all points to higher chances of getting into financial difficulties, financial stress, missed payments and even contract defaults.

So we find a dilemma: liquid, dynamic, financial markets need significant exposure to housing to reflect the asset base of the economy, yet the households that own, purchase or rent the housing are not liquid, and often not financially dynamic.

In this setting there is a demand in financial markets that some significant portion of household-based assets be deemed, or somehow made, 'safe' (low risk or a low probability of default) and, more generally, that the risks of these household-based assets and liabilities be calculated with maximum precision.

By and large, the payments by the top quintile of households are safe – they have the assets to service their various financial commitments. But in order to achieve sufficient scale, the supply of safe MBSs and ABSs has to reach beyond the payments of the top quintile and into the 'middle', with its high leverage and high exposure to labour and housing markets, and where risks are not well diversified.

This means that households become increasingly subject to more and more detailed financial monitoring so that household-based assets can be readily compared with other classes of financial assets, like government bonds and company shares, for their risk/return characteristics. In the riskier and financially fraught circumstances facing households, lenders and the issuers and purchasers of MBSs and ABSs need to know as precisely as possible the risks of contract default so as to protect their revenues. The state (especially the RBA and Australian Prudential Regulation Authority (APRA)) also wants to know the potential threat of large-scale defaults to overall economic stability.

In this chapter we identify how household finances are now being monitored by financial institutions, credit rating agencies and the state. Our goal is not to pronounce on whether Australian financial markets are safe or unsafe, but to highlight just how carefully or at least systematically risk shifting to households is being planned and managed. The point to emphasise is that risk shifting is deliberate and concerted; not simply a byproduct of the evolution of 'market forces'. We want to show, as the IMF (2005: 5) expressed it, how households are playing the role of financial market 'shock absorber of last resort', and in so doing are providing a new frontier of financialised profit-making.

But it is in the nature of financial competition that, at the frontier, things get pushed to the limit and sometimes beyond. The limits are constantly being tested. From a lender's point of view, lending to households isn't about being completely safe, for there would not be enough business if they lent only to completely safe customers. There must always be some default risk. Lending is about finding household payment limits. It means knowing just how much lending to and financial contracting with households can be undertaken that keeps default risk (and actual defaults) within acceptable predicted limits.

So our objective in this chapter is to explain that calculative process, to highlight how dependent financial markets are on households performing in financially predictable ways. A corollary therefore arises, which we address in the following chapter: what would happen if households decided to perform in financially unpredictable ways?

Financial markets 'rediscover' household lending: a short history

One of the keys to finance's (re)discovery of households is the changing lending practices of financial institutions in Australia. In the postwar period banks lent on the twin principles of minimum equity and a debt servicing ratio. The idea of minimum equity was that if a borrower defaulted on repayment, there would be enough equity in the house for the bank to recover the value of its loan, even allowing for a discount on a forced sale. The repayment ratio, on the other hand, meant that only a certain portion of household income should be permitted to be allocated to debt repayments. Implicit here is the notion that debt repayments must be 'affordable' in the context of a household's circumstances, although we will show that there has been a shift in what is being measured, from affordability to riskiness. Until the 1980s, the established convention was that around 30 percent of income was an upper limit before financial stress became likely (Senate 2008: 35). Thirty percent was initially applied to the income of a male 'breadwinner' only, converting to a household income measure in the late 1960s. The 30 percent figure is adjusted for income range by the Ontario or 30/40 rule where the stress threshold of 30 percent is confined to the bottom 40 percent of households by income distribution. This adjustment excludes higher income households who have the capacity to service higher debt to income ratios without experiencing undue hardship (Stevens 2008), or have the option of downsizing their housing without the need to leave home ownership completely.

As financialisation developed, these conventions of affordability proved too restrictive on the expansion of lending. By the 2000s there was a shift away from both minimum equity and debt servicing ratios in favour of models based on 'net income surplus assessment'. In part this shift away from a *minimum equity* approach is related to research evidence showing that people may continue to repay their mortgages even after they have lost all the equity in their house (and have entered negative equity).

In financial terms, default is like an 'option' which households exercise when the costs of continuing to repay exceeds the strike price of exercising the option. However, the evidence that households don't tend to exercise that option leads to another theory of default: the *ability to pay* approach. In this proposition, households will attempt to keep paying their mortgages despite equity considerations and only default when their incomes no longer cover the repayments and subsistence consumption expenses. The ability to pay proposition underlies the net income surplus assessment. It focuses on household liquidity constraints and credit market imperfections (see for instance Read et al. 2014).

These income surplus models involve a calculation of how much weekly income a household needs to live on, so that the rest (the 'income surplus') can potentially be allocated to loan repayments. As described by John Laker, then Chairman of APRA (Laker 2007: 3):

> These models require the borrower to have a minimum surplus of net after-tax income after taking into account debt servicing, other fixed payments and a basic level of living expenses. In contrast to the debt servicing ratio method, these expenses do not vary with the borrower's income ... At the same time, net income surplus models can in principle allow a higher level of borrowing than the debt servicing ratio method for borrowers with the same characteristics.

The growth of mortgage securitisation followed this shift in lending practices. From the mid-1990s, non-bank mortgage originators like Aussie Home Loans and RAMS started to grow. Their mortgage lending was on a different business model from banks. These originators had no deposits from savers; instead they borrowed (often short-term) in international money markets and on-lent those international loans to house buyers in Australia. They then packaged up these mortgages into securities, which they sold in local and international financial markets as residential mortgage-backed securities (RMBSs). By cashing out the mortgage, they could repay their own international loan or indeed make their next loan. They made profits from fees rather than from collecting interest payments.

As we described in Chapter 4, with securitisation there is a transfer of default risk on a loan from the lender (or mortgage originator) to the buyer of the security, for it is the latter that is owed the monthly household mortgage payments. This gives mortgage originators an incentive to embrace the riskier net-income surplus method of calculating lending limits. In 1995, less than 5 percent of mortgages were securitised; but a decade later it was more than 24 percent, with the major banks making up just 15 percent of securitised mortgage issuance (Standard & Poor's 2012: 26–27). By 2010, with the effects of the GFC, the figure was below 10 percent (Debelle 2010b).

But what became the new limits on lending, and how are they calculated? The task for lenders (and regulators) in the income surplus approach is to calculate the basic living expenses for households: how much the household must spend on basics, and thus how much is potentially left over and available for debt and other contractual payments. Laker (2007) explained how lenders have calculated these basic expenses:

[M]ost ADIs [authorised deposit-taking institutions – registered banks, building societies and credit unions] use either the Henderson Poverty Index (HPI) or (the higher) Household Expenditure Survey (HES) data from the Australian Bureau of Statistics as the basis for their living expense calculations. Around 20 percent of ADIs add a margin to these calculations to account for error in the estimates. Our review indicated that many lenders were, at the time, using estimates of living expenses below the HPI or were not regularly updating their estimates.

In effect, the head of the Australian financial regulator was saying that the culture of lending had changed such that lenders would make loans with repayment levels that implied households may (and often would have to) live at or below the socially defined poverty line in order to make those repayments. This income surplus approach has become the new standard for 'responsible' lending and contracting with households.

Laker was speaking less than two months before the world became aware of the escalating defaults of many US households, the consequent insolvency of US mortgage-backed securities, and the broader economic and financial consequences of mass default. On 9 August 2007 BNP Paribas announced that it was ceasing activity in three hedge funds that specialised in US mortgage debt. This was the first public statement of concern about the value of US MBSs. Since then, lending practices have tightened somewhat, albeit that the form of tightening has focused more on the capital reserves of lenders than on the repayment capacities of borrowers. So the same concern remains: housing lending standards remain a key focus of APRA (see Byres 2015). The Governor of the Reserve Bank of Australia noted in early 2017:

[T]oo many loans are still made where the borrower has the skinniest of income buffers after interest payments. In some cases, lenders are assuming that people can live more frugally than in practice they can, leaving little buffer if things go wrong. (Lowe 2017a)

It remains the case that, with competitive imperatives for lending pushing some households to the point of subsistence as a strategic goal, it is likely that some households are going to default. For any household, it just needs an event like a temporary loss of income, a sudden large expense, or a change in household members (especially relationship breakdown) and the household can quickly lose its capacity to meet a range of contractual payments. This is the new riskier condition facing households in rental and mortgaged housing.

While mortgage repayments can take up a growing share of income, they are not the only household contract of financial interest. Apart from other credit providers (for credit cards, car loans etc.), phone companies, utilities providers, insurance companies and so on increasingly attach their services to time-based contracts. (And as explained in Chapter 4, the periodic payments in these contracts also form the basis of potential securitisations.) For the households themselves, these contracts look like their other formal debt commitments: yet another form of fixed contracted monthly payment. So just as there are concerns about households defaulting on their mortgages, so there are concerns about them defaulting on these other payments too.

Little wonder that credit rating agencies, financial institutions, issuers of securities backed by household payments and state financial regulators monitor household financial performance and especially default risk (variously defined) very closely. So our analysis turns to that monitoring process for, if it is done effectively, finance can indeed groom households for new sources of wealth making for finance, while at the same time ensuring households absorb risks of financial volatility.

Financial stress

The monitoring process involves looking for signs of actual or looming financial stress, where the first main symptom is late payment on a contract, perhaps leading to default. Financial stress generally, and especially mortgage stress, tends to be concentrated among those households with at least one (but usually combinations) of the following characteristics (Breunig & Cobb-Clark 2006; Headey 2007; Headey et al. 2005; Marks 2007):

- low or volatile income
- high initial loan to value ratio (leverage)
- recent purchasers of a home
- low assets/wealth
- low labour market participation (especially due to unemployment)
- jobs of lower occupational status
- lone parent
- young children
- living in low socio-economic status areas
- significant change in household income or costs especially:
  - job loss
  - significant health issue or
  - relationship breakdown
- loan supplied in low doc form.

Monitoring households 1: financial institutions and credit agencies

The key to the emerging household monitoring project is to work out both the normal limits of risk absorption and the early warning signs of possible impending default; the earlier the better. This means profiling people both before they borrow (or sign a contract), to see whether they have the characteristics of people who have a high propensity to default and then, once they have a loan or contract, to monitor individual households to ensure that they are complying with their predicted patterns.

Hence the starting point for this monitoring is the assembly of massive datasets (what is now called 'big data') about millions of households. At this point of the process, the monitoring institutions are not interested in you personally (unlike the marketing departments of the contract providers): just in discerning the sorts of characteristics of households which get into arrears in their contracts, and then what specific characteristics from the list above (and others) lead to actual default. The data are interrogated (algorithms built) to discern which combinations of household attributes (for it is unlikely to be just one) best predict likelihood of loan arrears, missed contract payment and ultimate default.

Once these aggregate data profiles are built, there is an exercise of seeing how any individual household compares with the 'at risk' profile. Organisations considering making a contract with households (lenders, insurers, utility service providers) now check out prospective individual borrowers by asking a whole series of personal questions about background and lifestyle so that they can match your personal profile with a general risk profile, and hence allocate you a risk identity. That then defines your general probability of default or some other risk. As a recent insurance company television advertisement noted, if households provide more fine-grained information about their personal circumstances, the company contends it can offer a better deal – a deal tailored just for you (they would have you believe) if your detailed profile is associated with lower risk (for example, driving your car shorter distances or less often).

Information for big data comes from diverse sources; often ones we don't expect. Many people think of big data in reference to advertisers monitoring our internet usage, and 'placing' ads in various search engines and websites we visit. People will complain of the intrusion into privacy and the issue is often posed as a matter of civil liberties. But accessing personal internet usage so as to peddle personalised advertising is rather trivial compared with the financial monitoring big data is also now making possible.

In 2014, changes resulting from the *Privacy Amendment (Enhancing Privacy Protection) Act 2012* came into effect so that credit reporting agencies (like Equifax and Illion who we mentioned in Chapter 1) and their customers can get access to what is now called *comprehensive credit reporting* of individuals and households. Before then, credit reports could only contain information on whether you had actually defaulted or had some other sort of serious credit infringement. Now, credit reporting agencies can collect and report on a much wider range of financial activities, including a list of all savings and lending accounts, the nature and limits of all credit accounts and all account 24-month payment histories (Office of the Australian Information Commissioner 2014).

Although utility providers without a financial service licence are currently not permitted to access this data, and the payment data of utilities is not currently available in Australia, it is available in the United States, and the frontier of financial monitoring is expanding rapidly. According to one leading credit reporting agency, Equifax (n.d.), the new comprehensive credit reporting system is good for individuals and households too because it gives them more capacity to 'demonstrate credit worthiness (to potential financial service providers) and manage their credit profile (improve their credit rating)'. The company goes on to list the positive benefits including:

- **Highlights good credit behaviour**: You will be able to demonstrate recent good credit behaviour because the new system records if you have made your credit payments on time.
- **Faster recovery from adversity**: You may improve your credit profile more quickly after an adverse financial event by showing good credit behaviour, potentially countering the impact of a default up to five years old.
- **Quicker to establish a credit report**: For individuals new to consumer credit, the use of comprehensive information means that you can build credit worthiness more quickly. For example, if you are a young person or a recent arrival from overseas.
- **A more balanced system**: It is a more balanced and transparent system for consumers who already have a good credit history, as well as those who previously had trouble meeting their financial commitments – as it may enable them to access quality credit where they may not have been able to previously.
- **A better deal with providers**: With more complete credit bureau information and monthly updates, having a credit profile and showing good credit behaviour will become important in accessing credit at the best price.

Apart from your debt and other repayment history, all the non-cash transactions you make at shops or online are recorded in data banks. It is pretty easy to build a profile of what you spend your money on (and where you spend it). Add to that the fact that your income is known (for it is paid into a bank account – cash economy aside), your mortgage is known, as is your employment (and unemployment) history, and an estimated value of your house can be and is being calculated almost daily. RP Data and Rismark International have a suite of Australian home value indices which provide daily capital value change measurement of house prices by suburb, city and state. According to the Australian Stock Exchange:

> The indices have been specifically designed to track daily value changes in the Australian residential property market and are constructed using the latest possible property sales information thereby avoiding the 6 to 8 week reporting lags present in other property indices.

A number of new services are also emerging to provide individual home valuations. One example is RealAs, which uses an algorithm developed by machine-learning and data-mining. The company claims it can use this algorithm to predict property values with an average accuracy rate within 5 percent. In the United States, this process is even more advanced with postcode property price indices and home price valuation services being longer standing.

In short, even if you are unaware of this data assembly, your household financial risk profile – income/expenditure statement and balance sheet – is becoming pretty much transparent to financial institutions and those prepared to pay for the data.

When it comes to individuals applying for credit or some other contract, someone who lives in the 'wrong' (i.e. more risky) location, works in the 'wrong' occupation (or is unemployed), is of the 'wrong' age, and is in the 'wrong' relationship/household profile, won't even get to the starting line, for they will be deemed to be too high a risk of default. In Chapter 1 we referred to the 18 percent of Australians excluded from financial contracts.

The rest of the population can be attributed some probability of missing payments or default, based on the repayment records of 'like' people. One effect will be that amounts lent, durations of loans and interest rates charged can get adjusted to reflect people's financial riskiness (default probability). Another effect will be that people with high default probabilities will be monitored more closely. In mid-2015, for example, NAB announced that it had targeted 40 postcodes with a high risk of default. According to a bank spokesman:

> We do have higher-risk postcodes, and we make calls on what we think is the appropriate loan-to-value [LVR] ratio in those higher-risk postcodes ... One of the things that we definitely factor in is where there is actually higher unemployment, or a risk of higher unemployment, given the reliance on single industries for a town or region. We will also look very closely at areas that have had very dramatic increases in property values to consider what is the right ongoing LVR ratio as well. (Eyers 2015)

So the collection and analysis of data on household balance sheets measuring the risk of default on contracts is itself now big business.

In Australia, there are a few organisations that lead in the collection and processing of these data. There are three sorts of private groups doing this:

- credit reporting groups such as Illion and Equifax, who obtain reports from credit providers on the repayment (and non-repayment) patterns of households,
- financial institutions like banks who analyse the records of their own customers, and
- credit rating agencies and other financial services providers such as Moody's, Experian, Genworth, Fitch, Fujitsu Consulting and JP Morgan.

There are also two government-funded research agencies:

- the Australian Bureau of Statistics, which produces a Household Expenditure (HES) Series, and
- Melbourne University's Melbourne Institute, which produces a Household Income and Labour Dynamics (HILDA) series.

Digital Financial Analytics – *The Property Imperative*
This biannual report is based on consumer surveys of over 26,000 households per year (compared with the Australian government funded HILDA survey of 9,000), and focuses on households that are active in the residential property market. The survey provides information on households' mortgage, personal loan and credit card repayment performance, and also seeks information on the precursors of financial stress and default (such as having to use a credit card to meet regular mortgage payments, having to sell personal property to meet payments, missed or delayed paying other bills, or having approached the lender seeking refinancing or repayment relief). In its analysis and reporting it first divides households into property active (owner occupier, investor, and those actively looking to purchase a property) and property inactive (those who rent, live with parents or are homeless). The report estimates that about one-quarter of households is property inactive and that this proportion has been growing over time. In focusing on the property active segment it then further separates them into segments based on motivation (for property ownership) and demographic attributes.

The survey that informs *The Property Imperative* analyses the property active group around their intentions and experiences across a number of variables, including likelihood to enter a new property transaction in the next 12 months, needing to borrow more, how lenders are selected and so on. DFA also conducts research in association with JP Morgan, which produces *The Australian Mortgage Industry Report*.

ABS and HILDA produce extensive, high quality and fine-grained data, but their focus is not oriented to the quantification of risk. Finance needs data that is more frequent and with larger sample sizes than these datasets. As we will see shortly, privately produced data is increasingly surpassing these government-funded datasets both in size, frequency and information content for risk management.

And there are two government regulatory agencies:

• the Reserve Bank of Australia (RBA), and
• the Australian Prudential Regulatory Authority (APRA).

It is useful to look at some of their data and reports.

One format simply profiles the household balance sheets of a statistically significant portion of the household population so that inferences can be drawn about probabilities of financial stress and contract default.

Illion – *Consumer Financial Stress Index*
This index is a monthly indicative measure of consumer financial stress in Australia. First published in January 2013, the index uses information contained on Illion's various credit databases containing millions of individuals, households, small businesses and companies to measure consumer activity, demand, capacity and confidence.

The index score is an indicator of those data, combined with other relevant external data trends including personal credit growth and employment rates. The index is bound by -100 to +100, with a score above zero indicating increased stress levels, while a score below zero indicates lower stress. These variables are representative of consumer themes covering 'confidence', 'desperation', 'awareness', 'cash flow' and 'business risk'. Weighted and combined, these variables provide two scores predictive of consumers' demand for and capacity to service credit contracts. Together, these scores create a final index of consumer financial stress that is aligned with consumers' ability to meet future credit obligations, and indicative of future business and economic conditions.

Another way of assessing the financial risks households pose to financial institutions and to financial stability more broadly is found in the actual record of household financial repayments, especially their performance in the repayment of mortgages and credit cards. While banks can and do measure their own repayment (and non-repayment) trends, several mortgage credit reporting organisations exist to provide more comprehensive positive credit reporting and modelling (including Fitch, Standard & Poor's, Perpetual Trustees, JP Morgan, Fujitsu, and Marq Services).

Once a contract is signed, it is in the interests of all parties (the lender and borrower; the securitiser and purchaser) to keep the household payments flowing. According to leading mortgage insurer Genworth Financial (2009: 5):

The key to keeping borrowers in their homes is early notification (by households to credit providers) – the earlier a lender is aware a borrower may have trouble meeting their repayments, the more options can be implemented to keep them in their homes.

Hence the key issue for lenders is to know, with as much warning as possible, who is likely to go into arrears in their payments – what

---

NAB – *Consumer Anxiety Index*

Since 2014 NAB has been conducting a quarterly survey of about 2,000 households in conjunction with a Consumer Wellbeing Index. The anxiety index gauges households' concerns about their future spending and savings plans arising from what may be seen as risk factors, including job security, health, retirement, financial security and government policies. The index is based on survey participants' responses to five questions related to concerns about their future spending/savings plans arising from potential future changes to:

- job security
- health
- retirement security
- financial security
- cost of living and
- government policies.

This survey has the merit that, by asking households of perceptions of stress, it is intended to be a forward-looking indicator.

There are similar public reports on household financial issues published by other major banks, such as ANZ, ME Bank, Westpac and the Commonwealth Bank.

---

attitudes and circumstances are likely to lead to mortgage stress – before the non-payments actually occur. Hence, beyond balance sheet data, there is a constant monitoring of the perceptions of households.

The private (and public) monitoring of household finances is much more advanced in the United States, partly because of the damaging effects of the subprime mortgage meltdown that led to the GFC, and partly because the collection and use of big data is larger scale than in Australia. Here we provide one example of the frontier of household financial monitoring, to give some indication as to how monitoring will likely develop in Australia. JP Morgan's recent publication of a series *Household Financial Volatility Project*[1] applies large samples of detailed transaction-level analysis of households to produce a comprehensive report on household income and expenditure volatilities.

---

1   See www.jpmorganchase.com/corporate/institute/institute.htm.

JP Morgan Chase Institute – *US Household Financial Volatility Project*
The JP Morgan Chase Institute publishes regular reports on households and financial volatility. Its most recent report is 'Coping with costs: big data on expense volatility and medical payments', published in 2017.[2] This Household Financial Volatility report is specifically built on the basis of the availability of big data on individuals and households. From its 35 million accounts, JP Morgan samples the accounts of 2.5 million people, out of which 250,000 'core' customers (who use their checking account extensively) are subject to detailed analysis of their transactions involving mortgage and auto loans, checking and savings accounts, and credit card accounts. The Institute contends it can categorise at least 80 percent of household expenses.

JP Morgan's data show the amount, day, postcode, merchant and channel of each transaction. Additional data come from credit bureaus (on monthly credit payments, as well as outstanding balances and any non-repayment events) and various de-identified individual and demographic characteristics (including age, gender and location).

The research is currently used to produce three sets of measures:

1. month-to-month (and year-to-year) volatility in income and expenditure (by quintiles), segregated by various attributes such as income and consumption,
2. the patterns of income and consumption volatility, and
3. estimates of the financial buffers households have to weather these volatilities.

JP Morgan announced an intention to break down financial volatility by state, region, city, zip code, and age, gender and household type. They also expressed a plan to examine the patterns of people's expenditure during periods of financial stress (e.g. spending on restaurants versus groceries). To do this, the company intends to supplement the income and expenditure data with household asset and liability (balance sheet) data, i.e. to (re)build an individual household's balance sheet.

Monitoring households 2: governments and central banks

In the past, any government monitoring of household financial stress (and associated income poverty levels) was mostly a way of forecasting

---

2   The report is available at www.jpmorganchase.com/corporate/institute/
report-coping-with-costs.htm.

likely calls on government and charitable welfare services. It was a measure of social rather than financial stress and dislocation; not designed to evaluate risks households might pose to the financial system. The evaluation of wider financial market risks occurred via a broad monitoring of the balance sheets of the regulated savings and trading banks, which undertook mortgage and other lending.

Around the world, this agenda has changed, especially since the GFC, where the crash of subprime lending showed how household finances can impact directly and profoundly on financial stability. The monitoring of bank balance sheets still occurs, and in a more intensive way, but central banks no longer rely on the financial assessment of lenders themselves to monitor financial stability risks.

Reserve Bank of Australia Financial Stability Reviews now consistently nominate the residential real estate market and associated mortgage lending as the major risks to the financial sector. These risks are in turn linked to the labour market conditions. The RBA makes use of the greater level of granularity available from performance of securitised mortgage loans. Also, in a recent APRA stress testing of banks it was found that:

> All of the capital assigned to protect the major banks' $1.25 trillion mortgage books would be wiped out by a 'severe downturn' in the housing market. The four majors were only able to pass APRA's stress tests after drawing on extra capital allocated to other areas of their business and through profits generated in some years of the test. (Joye 2014)

The report has seen APRA impose higher capital adequacy rules on banks and this has led to them having to raise more equity capital, which would act as a buffer if a wave of defaults were to occur.

The change is that lending and borrowing have become altogether more complex. Households, as we saw in Chapter 5, are now more leveraged and the lenders themselves have transformed into broader roles of risk management, trading in insurance and derivative markets. They now have their own risk exposures that are more than the risks of their borrowers. Moreover, with households so integral to financial stability, government regulators are focusing on monitoring household financial experiences directly.

The regulation of financial stability, in Australia involving the RBA and APRA, is now as much centred on the performance of households as it is on the banks that lend to them, manage their superannuation and insure them. The RBA now undertakes regular direct monitoring of households, including 'stress testing' them: they model what would happen to household finances in response to significant changes in unemployment, interest rates and asset prices. They want to make sure that households do not destabilise financial markets and the economy, especially by defaulting on securities backed by household payments. As one recent RBA report explains:

> The Australian banking sector's lending to households accounts for a sizeable share of its total lending exposures and this share has increased over recent decades. Furthermore, recent international experience has emphasised the risks that the household sector can pose to financial stability and, consequently, to the broader macro economy. Therefore, it is prudent to continuously assess the household sector's financial resilience. (Bilston et al. 2015)

Additionally, household stress testing is reported biannually in the RBA *Financial Stability Review*, and a series of other publications on household finances and repayment performance.[5]

Because Australia's experience of the GFC was not too bad, the RBA has generally been upbeat about household financial viability and risks. But in other parts of the world, where the GFC hit harder, the focus on households has a sharper edge. For example, in the United States the St Louis branch of the Federal Reserve (the US central bank) now has a Center for Household Financial Stability,[6] which has as its goals the study of the determinants of healthy family (household)

---

5   For instance in an RBA research publication, Read, Stewart and La Cava (2014) used household loan level data to analyse the factors associated with entering 90+ day housing loan arrears; and explore the factors associated with households missing mortgage payments.

6   See www.stlouisfed.org/household-financial-stability/about-the-center.

> **RBA – *Securitisations Industry Forum***
> The RBA Securitisations Industry Forum[3] was set up in 2015 to share data between itself and financial institutions called in this context 'Information Providers' (IPs). The RBA uses data from IPs for policy purposes relating to what are known as 'repos' (repurchase agreements): instruments used in the short-term money market, in which the RBA is central. The RBA needs to ensure that the securities issued by IPs are of sufficient quality to be eligible as collateral in the repo market. The RBA claims its contingent exposure to asset-backed securities (ABS) is expected to increase significantly in coming years.[4]
>
> For each loan, IPs are required to submit monthly data on loan level, security level, transaction level, pool level, cash flow waterfall model and related data. A non-sensitive version of the data is made publicly available just a month after submission. As explained by the RBA's Assistant Governor Christopher Kent (2017):
>
> Currently, the dataset covers about 280 'pools' of securitised assets… The vast bulk of the assets underlying these securities are residential mortgages (other assets, such as commercial property mortgages and car loans, constitute only about 2 per cent of the pools).
>
> … The dataset covers information on 1.6 million individual mortgages with a total value of around $400 billion. Currently, this accounts for about one-quarter of the total value of home loans outstanding in Australia.
>
> … For each housing loan, we collect (de-identified) data on around 100 fields including:
>
> • loan characteristics, such as balances, interest rates, loan type (e.g. principal-and-interest (P&I), interest-only), loan purpose (e.g. owner-occupier, investor) and arrears status;
> • borrower characteristics, such as income and the type of employment (e.g. pay as you go (PAYG), self-employed);
> • details on the collateral underpinning the mortgage, such as the type of property (e.g. house or apartment), its location (postcode) and its valuation.

---

3   See www.rba.gov.au/securitisations/about-the-sif/background.html.
4   This expectation is expressed at www.rba.gov.au/securitisations/about-the-sif/background.html.

balance sheets, their links to the broader economy and ideas to improve them. In terms of household balance sheets, these are defined as what a family saves, owns and owes – in other words, its net worth. The Center even describes the GFC as a 'household balance sheet recession'. Given the disclosure of vast illegal practices in financial institutions, it is telling that the GFC can be framed in terms of household financial imbalance! But given the inability of regulators to prevent it, or prosecute any systemic financial institution imprudence, it is perhaps the place where regulators believe they can achieve most traction in regulatory reform for financial stability.

The Federal Reserve makes the following sorts of observations about both the structure of household balance sheets in the United States and its preferred behaviour of households:

- Most household balance sheets have not yet fully recovered from the 2007–2009 GFC.
- Households with older household heads have greater balance sheet health.
- Student debt has grown rapidly, is the fastest growing form of debt and, despite balance sheet health being linked to college completion, student debt is associated with lower levels of net worth.
- Households with diversified balance sheets have recovered best from the GFC. In particular, it argues that to achieve financial stability, families should aim for a 'diversified' balance sheet that includes investments in various assets (not just a home) and that should include high levels of liquid assets (especially emergency savings). It also recommends that families should only possess debts that are in proportion to their income and assets.
- The building of household life-course balance sheets should start as young as possible. College savings accounts should be established at birth or when entering kindergarten. (Center for Household Financial Stability 2016)

From the evidence presented in Chapter 5, it is clear that middle Australia (the middle three quintiles) is the most susceptible to these criteria.

Conclusion

Around 100 years ago we saw the rise of mass production, epitomised in Henry Ford's assembly-line car plant. The era of the production line ('Fordism') changed our idea of industry, and certainly changed what it meant to be an industrial worker at the frontiers of large scale, capitalist development.

But 'Fordism' did not arise out of thin air. Behind it lay the development of the school of 'scientific management', or 'Taylorism' as it became known in recognition of its originator Fredrick Taylor. Taylor's goal was to decompose production in a factory into a flow of carefully calculated, rational processes, so that worker, machine and management could coordinate for greatest efficiency and minimal waste. Part of his agenda was to redesign the organisation of work on 'scientific' principles; part was about incentives, both financial and moral, for workers to commit to this project.

The idea that a doctrine of 'scientific management' would provide all the answers did not last long: we keep on having to 'discover' that people are not like machines. But the culture of logistics, best practice, knowledge transfer and work ethic, and the use of measurement for verification, remain ongoing. They now seem like common-sense propositions in the workplace.

We are now seeing Taylorism move beyond the workplace and into the home, as a financial project. We see the household decomposed into its balance sheet and risks (the personal hedge fund) and subject to increasingly detailed monitoring of its logistics and efficiency. Along with the monitoring has also come a project of promoting a financial (responsibility) ethic. In this regard, financialisation makes the home more like the Taylorist workplace, just as we saw, in Chapter 3, that the workplace is itself becoming more financialised.

All the critiques of Taylorism – its authoritarianism, the alienated labour it implies and, most critically for our analysis, the way in which it treats workers like objects or machines – surely now also applies to the relation between households and finance. This is a theme we will develop in Chapter 7.

Our analysis also shows the lengths that are being gone to so as to make households financial risk absorbers of last resort, and financial product producers of first resort. Ultimately, of course, there must be some inconsistency and fragility in these expectations. The goal is *not* to create vast quantities of high-risk financial assets – the world is well endowed with these – but to create a safe risk spread, such that the financial risks going into households are greater than the financial risks coming out.

This spread requires that households systematically absorb financial risk. It is not unlike the recent experience of expecting workers to become more and more productive for less and less reward. Both the 'risk spread' and the 'income spread' have their limits. But in the intervening period, for capital there are massive risks to be shed and profits to be made, and the goal is to make that period long and the spread wide. Financial policies of literacy and cultures of personal, moral and legal responsibility to meet contractual obligations all serve to push the risk spread wider. Financial monitoring of households shows (or promises to show) for how long that spread can be maintained.

In workplace relations, union struggles of the 20th century sought to narrow the income spread; and sometimes even to challenge the existence of such a spread. In the 21st century, the financialised risk spread offers similar points of struggle. The following chapters will take up the challenge of identifying some of these opportunities.

7
Pushing back in a financialised way

The rise of financial calculation and the trading of risk is now intruding into some basic aspects of our social and economic relations – not just in business and banking, but in our working and home lives too. Risks are being traded and shifted in all sorts of directions and, if we look beyond the minute detail to general trends, it is clear that there is a systematic shift of risks to workers and their households.

For finance, there is a basic logic here. It is that successful risk trading in financial markets is about being liquid: a capacity to buy and sell rapidly as the pricing of risk changes. But people are not liquid. Outside of finance, we might even say that people look for 'social stability' – they want shelter to call a home; jobs to call a career; income to call a 'living wage'; social engagement to call a community; and a pension or income stream to call retirement. To the world of finance, this 'social stability' looks like illiquid positions in markets, and when finance finds someone (indeed, millions of people) with illiquid positions it means opportunities to shift risks and to make profit. The great innovation of finance in the past 30 years has been to work out ways to convert our desire for social stability into liquid assets for finance, and for profits to be made on the 'spread' (the difference between the costs of risks transferred to households and the yield on the assets built on household contract payments).

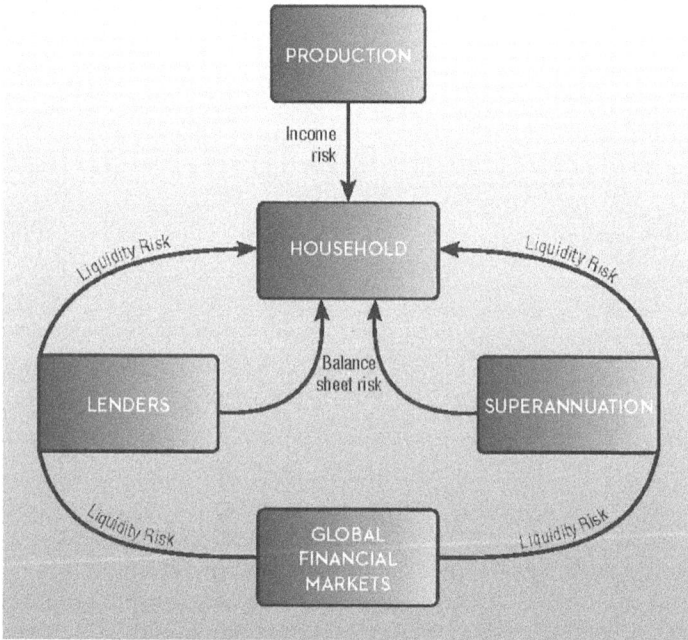

Figure 7.1 Financial flows and risk flows.

This great money-making invention of financial risk shifting to households has also produced one of our generation's great social and economic contradictions: developing financial ways to profit on our desire for social stability has itself generated enormous social and financial instability.

We have named this as a social experiment of risk shifting to workers and their households, and we can think about it in visual ways too. In Figure 7.1 we have reformulated the stylised model of household financial flows presented in Chapter 4, in terms of three types of risks that are being shifted to households: income risk, balance sheet risk and liquidity risk.

Income risk

The rise of liquid forms of employment and work identified in Chapter 3 (most notably casualisation and independent contracting) sees risks of work shifted systematically to illiquid workers. Households (workers) face increasing risks of precarious employment and income.

Balance sheet risk

Households are being framed and measured increasingly as if they are small businesses, small farmers or small financial institutions (hedge funds). Compulsory (illiquid) superannuation, higher education and the desire to acquire (illiquid) houses sees households saving and borrowing in anticipation that largely illiquid asset values will grow faster than their liabilities. This issue was explored in Chapter 4. Households face the risk that the long-term 'yield' on their superannuation, skills and house is less than the rate of interest on their loans.

Liquidity risk

The desire to have stability in housing and in lifestyle means that people sign long-term financial contracts for their subsistence items. You get locked-in and in financial terms that makes you illiquid. Households are legally required to meet these locked-in payments even though income risk and balance sheet risk mean that households' income and wealth are increasingly precarious (volatile). These issues were explained in Chapter 5. Moreover, while 'real' businesses can (and must) default and declare bankruptcy when their liabilities exceed their assets (and the USA has a president who has made this process an art form), households have no such option: they must keep up payments even if consumption levels fall below the poverty line. Financial market concern for household liquidity risk is seeing the production of more detailed financial risk profiles of households, as we discussed in Chapter 6, so that finance and financial contract providers can better determine and price the risks of each individual household.

Are trends apparent?

With so much risk shifting to households, there must be limits. Limits certainly showed in the USA in the GFC through the consequences of subprime mortgage lending, where households could not absorb the risks, and defaulted in large numbers. Subprime lending permitted quick, but unsustainable, financial revenue, based on aggressive and deliberately excessive risk shifting.

The lesson learnt from the US experience, by government and financial institutions there and in Australia, is not that risk shifting is socially destructive and should be reversed; just that it went too far. What we have seen in the wake of the GFC is that financial management of household balance sheets is intensifying so that risk shifting can be better calibrated. There is desire to monitor households for their contractual viability, and to do what is needed to keep those who do get contracts (for many do not) 'on payment'. Accordingly, we have seen a vast range of innovations and state policies designed to target this process. Since the GFC, economic policies in some countries, including Australia, have targeted households as their path to recovery. Where it has been done most successfully, such as in the US, the state has expanded employment and wage levels and underwritten the mortgage market (Yellen 2015). Where it has failed (like Europe), there has been no policy to alleviate household debt (Bryan and Rafferty 2017). We have also seen, around the world and in Australia, a growing surveillance of household balance sheets both in aggregate (by central banks) and individually (by financial institutions).

Further, and more subtly, we have seen the rise of a culture and moral project of contractual obligation (responsibility and reliability), ranging from compulsion in saving (superannuation) and insurance (e.g. health) to financial literacy education and laws restricting personal bankruptcy.

Where is it all heading? Surely no one really knows! The only answer we can confidently give is that we should never be surprised just how creative financial innovation can be to invent ways to turn ordinary 'things' of daily life into tradeable financial commodities, and not necessarily by trading the 'thing' itself, but by trading some derivative on the thing – risks of (bets on) the change in some measure of the performance of a thing. Accordingly, we feel confident that more and more forms of household expenditure will be converted into contracts, so that the revenues can be securitised, and that the surveillance of household expenditure patterns will intensify.

We can identify two other probable trends in Australia that are ultimately deeply at odds.

One is the ongoing government desire that people accumulate personal wealth to prevent reliance on state welfare payments, but it's a desire with a twist. The policy goal will become increasingly that people accumulate wealth in working life (mainly houses and superannuation) but in old age run down that wealth before they are permitted to access state-funded health, welfare and residential age care. Inheritance then becomes what is left over after a fully self-funded old age: it will return to being the domain of the higher wealth households. But set against this is the increasing costs and financial risks of getting to retirement age. More and more young people now enter the full-time workforce with (student) debt, and are required to pay into superannuation before paying off that debt, or saving for a house. They are likewise encouraged to take positions on utilities like phone contracts, health insurance and even income protection insurance.

In line with this trend, there are some future policy scenarios we anticipate round the corner in housing and superannuation.

Housing

Before you will be permitted to access welfare it is feasible you will first require compulsory use of financial products like reverse 'equity'/'equity unlock'/ 'equity release'[1] where financial institutions give home owners cash in return for a share of equity or a loan against equity. It used to be that you had to demonstrate a lack of means (i.e. wage income) and that meant showing you had no job, or perhaps minimal savings in the bank before getting welfare. But increasingly you will need to show asset poverty as well. So running down any housing equity may then become the precondition of access to state welfare.

A new industry in the United States involves companies buying an equity stake of about 10 percent of the current value of a home in

---

1   See Ong and Wood (2014) for a neat summary of the trend.

exchange for cash. They claim a much higher percentage of capital gain and require that the house is sold within ten years (See Geron 2017). Already the federal government offers age pensioners a pension loans scheme where they can top up their pension via a loan secured on their real estate holdings. The Department of Human Services registers a charge with the Land Titles Office on the title deed of the property offered as security.[2]

Superannuation

Following the example of a number of European countries, we may see superannuation payouts be compulsorily taken as annuities (an income stream based on your superannuation savings, discounted by the expected time you have to live – which, without irony, finance calls your 'longevity risk'). The *Financial System Inquiry Final Report* (Murray 2014b: 120), citing the OECD, reports that:

> The size of Australia's annuity market is only around 0.3 percent of gross domestic product, compared with 28.8 percent in Japan, 15.4 percent in the United States and more than 40 percent in some European countries.

However, it should be noted that in 2014 the British government abolished compulsory annuities, although there remain very strict limits on cash draw-downs from retirement savings.

Annuities convert a lump sum payment into a lifelong stream of monthly payments that expire at death. They eradicate risk of income volatility in old age (though not the risk that the company providing the annuity goes broke) so they look like a privately funded pension, but providers of annuities demand a big 'cut' from the lump sum to take on both income smoothing and longevity risk. Governments will be drawn to annuities so as to prevent 'profligate' spending of lump sum payments and to ensure that superannuation cannot be preserved for inheritance (Murray 2014a, 2014b).

---

2   See www.humanservices.gov.au/customer/services/centrelink/pension-loans-scheme.

Federal Social Services Minister (now Treasurer) Scott Morrison expressed a similar view: 'The purpose of providing tax incentives to encourage people to build up their super is so they can draw down on it in their retirement, not maintain it as a capital pool to be passed on as an inheritance' (Tingle 2015).

Proposals that first home buyers might 'borrow' from their superannuation to provide a deposit for home purchase draw the connection of home and post-retirement income into the same framework. If superannuation can become part of home equity, then home equity can become part of superannuation, to be drawn down to fund retirement!

The second, and potentially opposed, trend is that we can see securities backed by household payments becoming an increasingly important asset class in global financial markets. More generally, global financial markets want access to a large pool of 'safe', but high yielding, financial assets. Recent history reveals that government bonds are not particularly safe (in Europe it was not just questions about default in countries like Greece, but also negative interest rates) and, with interest rates low, many government bonds now have low yields. So there is a widespread shift out of government bonds and into infrastructure and housing investment (OMFIF 2015).

In Australia, demand from financial institutions like super funds for access to infrastructure investments seems unlimited. What do housing and infrastructure have in common? Both, if appropriately managed (and here the state's role is critical), offer stable returns that (finance hopes) do not cycle very closely with the stock market. In this role, as the basis of assets that can occupy the 'safe' end of superannuation fund and hedge fund asset portfolios, it is critical that households stay 'on contract'.

We have discussed the management of securitised household payments at length, including the central role of the state's regulators. The same applies to infrastructure. Public services are now undertaken not simply for wider social need, but as a way of producing future financial assets which, having been constructed and proven their demand (potential profitability), are ideal for later privatisation as low risk assets for financial institutions to invest in. Privatisation of state assets is preferable to new projects for infrastructure investors because the latter carry what is now called 'completion risk'. The rolling out of infrastructure assets is the state's new contribution to the diversification of risk in financial markets. Indeed this new role for governments now has an appropriate financial name – 'asset recycling'. In 2014 the Australian government announced the establishment of an Asset Recycling Fund:

> The Asset Recycling Fund will be used to make payments to states and territories under the Infrastructure Growth Package. These payments will be used to assist states and territories sell existing assets and recycle the capital into new productivity-enhancing infrastructure as well as expedite nationally significant infrastructure projects across the country. (Australian Government Budget 2014–15)

Notice that in these two possible trends there lies a deeper, systemic source of instability at the heart of financial change: households are being looked to increasingly to both absorb social and financial risks and run down lifetime assets and, at the same time, to anchor financial stability. It is an increasingly fragile balance.

How this tension of objectives is played out in the future cannot be known now, although it is not hard to see implications for financial instability, and perhaps even dramatic ones.

But what is also clear to us is that the growing centrality of households to systemic stability is a source of increasing potential for political responses to risk shifting.

New responses beyond conventional unionism

Those of us on the 'left' of politics have grown up with an understanding of 'class' centred on structural tensions and conflicts based on relations in the workplace. Trade unions have been central to that politics of class. Other political organisations on the left that cast themselves as broader in political vision than trade unions have still often centred their organisation and activism on workplace mobilisation.

A 'left' politics for the future needs to re-evaluate that focus. As well as industry unions addressing enterprise bargaining, national wage cases and industrial action, we propose an agenda that also addresses the class aspects of financial risk shifting. We can think about these responses in terms of 'household unionism', 'liquidity refusal' and strategies to 'block capital's liquidity risk spread'. We will explain these terms as they arise.

Whether this agenda should be seen as additional to or a substitute for industrial unionism is up to the reader to decide. What we observe is that, as the effectiveness of industrial unionism is diminishing for all sorts of reasons, new spaces of systemic conflict are opening up, calling forth new forms of political response. We can pose them, schematically, as the traditional-industrial framing of strategic action and the financialised style of response.

In Table 7.1 we capture the core differences between the industrial framing and our alternative, financialised depiction.

Of course whenever things are reduced to phrases in a box there is the danger of being overly simplistic, but Table 7.1 can help facilitate some telling points for opening up discussion.

Compatibility: deepening analytics

The industrial, workplace-centred view and the financialised view are compatible in many ways. People work for wages or income and produce a surplus and also live in households and absorb risk. In this dimension the financialised view is just adding a new emphasis.

We can extend this complementarity to the way each frames labour's/ households' connection of production and consumption: an issue we addressed in Chapter 4. For the industrial view the household earns wages, which are then spent on a bundle of goods for consumption – labour's subsistence goods and services. That spending is also demand for future output so, contrary to the proposition that capital always wants to cut wages in order to cut costs, there is the standard 'Keynesian' response that wages are also the source of demand for output. But what applies to all employers doesn't apply to every employer. Moreover, we are in a global economy with global demand, so this argument has limitations.

There is no obvious financialised dimension here – no recognition that many households have to spend more and more income on debt

	Industrial	Financialised
Structural class relation	Labour and capital	Households and capital
The subordinate class	'Labour' is people who work, but excludes high paid managers who are paid out of the surplus produced by labour. Also excludes unpaid domestic labour.	'Households' are people who cohabit, but excludes high wealth households who have the means to lay off risk. No differentiation of paid and unpaid labour.
The dominant class	'Capital' is conceived as ownership and operation of the means of production (workplace, technology, etc.). The class project is to universalise the conditions of wage labour.	'Capital' is conceived as a fund of mobile finance for 'investment' in whatever generates the best risk-adjusted expected yield. The class project is to preserve market liquidity.
Mode of 'exploitation' (contribution to profit)	Labour produces more value in output than it receives as a wage (surplus value as a spread between the wage and the value added created by labour).	Households absorb risks from capital and carry more risk than they can lay off (a liquidity spread between the risks absorbed by households and the risks of the financial securities backed by household payments).
Reproduction of the subordinate class	Workers combine wage and unpaid labour to reproduce themselves in households. Their consumption expenditure is part of the income of 'capital'.	Household consumption expenditure in their reproduction is part of the production of financial assets that become 'capital' (financial fees and asset-backed securities).
Reproduction of the dominant class	Profits are reinvested in acquisition of new production capacity for the creation of future value. They might also be invested in speculative financial acquisitions which may be profitable but create no new value.	Assets are constantly traded to balance risk and return in a portfolio with diverse risks. This may include the buying, holding and selling of 'production capacity' but it is not a privileged investment category.

Table 7.1 Industrial and financialised class relations.

repayment or various financial buffers against unforeseen circumstances. Indeed, until the 1980s bank lending to households was controlled and other social risks tended to be managed collectively at the workplace level and by governments. Further, there is no engagement with the process of securitisation: that many of the subsistence and other expenditures on goods and services by workers and their financial dependants are now being reconfigured as inputs into globally traded securities.

Conversely, the financialisation framing focuses on household balance sheet issues and on the securitisation of subsistence expenditures, but it does not itself explain where households get their income from. Yet the financialisation framing opens up the argument that, while demand for industrial output may be global, so is demand for securities, and the reputation of securities backed by Australian household payments requires that households have sufficient income to keep meeting their contractual payments. The industrial and financialised version can each speak to the other.

In June 2017 the Governor of the Reserve Bank of Australia called on Australian workers to demand higher wages from their employers. While framed in the context of the need for stimulus to aggregate demand (our industrial view), it was perhaps also a concern that households secure higher incomes to reduce their default risk (our financialised view; see Greber 2017).

Accordingly, new agendas surely open up about labour's subsistence consumption. The industrial view focuses on this consumption as a bundle of goods and services, and seeks, including via strategic actions, to ensure that the bundle is sufficient to secure 'reasonable' living standards for workers. The financialisation view highlights that these subsistence goods and services are increasingly sold on contract, and they are thereby the actual or potential bearers of relations of securitisation. Subsistence for workers is increasingly becoming a financial asset for capital and this opens up possibilities for new forms of strategic action, as we will see shortly.

Moreover, financialisation highlights that new forms of risk have entered households, especially in relation to the stability of income and home affordability. Risk and volatility have to be seen as costs to households, yet these costs are ignored in the 'industrial' version of class relations.

As we saw in Chapter 6, surveys by financial institutions and governments consistently show that financial stress is increasing and that people report that the 'cost of living' is rising rapidly. This is an observation not consistent with standard measures of either inflation or wage rate growth, which, by conventional analysis, suggest that the cost of living is pretty stable. So why do people so consistently report cost of living stresses when the data seems to show the contrary? Partly, it is because conventional measures adopt an industrial framing and neglect a financialised framing.

Posed differently, people *do* put a price on risk and volatility, although there are not the data produced in Australia to verify it. But in the United States, US Financial Diaries is an organisation that closely monitors the budgets of a large sample of lower and middle-income households. They recount:

> When asked whether 'financial stability' or 'moving up the income ladder' is more important, 77% of the participants in the US Financial Diaries (USFD) research study chose 'financial stability'. (Morduch and Schneider 2013)

This is significant. Financial instability should be seen as a cost for households, which needs an explicit pricing in a risk/return trade-off. But it isn't. Nowhere are living standards being measured in a way that clearly puts a price on the risks and volatility of income or subsistence costs. Of course, one reason for there not being such a price is clear: if there were attempts to put a price on increasing household financial stress and volatility, that would only encourage households to put a claim on capital for compensation via wage increases.

For the class of capital, by contrast, the trade-off of risk and return is definitional and axiomatic. There is the basic understanding in finance that the higher the risk, the higher the expected/necessary average rate of return – all investment decisions by firms and banks are made on this principle. No one questions this trade-off for investors, yet no one yet raises it as a question for workers!

Indeed when the Australian Treasury compiled a 'Wellbeing Framework' (Gorecki and Kelly 2012) in recognition that wellbeing is broader than simply dollar income, it identified increasing levels of financial risk and complexity in daily life as two of the five key determinants that affect wellbeing. But rather than pricing this risk and proposing that it warrants financial compensation to households, as would be expected in capital markets, Treasury simply advocated a policy of financial literacy to assist better household financial decision-making (Bundey 2015)!

Financial literacy education should, if well taught, make the transfer of risks to households transparent, though it cannot eradicate the shift, for it is systemic. But current notions of financial literacy are all about training people for compliance with, and resilience in the face of, a still un-named process of risk shifting. If we reframe financial literacy politically, resilience is also a program to 're-silence' households in the face of growing risk in markets for employment, housing, retirement income, credit and so on. Its effect is to keep the household payments coming and to keep the consequences of financial failure private, as a statement of personal financial incompetence; not a systemic social failure. The wider social processes of financialisation are kept as individualised processes, and thereby socially normalised as 'personal' matters. In short, capital is compensated for risk; labour's new risks are largely un-named and uncompensated.

Yet volatility and contingency *are* a cost to households, and impact on living standards in ways that parallel how volatility impacts on returns to capital. Uncompensated, it is bad for households and for the overall economy. The Reserve Bank of Australia (Berger-Thomson et al. 2009) has found that for any given level of income, households that are worried about their future employment status consume less out of their current income, and so have lower living standards than households that are not concerned about employment.

In policy terms, this sort of evidence points to the need for financial regulators, as well as employment regulators, to monitor and measure the transfer of risks to households. The problem is that our society is using data sources that are predicated on an industrial view of the world: not a financialised one.

Conventional indices of living costs, like the consumer price index (CPI), have to be understood as indicators of a pre-risk-shifting world. The CPI is designed to measure changes in price of a certain range (a 'basket') of household commodities; not the cost of volatility nor the full cost of new additional commodities, which have now become a requirement of subsistence in the risk-shifting era. In particular, it ignores some of the forms of insurance many people now require (Bundey 2015) – like income protection – and the full cost (not just annual change in the cost) of professional financial advice.

The emphasis here on full cost is that the cost of financial planning is a new need for households: in principle, when it first enters the index it must be seen to add to the cost of living at its full cost and only thereafter at its annual increase in price. We contend it must first enter at full cost because until the 1980s no one 'needed' a financial planner because so many risks were held by the state and employers, and hence provided to households free of direct charge. When those risks shift, the cost of managing them shift, and add to the costs of living.

In short, therefore, the 'real' (financialised) costs of living for households today are largely unknown. That is not to say that there is not detailed financial monitoring of households. There is, and in historically unprecedented ways, as we showed in Chapter 6. But that monitoring is currently targeted to estimating the (default) risks that households pose to finance; not the (wellbeing) risks that finance poses to households.

The state's collection of detailed, up-to-date financial data on households in Australia is currently only a high policy priority in two areas: access to welfare (see Chapter 3) and default risk on securitised household payments.[3] In both cases the objective is household discipline: restricting access to publicly funded consumption and ensuring households stay on contract.

But what about the wellbeing risks that finance poses to households? To find about wellbeing in households, the RBA produces no data of its own. It currently relies on the household attitude data mainly coming out of corporate financial institutions and the Household Income and Labour Dynamics in Australia (HILDA) surveys. In this study, we have we have utilised these same sources, for these are the data available. HILDA surveys are funded by the Australian government and designed and managed by the Melbourne Institute, Melbourne University. Surveys are held only every four years,

---

3   The RBA-runs Securitisations Industry Forum to give up-to-date data on household default risk (see box in Chapter 6).

and data released two years after the survey. At times, therefore, 'current' data on household wellbeing that inform the state's financial and social policy are up to six years old! Conversely, the securitisation default risk data produced by the RBA are updated monthly. This data neglect by financial regulators of household wellbeing is itself a statement of policy neglect.

To redress this neglect, as a starting point we would propose the formation of a suite of state-administered datasets as an official alternative to those currently provided by large financial institutions. These institutions are players in the market and have a vested interest in policy outcomes and so should not be looked to by the state as the principal providers of household survey data. This is not a suggestion of corporate corruption of data; simply that it is well understood that data do not 'speak for themselves': they are always assembled to frame issues in particular ways. What suits financial institutions may not, and we contend does not, suit social policy agendas. We know the state would not look to trade unions to provide its labour market data!

The sorts of datasets we propose relate household financial risk indices that could be used in social policy related to living standards and the impacts of market volatility, and in public and workplace debates over household payments such as wages and welfare. We would also propose something akin to the *US Financial Diaries* that monitors the actual household life experiences of income volatility and lack of discretionary expenditure; not just statistical averages of income and spending patterns.

Such data would be more than a pretext for higher payments to workers/households, although, as those who have studied income inequality have shown, we have seen a large proportion of national income shifted away from wage and salary earners toward asset owners. Such data has potential to inform and shift public understanding of both the personal and economy-wide impacts of financial risk. At least there could then start an informed debate over the structural ramifications of financialised daily life.

Risking together

Divergence: thinking strategy otherwise

There is a critical point of difference between the industrial and the financialised relations shown in Table 7.1. Central to the conventional industrial depiction is that producing goods and services for the market in workplaces (or at home) is 'real' and 'productive', but finance is fictitious and speculative. Hence, for the industrial perspective, the politics of finance is about taming it – restricting its growth and regulating its activities to rein in speculation and greedy bankers – so that the focus can be on 'real' production and 'real' jobs.

This dichotomy is, we believe, politically unhelpful. There is no longer any clear differentiation between industry and finance. Whether we identify the increasing blending of activities of producing and consuming in the domain of conventional 'consumption' (such as packing your own groceries at the supermarket, renting a room in your home on Airbnb, and providing metadata to companies while you surf the net), or the domain of conventional 'production' (for example, that individual companies are increasingly undertaking integrated processes of making commodities and funding their creation and purchase), the conclusion is the same. Attempts to contrive a separation seem to be driven by old theories, from past eras, that cannot countenance the very blending process that finance has ushered in.

Moreover, a 'progressive' politics conceived in reining-in finance invariably leads to forms of state paternalism, like compulsory superannuation, financial literacy and even income management, designed to help people resist the temptations of borrowing to consume and of quick speculative investing. It involves an advocacy of state management of households and their financial relations that is, we believe, disempowering.

Our alternative position seeks to make no such judgements about one domain being 'productive' (virtuous) and the other 'unproductive' (parasitic). Accordingly, our agenda is not to place emphasis on taming finance, for it feels like a political distraction to focus on this agenda beyond what is already being advocated in mainstream politics and delivered by way of 'taming'. There is already established advocacy of such taming. For example, the 2014 *Financial System Inquiry, Final Report* (Murray 2014b) recommended that banks be required to hold higher reserves as security for when the next financial crisis comes. The ASIC's *Future of Financial Advice* (2014) and *Review of Remuneration of Mortgage Brokers* (2017) are further instances of regulation curtailing illegal fees collected by banks and other financial institutions. Whether such regulation is ever sufficient to eradicate fee gouging by financial institutions is a moot point. After a series of reports by investigative journalists into financial malpractice, a royal commission into banking was finally announced in December 2017.

Instead, our proposition is to look to the growth of finance and, most importantly, to financial calculation, coming to dominate more and more domains of social and economic life, and try and find the scope for political debate and action in response to this change.

The impacts of financialisation, both direct and indirect, surely need to be recognised and incorporated by trade unions: their members' relations with 'capital' have moved far beyond the conventional industrial depictions familiar to unions. Put simply, our working lives have become not just more unequal but financially riskier, and that relates not just to the world of paid work. We are proposing here a need for unions to shift focus: to become 'household unions', addressing their members' absorption of financial risks outlined in this book, as well as their established workplace roles. Household unionism in addition to industrial unionism would constitute a significant cultural shift for unions, but one we believe would take them to the frontier of their members' concerns, for it addresses the wider set of issues that determine people's standards of living. Some will say that unions are not capable of this shift. We see it as a historical challenge to Australian unionism.

Re-thinking

We take as our starting point that the juggernaut of financial calculation is in full motion, relatively undaunted by a financial crisis, and immune from calls for contrition; indeed it is now assured that it has the weight of the state behind it, and has itself come to set agendas within state policy.

We can frame a mode of resistance to such a force as a process of turning that force back on itself. It needs some clarification. Industrial capitalism, as the form of capitalism which has historically been most extensively analysed, involves the identity of the industrial factory and the process of turning inputs into outputs, in which industrial workers are central. One of labour's key threats is to stop that process. The withdrawal of labour from the workplace stops the transformation of inputs to outputs. Therein lies the political capacity of organised industrial labour (trade unions) to turn the momentum of capital back on itself, by stopping production.

Finance does not obviously fit into this sort of model. There is no 'factory' for many financial processes, and even where there is something analogous, such as in trading rooms, data entry and call centres, the withdrawal of labour is an improbable scenario: workplaces in finance are completely different from industrial workplaces; they are globally dispersed and they lack an 'industrial' culture. Similarly, to treat finance as a 'sector' of the economy (alongside 'industrial manufacturing') is to completely misunderstand the pervasive presence of finance across all 'sectors'. The evidence is clear that union densities are extremely low in the so-called 'finance sector', but our critical point is that finance is not limited to a 'sector'.

Finance may not fit the industrial model, but we can reframe the industrial model to fit finance. Strikes in 'industrial' workplaces were about slowing or stopping the process of turning inputs into outputs and thereby profits. Strikes were, in financial terms, about choking productive liquidity of employers. As business logistics and 'just-in-time' technologies entered conventional industry, so too were strikes about leverage: that stopping one component of production could stop the whole show up and down supply chains. So a reason for capital's development of contracting out, contingent employment and global supply chains was precisely to deny industrial workers their capacity to exercise leverage to choke off liquidity.

To many, this has been disempowering: if workers got outmanoeuvered in relation to industrial capital, how do you challenge something as fluid and as nebulous as finance, which cannot be pinned down and corralled in a specific place? Finance, it seems, is almost untouchable on those industrial terms.

But our concern is finance as a process of calculation and logic, and one that pervades all 'sectors' of the economy, households and government too. In fact, finance and financial risk shifting is both an economic project of realigning economic power and a political agenda of normalising and enforcing it. As an economic project and political agenda, finance also has vulnerabilities. It is an activity built on liquidity and leverage. Neither of these attributes is immune from political contestation.

Leverage and liquidity are closely related. Leverage means holding financial positions in excess of actual wealth – be it by borrowing and purchasing assets with debt, or purchasing assets with higher risks that you can directly afford to hold. Anyone with leverage is vulnerable to asset prices going in unexpected directions.[4] The key to holding leveraged positions is that markets have to be liquid so that assets can be quickly turned back into cash as a way of bailing out of a vulnerable position. That is, there needs to be the capacity to sell out of leveraged positions into a market that will buy those positions at a 'fair' price, not one shot down by panic of market failure. Runs on banks are the classic image of illiquidity in relation to debt. Crashes in mortgage-backed securities and credit default swap markets, as occurred in 2008, are the image of illiquidity in relation to risk holdings.

But leverage and liquidity are their own vulnerability and therein lies the political capacity of an alternative politics to turn the momentum of (financial) capital back on itself. They are fragile. They rely on market players holding their nerve and on confidence in a constant, high level of turnover (churning) in markets. That's what failed in 2007 and 2008. The details of that fragility may have changed, but what remains are leveraged players with a vulnerability to sudden illiquidity.

Challenging these assumptions was the symbolic success of the 'Occupy Wall Street' movement. By blocking the physical spaces around the New York financial district there was a challenge to the assumed knowledge and confidence of Wall Street traders and a challenge to the liquidity of the market – albeit that obstructing bankers and traders in their daily movements is no more than a symbolic gesture. So protests like 'Occupy' could not last, at least not in the form of occupation of physical places, because they were obstructing and calling out rather than challenging logics. Moreover, as symbolic

---

4   It would be simplest to say 'down', but there are derivative products that make profits when prices fall. Finance trades volatility; the ups and the downs.

challenges, 'Occupy' was about holding ground space as a point of resistance to something that is essentially in outer-space (in satellites!). This is what makes traditional forms of protest so difficult.

But leverage offers other political potentials. Precision of measurement is critical when trades are made on the smallest margins of gain. If these small margins cannot be accurately and reliably measured, the momentum of finance is severely undermined. The big profit comes from holding leveraged positions in those trades, as we saw in Chapter 5 in relation to hedge funds: a trader may have $100 of underlying wealth, but be highly leveraged with $700 of loans, and so trades on a book of $800. So every gain (or loss) on a $800 book is carried by the underlying $100 asset position. A 1 percent gain/loss on $800 expresses an 8 percent gain/loss for the underlying $100. A mere 12.5 percent loss sees the trader lose 100 percent of underlying wealth!

Precision of measurement relates directly to households, for households are critical to finance as borrowers (debtors), as asset holders (via superannuation) and as the providers of the payments that go into asset-backed securities. The fact that so much effort goes into measuring and managing household financial risk, as we saw in Chapter 6, is testament to the power of households to challenge this precision. As we have mentioned several times, the 'subprime crisis' in the USA was a clear demonstration of this power. Many mortgage holders stopped repaying their debts, and in largely unpredictable ways. There are indeed parallels between a mass strike in a factory and a mass failure to repay mortgages. The trouble was that there was nothing organised or strategic about those mortgage defaults, so the analogy is limited. Those people who stopped paying their mortgages did not do it conceived in collective political strategy, but as a mass of discrete individuals.

The key here is the capacity to act unpredictably in an organised way: to treat unpredictability as a financial option. The 'right to strike' is an option, and the right to not pay bills in accordance with predicted default risk is also an option.

Re-acting

Here we offer a broad reframing of the possible politics, borrowing the terminology of our colleagues Randy Martin and Bob Meister.

In industrial capitalism, the working class's capacity for mass strikes was, in financial language, the 'option' to create an industrial liquidity crisis – a 'dis-accumulation' of capital. The welfare state and risk sharing arrangements at work were the political price exacted for the working class *not* exercising the option of a General Strike in the early 20th century. In financialised capitalism, households' capacity to withhold contractual payments is the option to create General Illiquidity. So what is the financial price to be extracted for *not* exercising that option? What is the financial equivalent of a welfare state?

Part of the answer surely has something to do with acceptable and stable standards of living for all, as the minimum social priority that must be met before returns on capital (profits, interest and rent) become the drivers of economic and social policy. That is, our proposition is not just a one-off redistribution of income, but a redistribution of control over access to income. This would be the exact inversion of what we are currently seeing, where basic elements of living standards – universal provision for health, education, pensions, housing, transport, and various forms of social inclusion – are all being reduced in the name of being 'unaffordable' if profits are to be guaranteed. Yet, as we saw in massive bank bailouts in 2008, the 'unaffordable' suddenly becomes 'affordable', including by capital, if the alternative is the threat of rapid dis-accumulation. This potential threat to capital awaits an organisational form and strategy, but we can name it here as capital's new exposure to labour.

There is no single politics that follows from this framing, for people have different images of good strategy and good outcomes. But we want to present a few agendas we believe worthy of consideration.

One possible agenda is centred on a reframing of debt. The principle critique of debt is that ordinary people find themselves in more and more debt and, with growing interest payments, less and less discretionary income. A vicious cycle of debt growth can follow.

A growing level of debt has also generated the emergence of a politics of debt refusal, growing out of the Occupy Wall Street movement, and the analysis of debt by David Graber (2011). In the Bay Area (San Francisco), for example, an organisation called Strike Debt, now nationally expanded as The Debt Collective, campaigns under the slogan 'you are not a loan', and advocates debt refusal.

Debt refusal is a statement that, for many people, personal debt has grown so high as to become incompatible with socially accepted minimum living standards; that this debt is now socially destructive. The politics which follows is that, as with a strike at the workplace, there is scope for financial strikes. Instead of feeling personal shame because of financial incompetence, there can be a collective politics of insolvency that announces that debt levels are unreasonable and unsustainable; indeed perhaps that finance knows this to be the case and that such strikes can 're-balance' financial relations with households.

It is an interesting politics, yet it is also a strangely antiquarian one, for the burdens of debt, and the life of indenture which follows has, as Graber's history of debt reminds us, a multiple thousand year history. Campaigning against debt may be a protest against capital in one of its oldest and most important financial forms, but it does not fully engage capitalism at its 21st-century frontier. A politics centred on debt is an engagement with the state of household budgets (a protest against financial imbalance); not a protest against risk shifting.

Moreover, there is the concern that debt signals a common, but not a shared, point of political resistance. Debt represents the private, individualised form of subordination to finance: each person renounces his or her own debt. It would be a politically brave act for the individuals who participate, for they damage their personal credit scores. But this denial does not constitute a collective politics (as, for example, a strike in a workplace does) except in the sense that multiple individuals, acting simultaneously, constitute a mass rather than collective social statement of protest.

There needs to be an alternative political response, in which the political action is innately collective. The process of securitisation of household payments (see Chapter 4) sees the repayments on household loans and other contracts bundled together, and sold as a financial asset (asset-backed securities). So unlike debt, which is defined in terms of individual payments, each of these securities innately involves bundles of collective household payments. This form of subordination to finance is social in a way that debt per se is not.

An alternative politics opens up around rights and conditions of access to household expenditures that are already being drawn through financial markets or are potentially securitisable: to things like housing, health care, education and utilities. These have long been considered sites of struggle for social justice and minimum standards of living, but they now take on a new potency as a site of conflict with capital; a conflict based on payment refusal and risking together to block capital's liquidity risk spread.

In general, we know that households are reluctant to default on contractual payments: we saw in Chapter 5 that almost all securitised household payments are based on non-discretionary expenditures; most of them rightly classified as subsistence needs. To default means to lose access to subsistence consumption (housing, water, gas and electricity, a car, etc.). Household reluctance to default is key to the financial market desire for securities backed by household payments.

But if it became known that households might default or stop repaying in strategic ways, even partially, in concerted forms and unpredictably – inconsistently with their ascribed role as low default risk – this would profoundly challenge the securities markets.

An alternative politics involves starting with the claim that the highest social priority is the subsistence requirements of households rather than the yield on securities: that the liquidity of the securities needs to be seen as resting on the satisfaction of household subsistence.

So a politics opens around what we might call 'liquidity refusal': a strategy to block or challenge capital's risk spread, or the difference between the risks faced by households and the risk of securities built on household contract payments. This could be a politics exercised by unions or by other social movements.

Imagine the following. We conceive of a household budget that meets a socially acceptable minimum standard of living, and identify within that budget the range of non-discretionary expenditures (it will be most of them) integral to that minimum. But how affordable are these expenditures? Analysis in Chapter 6 shows that a significant portion of the population is either currently in some degree of financial stress, unable to meet basic payments without some significant sacrifice, or at risk of stress should small changes in income or expenditure occur. For financial markets and central banks, this 'significant sacrifice' is only a concern if it leads to actual default or non-repayment. Yet for social analysis, the 'significant sacrifice' is a concern in itself. These households, for whatever reason, lack sufficient or stable income to consume at a socially conceived adequate level. Either incomes must go up and be stabilised, or the prices of targeted subsistence items need to go down.

Of course there is a political agenda of pursuing higher wages and/ or social security payments to enable households to meet payments. Perhaps, alternatively, a politics lies in the option of mass (partial) default or 'liquidity refusal' – a widespread and targeted refusal to pay (or even delaying payment) some part of bills on subsistence contracts. A union (or collection of unions and/or other social movements) may, for example, take on the role of agency for their members' utility contracts; in effect as a payment intermediary for members. The organisation holding the contracts might then declare that it would not pay a particular sort of bill during a particular month or period. They may declare a partial and temporary non-payment, because, when markets are liquid and leveraged, even partial and temporary non-payment is a threat to asset values.

The effect would be to undermine the value of securities backed by household payments, creating a liquidity crisis in those products, and losses for the owners of these securities and insecurity for financial markets generally. Indirectly, such a strategy targets the providers of subsistence items whose financial strategy requires that they securitise their contracts, and in so doing put the rate of return on the security as the preeminent determinant of service delivery. Of course, there may and probably will be contractual penalties for participants in a 'strike' or financial action, but nothing like the losses incurred by withdrawing wage labour for days or weeks to win a pay rise.

Perhaps the response will be that it is not as simple as this, and indeed it is not. But it is worth exploring, and if our analysis is sound, it may be necessary to do so in some form or another. What we are really trying to do here is to create a language in which the experience of living in a world in which financial risk is being driven down to individual levels can be discussed, understood, and contested. Our framing here is a way of thinking issues of risk, finance, leverage and liquidity differently, so as to wrest the initiative of financial change away from capital and the state, and claim it for a progressive politics; a politics conceived in risking together.

8
Short cuts: lean, prime propositions

In a world increasingly driven by finance (financialisation), households face many sorts of financial and economic risks. There always were risks, but in the past few decades they have increasingly been passed from employers to workers and from the state to households. These risks are now the jobs of workers and households to manage. Our project was to identify what is systematic about these risk transfers, in the hope of giving the process a name and framing some collective responses.

Those responses need to be different from any previous responses. The key to an effective response in the current era is to find capital's evolving frontier of change, for at the frontier there is always vulnerability. The frontier we have identified is around households, risk and liquidity and we look to ways to frame the potential for turning that change back on capital, as a means to advance progressive social and economic goals.

We will work our way through these frontier issues as we go. We focus first on three domains of risk transfer in financialised society: income risk, household balance sheet risk and household liquidity risk.

Income risk

Once this could have been termed workplace or employment risk, but now so many people don't have a specific place of work, or even an 'employer' as such, that the terms 'workplace' and 'employment' are not sufficient. The term 'income risk' thus also enables inclusion of 'gig economy' jobs like driving for Uber or renting a room on Airbnb, and production occurring within the household. It also includes the myriad new forms of seemingly incidental and social activities that are being variously called 'shadow work' or 'prosumption' (production by consumers, both deliberate, like scanning and bagging your own groceries, or incidental, like the data you provide via your internet use). But here we seek to identify not just new forms of work or value creation, but how 'workers' now have to manage new forms of risks in accessing income from production.

Income risk is pretty well understood, so needs only a brief mention. It is about processes like the casualisation and subcontracting of work (where people are nominally self-employed, but in effect work under the direction of a manager), cashing out or trading away working conditions and lengthening unpaid overtime and working life too. These contractual changes are said to make employment more precarious for workers because many of the risks of variability in work – its amount, time and delay in payment – are all being systematically passed to the workers. Workers are managing risks and costs that were once the responsibility of employers or the state. Household incomes are, as a direct consequence, now less predictable (more volatile).

These growing income risks carried by workers are generally not explicitly compensated (especially as casual work generalises, and the casual 'loading' is undermined). Once the measure of a minimum weekly wage gave way to a minimum hourly rate (making workers adjust their working weeks to secure living standards [or not]), our society gave up connecting paid work to minimum and stable living standards. In debates about wage levels – for example, the Fair Work Commission's 'Annual Wage Review' – there is no reference to compensation for increased risk. Capital, on the other hand, has a deeply embedded and explicit understanding that it demands a trade-off between taking on more risk and expected higher returns: it is argued that riskier investments require a higher yield to justify taking the risk.

What's the difference here between investors and workers? Social convention says that investors are entitled to be choosy – they must be seduced into investing – while ordinary people require no such compensation. They have no choice but to work. So the effect is that workers absorb risk and by that absorption investors achieved higher yield at lower risk.

Part of the problem is that no one is really measuring this risk transfer and its costs for workers. In measurement, we use old, not-financialised, measures like the consumer price index (CPI) or average wages: measures that don't take account that a risky income entails costs that a safe, stable income does not, and that there are now forms of insurance that households have to undertake to avoid excessive costs of some life-course risks.

We need official, detailed measures of household risk, and a social debate about how to price them. It is analytical negligence that sees the Reserve Bank and other financial and economic regulators pay attention only to default risk and ignore living standard risk. This is an urgent debate and one in which unions and other NGOs should be taking the lead.

Balance sheet risk

Households are now also borrowing more than ever to buy houses, cars, education and consumer goods. This growth in debt is especially tied to increasing mortgages, with more and more of household income being allocated to mortgage repayments. (The same applies to rent too.)

Many people talk about mounting household risk from so much borrowing. There are also predictions that this mounting debt is unsustainable when interest rates rise, or unemployment occurs and house prices fall. Some predict an imminent financial crash. They may be right, for who can predict the future, but we believe that things are more complex than simply the growing level of debt.

Households are borrowing more and more, but they are also saving more and more, especially via compulsory superannuation. And they are accumulating more assets – many now own (fractions of) houses which have escalated in value. Borrowing has facilitated many people, accidentally or intentionally, to be property speculators. For many younger people, on the other hand, the prospect of entering the housing market now requires two incomes and an increasing proportion of that income to be allocated to debt repayments, and even then there may be insufficient funds.

But the issue goes beyond experiences of debt to the associated issues of risk. It is, more broadly, about households as pseudo-businesses – the income vs expenditure and assets vs liabilities positions of households. The critical issue is household capacity to service debts, rather than simply the level of debt per se, and about the volatility of income and asset values. Different households have different financial exposure positions. Some households are in the red; others are in the black. Predictably, high wealth households are in the black, but from there down it is quite complex. Young households are likely to be in the red, as are rural ones. Middle-income households are more likely to be deeply in the red than low- or high-income households – because low income households without a mortgage carry lower debt levels, and high income households have the capacity to service higher debt and have substantial equity in their homes as well as other assets.

These household specifics we will return to shortly. Our proposition to this point is that there has been a critical shift in the financial market expectations placed on households: they are expected to use their 'balance sheets' to manage risk and chase yield (returns) outside of paid work. We can depict the household as a sort of hedge fund (we call it a 'household hedge fund'). Households are expected to borrow, and use the borrowed money to take 'long' and 'short' positions (just like the original hedge funds). Long positions are investments expected to generate long-term returns. The obvious ones for households are investments in a house, a car, increasingly in education and training, and, whether you want to or not, in superannuation. Short positions are where (or whether) you cover or 'hedge' your exposure to the long ones. The main short positions of households are insurance policies – mortgage and home insurance, income protection and life insurance as well as car insurance, but bank savings deposits and working longer hours also fit here.

What can we observe about these household as hedge fund positions?

1. They are increasingly leveraged. Because people are borrowing more, the stakes are getting higher and higher – there is greater vulnerability to a downturn in the economy, but also even to an upturn if it manifests as rapidly increasing interest rates.
2. For most they are illiquid (they cannot be easily sold). The long positions are, for most people, very narrow and fixed in scope. The assets they hold are: their skills (human capital), equity in a house and a car, some superannuation and home contents. On the other hand, further up the income scale are investment properties and other assets in shares, trusts, etc. and these people hold much more diversified and liquid long positions.
3. For most they are under-hedged (over-exposed to risk). Households tend to underinsure – their 'short' positions often do not adequately hedge their 'long' ones. For poor people it is about affordability; rich people can afford to gamble. But for the middle it is a major risk.

In the search for yield, households have few choices. They have to invest in skills and in home contents (and often a car) and our culture (and social contract) says they should aspire to invest in housing too. It is innate to being a household that they have their major investments tied up in these assets, but none of these is easy to sell – skills are impossible to sell, for they are part of the person.

Liquidity risk

Balance sheet risk leads to liquidity risk, and here there is a contrast with 'real' hedge funds. Except for the households towards the top of the wealth profile, household assets are incredibly undiversified and illiquid, because their assets are the essential means of subsistence. Households can't sell out of the asset class of housing (they can sell particular houses, though it is heavily taxed, and move between owning and renting, but they need housing). Nor can they sell out of utilities or health insurance. These are things that are either legal requirements or that people need for daily life. So people don't trade them willy-nilly as market prices go up and down. Illiquid and undiversified assets make households especially vulnerable to economic and financial shocks – especially unemployment or income drop, and to falls in house prices, or to rising rents.

Yet other asset holders like (real) hedge funds, investment banks and superannuation funds are liquid, and they trade their assets actively – often many times a day. They can trade out of risk in a way households cannot. What's more, households can't declare themselves bankrupt as easily as companies can. Households have to keep paying and paying till they meet their contractual obligations, even if their debts and commitments exceed their assets.

So this is the sense in which households systematically carry liquidity risk in the same way that they systematically carry income risk: in both cases the risks are the penalty of being a person (labour in production or a household in liquid financial markets) whose life inevitably involves both using their skills to earn money and spending money to acquire the basics of life – food, shelter, heat, etc. In the market for risk trading, households are sitting ducks.

On the other hand, the assets built on those illiquid household payments – mortgage- and asset-backed securities – are themselves highly liquid: they are actively traded in global markets. The difference is critical. In their daily lives people hold illiquid positions, and make regular rent, mortgage and other contract payments. Financial institutions which buy the securities backed by these payments hold highly liquid positions: they hold exposure to the performance of household payments, but they don't own the house or the rental or other contract. They can trade in and out of this asset class in a way that households can't.

What follows?

So what political issues follow from our depictions of the three risks?

Confronting households' income risk is an area where trade unions have struggled for well over a century and a half. Their long-term successes are well understood in creating safer workplaces and better and more securely remunerated terms of employment (the living wage). Their more recent successes have been at best modest, and largely focused on holding ground against attempts to shift more and more risks onto 'workers'. Some will even say trade unions have been defeated over the past 30 years, and that this acknowledgement has to be the starting point of rebuilding.[1] Nonetheless, unions will keep playing their historic role, though we have already identified an area of data gathering and measurement of the costs of risk where they can take a lead.

Perhaps also their focus needs to shift to other sites of relations between households and capital, in recognition of the expanding frontiers of that relationship.

The domain of household balance sheet risk is a difficult one politically, for it potentially divides rather than unifies people. Home owners want house prices to increase; prospective buyers want them to fall. Workers want a bigger claim on company revenues; shareholders (including those workers with superannuation savings) want profits to be bigger. The only general social observation we can make here is that people are effectively forced to become players in the market for balance sheet risk. If you don't borrow to invest (in your education, in housing etc.), chances are you will find yourself in more precarious forms of employment and earning a lower lifetime income. It may also mean that you retire later and on a very meagre state pension – a pension increasingly conceived as being for those cast as failures in balance sheet management.

Here is a broader social and cultural politics of challenging the social and economic order that has turned all of us into gamblers and risk traders in our household hedge funds.

Liquidity risk is really important politically, and herein lies our distinctive contribution. If it sounds surprising that we see a politics in financial liquidity, just recall the United States subprime crisis of 2007 and 2008. Key to it was that large numbers of households in the USA stopped paying mortgages (mortgage contracts they were never in a position to repay). This payment halt crashed the mortgage-backed securities market, and this cascaded into a massive global crisis.

---

1   Sam Gindin's analysis is critical here, and we appreciate personal communication on these themes. See, for example, Maisano (2013).

There are two key points here. First, subprime was a demonstration that households are critical to financial market stability, and to the wellbeing of the global economy at large. We saw this power expressed negatively and unintentionally. But it *was* revealed.

Second, the key reason the crash spread beyond those holding mortgage-backed securities and into a full-blown crisis is because broader financial market liquidity dried up. Everyone in the market who thought these securities were very liquid and low risk suddenly feared they had exposure to 'toxic assets' and would be unable to sell them, so they engaged in panic selling, but no one wanted to buy!

So what is the political possibility here? We need briefly to explain securitisation to push our argument on. Securitisation is where a financial institution converts a future stream of income into a financial instrument in return for current cash. The most recognised thing to sell is a set of monthly mortgage repayments (mortgage-backed securities) – not just the mortgage payments of one household, but the payment streams of thousands of households bundled together. And it is not just mortgages that get securitised. It is all forms of debt (car loans, credit card and student debt too) and it is not just debts, but increasingly also other contracts, especially electricity, gas and mobile phone bills, and insurance contracts like home and health insurance (notice that for households these contracted, regular bill payments manifest no differently from debt repayments).

Financial markets love these types of products because they are thought to be safe, and in a world conspicuously lacking yield-generating safe assets (unlike Treasury bonds which are becoming less safe and with low, even negative yield), the expanding asset class of household payments is a godsend.

Why are they considered safe, when they crashed in 2007? Because a concerted effort is being made by financial institutions and governments to make them safe, or at least to clearly differentiate those which are and are not safe. Financial markets believe if you target the contracts and monitor payments carefully, people *will* keep paying. After all, to not pay the electricity or the mortgage means you lose your means of subsistence. But to be sure, financial institutions monitor and manage household balance sheets really closely. They are getting to know far more about the accounts and financial viability of households than they do about corporations and other businesses.

They have ready access to all our financial, income and spending data, and they build profiles of the sorts of people at high risk of default – what suburbs they live in, their employment and credit histories, what they spend money on, etc. They know who fits this profile (who is 'at risk') and who is actually running behind in contract payments. So we find targeted monitoring (the 'at risk' versus the 'risk managing'), as well as financial exclusion, to make sure the securitisation process focuses on payments by 'safer' households.

As households, we are being classified in terms of our repayment riskiness (a process known in finance as tranching) and monitored on the basis that what really matters about us is not our standard of living or general wellbeing, but our reliability and dependability as contract payers: our success as household hedge funds.

Herein lies a politics at the frontier of financial innovation. There is collective power in being treated as, or expected to play the role of, safe players in a liquid market, for, if households become 'unsafe', securities prices crash and financial markets freeze up. We would see 2007 all over again. The key is how to transfer or shift liquidity and balance sheet risk back to finance (to be – or threaten to be – financially 'unsafe'), and how to make this capacity a point of effective bargaining.

Thinking in novel ways about how to find the political potency of mass bill-paying may well turn out to be a critical frontier. It is an exciting potential direction of unionism. Political potency needs coordinated, large-scale decisions to act unpredictably – or not in accordance with their allocated, tranched risk profile. This would manifest as concerted, organised refusals to meet (some part of) contract payments over some time period. Perhaps a response is that this is simply irresponsible. But think of it this way. If people unite to appoint a collective organisation – like a union – to manage for them their bill payments, the capacity exists. We've termed it 'household unionism', in recognition that households' relations with capital now cover many more facets of life than just paid work.

If a union contends that a wage is not sufficient to meet basic living standards, it may call a production strike. Alternatively, it could say that mortgage, electricity, phone and insurance costs are too high to secure reasonable living standards, and declare a partial strike on contract payments: a liquidity strike. Because these contract payments are securitised in one way or another in liquid financial markets, there can be a really big impact – potentially much bigger, quicker and less costly than a production strike. (In financial language this would be framed as exercising 'leverage'.)

How might this be coordinated? How would it work? Of course we understand that readers would like concrete answers and a clear program of action. And we are indeed working with others on practical initiatives to promote alternative strategies. Those particular initiatives may eventually be enacted; they may not.

There are two points to make. One is that we don't want the significance of our analysis in this book to be reduced to our personal opinions about goals and strategies. Many goals and strategies could be built on this analysis. They should and must develop separately from us. The second thing is that strategies require organisations to advocate and enact them and, when it all boils down, the politics has to be played out by organisations that will have particular circumstances and distinctive problems to address. They will have their own take on strategy.

We are therefore intentionally not presenting our own manifesto for change. It is too easy for scholars to be advocates of 'effective' policies and 'desirable' outcomes, then sit back hoping that good ideas will somehow be enacted. The process of change is more serious, complicated and exciting than that!

Appendix 1
Types of derivatives: futures, swaps, options and securities

For those interested in looking further into the nature of financial derivatives, in this Appendix we introduce the three key categories of derivatives: futures, options and swaps, and securities as a key derivative-based financial product. Remember that they are about different ways of trading risk exposures, enabling parties to the trade to take-on or sell-off risk.

Futures

A futures contract is fairly straightforward. It is about agreeing to trade something at a price determined now, but to be exchanged or settled at a time in the future. It could be a barrel of oil in three months, or a government bond in three days. What is critical here is that it involves trading on where the price will move between the time the contract is signed and the settlement time in the contract. If you think the price of oil will increase (or you fear it will increase) over three months, you could lock in a price now, for a transaction in three months. If you guess right, and the price of oil goes up, you have a win – the person on the other side of the contract has to buy oil in the spot market in three months at the higher price and sell it to you at the agreed lower price (although these transactions are generally settled in cash, not the transfer of barrels of oil per se). Conversely, if you guess wrong, and the price of oil falls, you make a loss – you will be buying oil in three months at a price above what you could get it for in the spot market.

It can be seen immediately that this is a good activity for speculators who want to bet on the price of oil, but it also provides heavy users of oil, like airlines and trucking companies, and suppliers of oil, with an ability to lock in future prices, for their budgeting may benefit from the certainty, even if it may sometimes result in buying/ selling oil at a less than the best future price available. This latter role is called 'hedging'. It involves using such contracts to cover exposure to market volatility. But whether any particular futures transaction is actually a speculative position or a hedge is often impossible for an outsider to tell.

For our study, we can see that there are elements of a futures contract in employment: it locks in a price of labour for the duration of an enterprise agreement or other contract. The speculative element for the worker is that they are locking in a wage when their bargaining power might go up or down over the life of the agreement. The employer's speculative exposure is that they are not sure how much profit workers at a particular price will contribute. If profits fall, they will make a loss on employment; if they go up, there will have been something akin to a speculative gain. We can see why employers would want to shorten the duration of employment contracts, to reduce this form of speculation. Other contracts, such as for mobile phones, can also be seen to have similar futures-like attributes.

Swaps

The form of derivative which warrants our next focus is an option, but because we want to develop options theory in more detail, we will jump straight to swaps. Swaps are, as the name suggests, where two parties to a contract swap exposure to each other's asset but without normally swapping the underlying asset itself. The most common swap is an interest rate swap, where one party may borrow at a fixed interest rate, but would prefer to repay a variable rate loan. (They may borrow at a fixed rate because they get a better deal; they may prefer to repay at a variable rate, because their revenues vary with the rate of interest, such as with a bank.) Conversely, there will be another party that has exactly the opposite conditions. So they agree to swap their loan repayment terms while retaining formal ownership of their original repayment terms. The holder of the fixed rate loan repays the variable rate loan and vice versa. So if interest rates go up, the owner of the fixed interest loan, who now holds exposure to the variable rate loan, has to make higher loan repayments. It all sounds arcane, but the Bank for International Settlements calculated that at June 2016 there was $US327 trillion globally tied up globally in interest rate swaps measured by notional amount outstanding (BIS 2016: 13). For the Australian market the figure was $US12 trillion (Garner, et al. 2016).

There are swaps of many more things than interest rates – currencies and equities are prevalent other swaps. (With an equity swap you retain ownership of the shares, but swap exposure to share price appreciation and/or dividend payments.)

The idea of swaps – of exchanging exposures to assets but without exchanging ownership of those assets – is a powerful analytical device. It is in fact one way that finance has been able unlock the capacity to access your attributes and exposures, and find ways of trading them.

Options

The form of derivative we need to understand in a bit more detail is called an option. Options are like insurance policies, but they apply to many more contexts than we would usually associate with insurance.

In simple terms, an option gives its holder the right to buy an asset (say a barrel of oil) at a certain price at a certain future time, but not the obligation to purchase. (There are also options that involve the right but not the obligation to sell at a certain price and future time.) Think of the oil option and you will see that it puts a cap on the price you'll have to pay for oil. If the option is to buy oil for $150 (the term used is that the option has a 'strike price' of $150) in three months, and the actual price goes to $160, you exercise the option, and buy oil for $150 (plus the price you paid to purchase the option). But if the price of oil turns out to be less than the strike price, you do not exercise the option – you tear up the contract. It is immediately apparent that such a contract enables you to cover one direction of risks on the future price of a barrel of oil (in our case, it involves selling off the unwelcome risk of a price rise, but retaining the welcome risk of a price fall). It is a form of insurance against an oil price rise. Notice also that, because these option positions are generally settled in cash, not in deliveries of barrels of oil, it is risk positions on movements in the price of oil being traded, not oil itself.

How does this apply to daily life when hardly any of us are financial market traders? We observe that an increasing range of aspects of daily life embody the principle of an option. The obvious cases are various forms of insurance: the car, home and health. These can also be understood as options contracts: paying an insurance premium gives you the right to car, home and body 'repairs' over the year, as stated in the contract, but not the requirement of the smash repairer to work on your car even if there are no dents, or the surgeon to operate even though you have no ailments. You are buying a right to these things should certain triggers occur (a car crash/theft or an illness).

But our purpose is not simply to say that insurance can also be framed as an options contract: that may be analytically interesting, but of no real significance. Our purpose is to say that these sorts of contracts are spreading into our daily lives and the logic of some conventional practices can now be reframed as processes of risk transfer and risk management through options. Here are a few examples from the domains of consumption, work, finance and the state.

- When you see a good on sale in a store and put it on lay-by, you are effectively purchasing an option: the right to buy that good at the sale price in the future. If you choose not to buy, you must pay a small 'transaction' fee, which could be considered the price of the option.[1] One of the reasons you might not exercise the option is that the price may be even lower at a subsequent sale or in another store, but you have purchased protection against having to buy the good at a higher price.

---

1   See www.accc.gov.au/content/index.phtml/itemId/815403.

- A 'zero hours' contract is an employment contract that guarantees the worker no actual hours of work, but the obligation to work when requested. It is, in financial terms, an employer buying an option on a worker: the right, but not the obligation to set them to work at some time in the future.
- From the point of view of employers ('capital'), employment in general can be seen as an option: the right, but not the obligation to employ people. Employers pay taxes to have a trained and orderly labour force. This is the price of the option. By holding this option, employers may choose to offer work that will lead to production and profitability. If the going wage is higher than the 'strike price' (i.e. the wage is deemed too high and not consistent with profitability), the option will not be exercised. Self-funded education then appears as a free option to employers.
- When you take out a loan at the bank you have choice between the fixed and floating rate repayments. If you hold a floating rate, but then anticipate rates will rise, you can pay a premium (like the price of an option) to move to a fixed rate. It is something like purchasing an option in interest rate risk.
- Being the purchaser of a house or another asset in which you have little equity and a large debt is like holding a series of right-to-buy options (called a call option) on your own house. If the house price falls below a strike price, you don't exercise the option (you are insolvent) and you foreclose. If the strike price goes up, you exercise the option and continue loan repayments. Financial legislation seeks to make non-repayment harder and the consequences of any non-payment or foreclosure more onerous. This makes the cost of using the foreclosure option more expensive.
- There has been a shift in the state's welfare system from unemployment benefits (seen as a subsistence payment) to 'workfare' (seen as the requirement to undertake training as a condition of 'welfare' and penalties such as loss of payment for those who do not apply for jobs). It looks like the state buying an options contract on unemployed people: having the right, but not the obligation to require someone to work.
- Superannuation similarly has option dimensions for the state. The state has a contingent obligation to pay you a pension. The 'strike

price' is the minimum income you draw down from your superannuation that precludes you from accessing the aged pension. Above that income, the option is not exercised, and you receive no (or a partial) pension. Below that income, a pension is paid. In policy terms, the state is seeking to compel people to save in ways in which they will not permit you to exercise your public pension option.

Securities

Technically, securities are the application of swaps and futures, and so formally do not warrant a separate heading, but it will add to clarity if we consider them discretely.

Securitisation is a process of bundling together a large number of contracts that generate income streams through periodic (often monthly or annual) payments – things like loans, insurance policies, council rates and purchases with periodic payments (like phone bills) – and selling off the regular payments, but not selling off the contracts. Because they involve sale of exposure to the 'performance' of the contract, but not selling the underlying asset, we can think of them as derivatives. The owner of mortgage-backed securities (MBSs) (securities which generate an income stream based on regular mortgage payments) does not own any mortgages, and certainly not the houses that underlie the mortgages.

The person who sells the security – say a bank – wants cash now (for example, to make new housing loans) rather than the regular payments over five or ten years. The buyer of the security has cash, but wants to acquire a regular flow of payments (for example, a superannuation fund which receives regular money from wage deductions, and is paying out monthly pensions). In the process, it will be noted that there is not simply a trade of future income flows for cash; it is also the case that the risk of default on those regular payments has transferred from the owner of the underlying asset to the purchaser of the security. In the case of MBSs made famous in the GFC, the buyers of the MBSs had bought the risk of mortgagees defaulting on their payments, and when defaults started rising, the value of the MBSs started crashing. The owners of the MBSs, as owners of a financial exposure, have no recourse to the value of the houses that underlie the mortgages.

The lesson learnt was not so much that these risks were too financially and socially dangerous, but that the risks of default must be carefully monitored. People may be prepared to buy risky MBSs (with higher probabilities of default), but only if there is a much higher expected return on the security to compensate for the higher risk. But the critical issue is that buyers want to know the risk of the security they are purchasing. We explored this issue further in Chapter 6 in identifying how household finances are now being more closely monitored (or is it surveilled?).

The explanation of these essential derivative products, while not as technical as you will find in a finance textbook, is sufficient to understand the core logic of risk trading as a social as well as economic process.

Appendix 2
Data sources and calculations

Chapter 5 included data drawn primarily from the Australian Bureau of Statistics (ABS) – Cat. 6530.0, Household Expenditure Survey, Australia, 1984 to 2015-16 and Cat. 6523.0, Household Income and Income Distribution, Australia, 1999–2000 to 2011–12, and the Household Income and Labour Dynamics in Australia (HILDA) Survey 2015. While the ABS data is cross-sectional, the HILDA data is a household-based panel study that enables the same group of households and individuals from those households to be tracked over time. The HILDA survey began in 2001 and surveyed 7,682 households covering 19,914 individuals. It collects information about economic and subjective wellbeing, labour market dynamics and family dynamics. At the time of writing, the most recently available data were for the year 2014.

There are six statistical issues in Chapter 5 that require further explanation.

1. Quintiles of income and wealth

Much economic data relating to wealth, income and expenditure of either individuals or households is analysed by stratifying the sample into subgroups based on their level of either income or wealth. These groups may be called quartiles, quintiles or deciles – the name simply reflects the number of subgroups or strata under analysis. The rationale for stratifying on this basis is an often well-founded assumption that both households and individuals of similar wealth or income level behave financially in a similar manner. The analysis within this chapter is based on quintiles – five subgroups which differ in their level of income or wealth. We have used both income and wealth in our analyses, as income does not always translate into wealth and is not necessarily a good indicator of an individual's or household's ability to translate income into a favourable ratio of assets to debt.

The charts in Chapter 5 display three quintile groups: the lowest quintile representing the poorest 20 per cent of households; the highest quintile representing the richest 20 per cent; and the average of the second to fourth quintiles representing the middle 60 per cent. Researchers and financial analysts will often use either the 3rd quintile – representing the middle 20 per cent, or the average of the second to fourth quintile – representing the middle 60 per cent, to indicate the wealth or income for the middle of the population or sample. (The US Federal Reserve Bank often uses this latter method.) Our rationale for representing the middle 60 per cent is primarily due to our interest in gaining an understanding of the finances for the whole of middle Australia, and secondly due to our focus on examining *patterns of difference* in levels of income, wealth and expenditure – not necessarily patterns of change over time. Preliminary analyses revealed that the middle 60 per cent, when stratified, had remarkably similar patterns of financial behaviour, and patterns of change over time, thus using the average of the second to fourth quintile was the more appropriate method.

2. Estimated data for 2015–16

At the time of writing, the ABS had released summary statistics for 2015-16 but not their detailed statistics. The detailed statistics divided categories such as *Household services and operation* into more specific expenditures on items such as childcare, gardening, house cleaning, telephones and repair and maintenance of household items. Without access to the detailed data, estimations were made on expenditure in these subcategories so that we were able to calculate figures for fixed, discretionary and securitisable expenditures (see items 3 and 5 below). Detailed expenditure for 2015-16 was estimated using the percentage change in the parent summary figure from the 2009-10 period to 2015-16. That is, to arrive at the estimate for childcare expenditure in 2015-16, we first calculated the percentage change in expenditure for household services and operation and then applied the same rate of change to the chilcare sub-category. Given the lack of detailed childcare expenditure data for 2015-16, this method of estimation is the best available.

In addition, the ABS updated their classification of household expenditure creating two new summary categories, *Communication* and *Education*. These changes were made due to the growth in expenditure on such items by Australian households. At the time of writing the ABS had not released their user guide identifying which items at the detailed level had been used to create their two new categories. However the ABS had provided backdated summary statistics for these new categories for previous years. Some estimations of detailed expenditure were calculated using the percentage change in expenditure for these two new categories. For example in the case of expenditure on telephone accounts, these could reasonably be expected to have been reclassified from *Household services and operation* to *Communication*, thus the percentage change figure for *Communication* was used to calculate the estimation for 2015-16.

3. Fixed and discretionary expenditure

The divide between fixed and discretionary expenditure is contestable. Spending on expenses such as housing (rent or mortgage), food, clothing and utilities etc. can be viewed as necessary expenditure essential to daily living regardless of income. However, for the wealthy much of this expenditure can also be considered discretionary. While still needing to eat, be clothed, and housed, wealth provides a greater latitude for expenditure and the option to shop for designer, luxury or boutique goods rather than budget basics.

Conversely, this same criterion cannot be applied to current contractual payments from past obligations. Wealthy people may not need to live in expensive houses, but once they have taken out high mortgages, they are obliged to meet those payments: they are non-discretionary.

Our model of fixed and discretionary spending takes these differences into account in three ways.

For fixed expenditures we start with Elizabeth Warren's (2003) model as a base. This model includes as non-discretionary expenditures: mortgage payments, childcare costs, health insurance, car payments and taxation as a base – the costs deemed necessary for a household to participate in ongoing employment.

For some expenditures, notably food, clothing and footwear, household furnishings and equipment, other household services, personal care and education, we identify the expenditure of the poorest 20 per cent (lowest quintile) as 'necessary' and hence as non-discretionary expenditure. All expenditure in excess of this lowest-quintile average we classify as discretionary.

'Pure' discretionary expenditures, in addition to these 'above-necessity' expenditures, include expenditures on leisure activities and properties other than the home. Our breakdown of expenditure items into the categories of fixed and discretionary spending is listed below.

Fixed
Current housing costs
Domestic fuel and power
Childcare
Telephone (Communication)
Medical care and health expenses
Transport costs
Income tax
Superannuation & life insurance
To the value of the poorest quintile
    Food
    Clothing & Footwear
    Household Furnishings & Equipment
    Other Household Services

Personal Care
Education

Discretionary
Fuel and power (other than dwelling)
Alcohol
Tobacco
Recreation
Miscellaneous goods & services
Communication (other items not yet identified)
Other capital housing costs
The value in excess of the poorest quintile
> *Food*
> *Clothing & Footwear*
> *Household Furnishings & Equipment*
> *Personal Care*
> *Education*

4. Net wealth

Net wealth is a measure of assets owned, less debt. These figures are not easy to measure. ABS uses two main methods. One measures household net worth as the difference between the value of the assets and liabilities. However, those data also include non-profit clubs deemed to serve households, and that includes churches and wealthy organisations like leagues clubs. So these figures may not tell a sufficiently clear story. The other measure, the ABS Survey of Income and Housing, offers less recent data, but they are more detailed (see ABS 2010b).

5. Securitisable payments

We define securitisable payments as payments made under contract for which the contracted income stream can then potentially be 'onsold' to a third party. While some household contracted payments are already bought and sold on securities markets, we contend that any contracted payment has the potential to be securitised. Our list of securitisable payments is compiled from ABS expenditure categories and is presented below. This list illustrates the potential scope for expansion of securities formation across household payments.

Contractable payments
Rent payments
Rate payments
House and contents insurance
Electricity, mains and bottled gas
Childcare services
Telephone accounts – fixed line and mobile
Household appliance repairs insurance
Accident and health insurance
Hospital and nursing home charges
Vehicle registration and insurance
Boat registration and insurance
Aircraft registration and insurance
TV hire
Pay television
Health and fitness studio charges
Internet account
Education fees for primary and secondary schools
Education fees other
Rent payments other property
Insurance other property
Personal belongings insurance
Travel insurance
Superannuation and life insurance

Insurance payments on loans
Mortgage repayments on principal dwelling and other property
Loans for alterations and additions
Motor vehicle purchases
Interest payments on selected credit services

6. Data analysis: aggregate, per household and longitudinal

The data presented in Chapter 5 were analysed using three different methods: aggregate, per household or longitudinally. The ABS data were limited to aggregate calculations. The ABS data provided pre-aggregated data at the household level and we were not able to pair responses to different items – e.g. expenditure on housing, insurance and total household expenditure – at the household level. The HILDA data, as a panel study, did allow for the tracking of all responses on a household basis. The difference between these first two methods lies in when the base statistic is calculated; for example, if we are looking at debt to asset ratios on aggregate, we would calculate the average debt for the sample, then the average asset value and then use these figures to calculate our mean or ratio. To calculate the same statistic on a per household basis, we would calculate the ratio (debt divided by asset value) for each household in the sample first and then calculate the mean ratio. The HILDA survey, as a panel study, also enabled us to track the same households over time, in longitudinal analysis.

References

Abhayaratna, J., L. Andrews, H. Nuch and T. Podbury 2008 'Part Time Employment: The Australian Experience', Staff Working Paper, Productivity Commission, Canberra, June. Available at: http://bit.ly/2BQQeuL

ABS (Australian Bureau of Statistics) 2010a Year Book Australia, 2009–10, Cat. No. 1301.0.

ABS 2010b Measures of Australia's Progress, 2010, Cat. 1370.0: http://bit.ly/2F1oQMF

ABS 2014 Australian Social Trends, 2014, Cat. No. 4102.0.

ABS 2015 Australian System of National Accounts, 2014–15, Cat. No. 5204.0.

ABS 2016 Australian National Accounts: Finance and Wealth, June 2016, Cat. No. 5232.0.

ABS 2017 Australian National Accounts: Finance and Wealth, December 2016, Cat. No. 5232.0.

ABS 2018 Managed Funds, Australia, December 2017, Cat. No. 5655.0.

ACCC (Australian Competition and Consumer Commission) 2015 'Information and informed decision-making in private health insurance: A report to the Australian Senate on anti-competitive and other practices by health insurers and providers in relation to private health insurance'. For the period of 1 July 2013 to 30 June 2014. Available at: http://bit.ly/2ESPT9C

ACTU (Australian Council of Trade Unions) 2011 'Voices from Working Australia: Findings from the ACTU Working Australia Census 2011'. Available at: http://bit.ly/2GJI3zn

AIRC (Australian Industrial Relations Commission) 1986 National Wage Case, June. Available at: http://bit.ly/2CIrXUx

Allon, F. 2008 *Renovation Nation: Our Obsession with Home*. Sydney: UNSW Press.

Anglicare 2017 'Rental Affordability Snapshot 2017: Greater Sydney and the Illawarra'. Available at: http://bit.ly/2oyqMSn

ASIC (Australian Securities and Investments Commission) 2014 'Future of Financial Advice'. Available at:http://bit.ly/2CFJTyR

ASIC 2015 'Buying a Mobile'. Available at: http://bit.ly/2EUdd6V

ASIC 2017 'Review of Remuneration of Mortgage Brokers'. Available at: http://bit.ly/2FvCBRx

ASX (Australian Securities Exchange Limited) 2015 'The Australian Share Ownership Study 2014'. Available at: http://bit.ly/2twWjZj

Austrade 2010 'Investment Management Industry in Australia', June. Available at: http://bit.ly/1qWEvS9.

Australian Government 2012 'Budget 2012–13. Budget Paper No.1, Statement 6'. Available at: http://bit.ly/2oqWNfX

Australian Government 2014 'Budget 2014–15, Establishing an Asset Recycling Fund'. Available at: http://bit.ly/2oxXl30

Australian Government, Office of the Australian Information Commissioner 2013 'Privacy Business Resource 3: Credit Reporting – What has Changed', June. Available at: http://bit.ly/2F2mjBM

Australian Human Rights Commission 2009 'Accumulating Poverty? Women's Experiences of Inequality over the Lifecycle: An Issues Paper Examining the Gender Gap in Retirement Savings'. Available at: http://bit.ly/2oxXpzM

Australian Securitisation Forum 2014 'Submission to the Australian Government's Financial System Inquiry 2014'. Available at: http://bit.ly/2GMUbjf

Australian Securitisation Forum 2015 'Submission to the Final Report of the Financial System Inquiry'. Available at: http://bit.ly/2HJrFQK

Australian Treasury 2015 '2015 Intergenerational Report'. Available at: http://bit.ly/2CIfIqW

Aylmer, Chris 2016 'Towards a More Transparent Securitization Market', Speech to the Australian Securitisation Conference, Sydney, 22 November. Available at: http://bit.ly/2BS4WBt

Bailey, Kirk, Michael Davies, and Liz Dixon Smith 2004 'RBA Financial Stability Review, September 2004', pp. 48–56.

Bank for International Settlements 2016 'OTC Derivatives Statistics at end-June, 2016'. Available at: http://bit.ly/2sUzY8X

Banks M and Bowman, D 2017 *Juggling Risks: Insurance in Households Struggling with Financial Insecurity*. Fitzroy, Vic: Brotherhood of St Laurence Research and Policy Centre.

References

Bankwest Curtin Economics Centre 2014 'Falling Through the Cracks: Poverty and Disadvantage in Australia'. Focus on the States Report Series, No. 1, October, Curtin University. Available at: http://bit.ly/2F1qz4B

Berger-Thomson L, E Chung and W McKibbin 2009 'Estimating Marginal Propensities to Consume in Australia Using Micro Data', RBA Research Discussion Paper No. 2009-07. Available at: http://bit.ly/2ox9EMT

Bilston, Tom, Robert Johnson and Matthew Read 2015 'Stress Testing the Australian Household Sector Using the HILDA Survey', Reserve Bank of Australia Discussion Paper RDP 2015-01. Available at: http://bit.ly/2GJaxcE

Black, Susan; Lamorna Rogers and Albina Soultanaeva 2012 'Households' Appetite for Financial Risk', RBA Bulletin, March Quarter. Available at: http://bit.ly/2HJs3yG

Boshra, Ray (Center for Household Financial Stability at the US Federal Reserve Bank of St. Louis) 2015 'Thrivers and Strugglers: The Balance Sheets and Financial Health of U.S. Families', Presentation at Assets Funds Network's 2015 Grantmaker Conference in Dallas, April 8. Available at: http://bit.ly/2EU83b4

Brenner, Chris 2003 'Labour Flexibility and Regional Development: The Role of Labour Market Intermediaries', Regional Studies, 37(6&7): 621–33.

Breunig, R. and D. Cobb-Clark 2006, 'Understanding the Factors Associated with Financial Stress in Australian Households', Australian Social Policy 2005, Australian Government Department of Families, Community Services and Indigenous Affairs, FaCSIA, Canberra: 13–64.

Brown, William 2013 'The Australian Accord from an International Perspective', Faculty of Economics, University of Cambridge, mimeo.

Bryan, Dick 2008 'Minimum Living Standards and the Working Class Surplus: Higgins, Henderson and Housing', Labour History, 95: 213–23.

Bryan, Dick, Randy Martin and Michael Rafferty 2009 'Financialization and Marx: Giving Labor and Capital a Financial Makeover', Review of Radical Political Economics 41(4): 458–72.

Bryan, Dick, Michael Rafferty and Chris Jefferis 2015 'Risk and Value: Finance, Labour and Production' South Atlantic Quarterly, 114(2): 307–29.

Buddelmeyer, Hielke, Felix Leung Duncan McIvar and Mark Wooden 2013 'Training and its Impact on the Casual Employment Experience', NCVER Research Report, Adelaide. Available at: http://bit.ly/2BQ4XWK

Bundey, Freya 2015 'The Financialized Household and the Consumer Price Index: An Anachronistic Measure?' Review of Radical Political Economics, 47(4): 625–40.

Burgess, John and Iain Campbell 1998 'The Nature and Dimensions of Precarious Employment in Australia', Labour & Industry, 8(3): 5–21.

Burgess, John, Iain Campbell and Robyn May 2008 'Pathways from Casual Employment to Economic Security: The Australian Experience', *Social Indicators Research*, 88(1): 161–78.

Byres, Wayne (Chairman, APRA) 2015 'Sound Lending Standards and Adequate Capital: Preconditions for Long-term Success'. Address to COBA CEO & Director Forum, Sydney, 13 May. Available at: http://bit.ly/1QHTur0

Campbell, Iain 2007 'Long Working Hours in Australia: Working-time Regulation and Employer Pressures', *Economic and Labour Relations Review*, 17(2): 37–68.

Campbell, Iain and Peter Brosnan 1999 'Labour Market Deregulation in Australia: The Slow Combustion Approach to Workplace Change', Working Paper no. 67, National Key Centre in Industrial Relations, Monash University, Melbourne, March.

Campbell, Iain and John Burgess 2005 'Casual Employment in Australia and Temporary Employment in Europe: Developing a Cross-National Comparison', *Work, Employment and Society*, 15(1): 171–84.

Castles, Francis 1985 *The Working Class and Welfare: Reflections on the Political Development of the Welfare State in Australia and New Zealand, 1890–1980*, Sydney: Allen & Unwin.

Castles, Francis 1994 'The Wage-Earners Welfare State Revisited: Refurbishing the Established Model of Australian Social Protection: 1983–1993', *Australian Journal of Social Issues*, 29(2): 118–32.

Center for Household Financial Stability 2016 'Rebuilding family balance sheets', CD1420 04/16. Available at: http://bit.ly/2or5w1A

Chopra, Rohit 2013 'A Closer Look at the Trillion', US Consumer Financial Protection Bureau, August 5. Available at: http://bit.ly/1v0FRss/

Claes, Lisa 2016 'Snapshot of the Housing Market'. Presentation to Australian Securitization 2016, Sydney, November 21–2. Available at: http://bit.ly/2ESsY2f

Collett, John 2013, 'GFC hits Australian retirees hardest', *Sydney Morning Herald*, 18 September. Available at: http://bit.ly/2EStc9B

Connolly, Chris et al. 2013 'Measuring the Cost of Financial Exclusion in Australia'. Centre for Social Impact for National Australia Bank, June. Available at: http://nab.co/2kU10JZ

Considine, Mark, Jenny Lewis, Siobhan O'Sullivan and Els Sol 2015 *Getting Welfare to Work: Street-Level Governance in Australia, the UK, and the Netherlands*. Oxford: Oxford University Press.

Cooper, Jeremy 2013 'Report on the Super Charter and Super Council' (Jeremy Cooper, Chair), Australian Treasury. Available at: http://bit.ly/2CInPUm

References

Coorey, Phillip 2014 'Retirement age will rise to 70 by 2035', *Australian Financial Review*, 2 May. Available at: http://bit.ly/2EStqxt

Cormack, Lucy 2017 'Energy Australia announces 19 per cent price increase to electricity prices in NSW', *Sydney Morning Herald*, 16 June. Available at: http://bit.ly/2uha3sy

Cowgill, Matthew 2013 'A Shrinking Slice of the Pie' ACTU Working Australia Papers No. 1 of 2013. Available at: http://bit.ly/2oAg5P4

Creighton, Adam 2014 'Retirement riches can't go on like this ... and yet, alas, they will', *The Australian*, 10 May. Available at: http://bit.ly/2EQQFDR

Davis, G 2010 'Not Just a Mortgage Crisis: How Finance Maimed Society', *Strategic Organization*, 8(1): 75–82.

Debelle, Guy (Assistant Governor, RBA) 2010a 'The State of the Mortgage Market'. Address to Mortgage Innovation Conference, Sydney March. Available at: http://bit.ly/2orU4mF

Debelle, Guy 2010b 'The State of Play in the Securitisation Market', Address to the Australian Securitisation Conference 2010, Sydney, 30 November. Available at: http://bit.ly/2HMbeTK

Debelle, Guy 2011 Address to the ACI High Frequency Trading Conference, Sydney, 12 October. Available at: http://bit.ly/2osacUX

Department of Education, Employment and Workplace Relations 2012 'Job Seeker Classification Instrument – Factors and Points', 1 July. Available at: http://bit.ly/2CH1dnj

Edey, Malcolm (Assistant Governor, RBA) 2013 Remarks at the Financial Services Institute of Australasia (FINSIA) Financial Services Conference 2013, Sydney, 18 September. Available at: http://bit.ly/2EUHHJK

Enright, Bryony 2013 '(Re)considering New Agents: A Review of Labour Market Intermediaries Within Labour Geography', *Geography Compass* 7(4): 287–99.

Equifax n.d. 'Comprehensive Credit Reporting'. Available at: http://bit.ly/2sUBjN1.

Eyers, James 2015 'NAB puts 40 postcodes on credit watchlist', *Sydney Morning Herald*, 18 August. Available at: http://bit.ly/2CJWukx

Experian 2010 'Balance Collections with Retention for Each Customer: Decision Analytics for Debt Management in Telecommunications'. Available at: http://bit.ly/2HKul0y

Fahrenthold, David and Scott Wilson 2012 'Cass Sunstein, Top Obama Adviser on Regulations, to Leave Administration', *The Washington Post*, August 3. Available at: http://wapo.st/2opXO7Q

FairWork Commission (2015) '4 yearly review of modern awards — Annual Leave' (AM2014/47) Summary of Decision, June 11, accessed at: http://bit.ly/1LcXRa9

Farnham, Daisy 2013 'Workfare, Neoliberalism and the Welfare State: Towards a Historical Materialist Analysis of Australian Workfare'. Honours Thesis, Department of Political Economy, University of Sydney. Available at: http://bit.ly/2GK2cp2

Farrell, Diana and Fiona Greig 2015 'Weathering Volatility: Big Data on the Financial Ups and Downs of U.S. Individuals'. JPMorgan Chase Institute, May. Available at: http://bit.ly/1O6EnoR

Finlay Richard 2012 'The Distribution of Household Wealth in Australia: Evidence from the 2010 HILDA Survey', RBA Bulletin, March: 19–27. Available at: http://bit.ly/2gLy0lZ

Finlay, Richard and Fiona Price 2014 'Household Saving in Australia', Reserve Bank of Australia Research Discussion Paper 2014-03. Available at: http://bit.ly/2oxOIoS

Frade, C. and I. Darmon 2005 'New Modes of Business Organization and Precarious Employment: Towards the Re-Commodification of Labour?', Journal of European Social Policy, 15(2): 107–21.

Fudge, Judy 2006 'Fragmenting Work and Fragmenting Organizations: The Contract of Employment and the Scope of Labour Regulation', Osgoode Hall Law Journal 44(4): 609–48.

Furman, Jason and Orszag, Peter 2015 'A Firm-Level Perspective on the Role of Rents in the Rise in Inequality'. Presentation at 'A Just Society' Centennial Event in Honor of Joseph Stiglitz, Columbia University, October 16. Available at: http://bit.ly/1Ga2qEI

Gannon, M. 2017, 'Debate: are doctors or insurers to blame for health insurance price hikes', Australian Financial Review, 23 August. Available at: http://bit.ly/2ESvqFZ

Garner M., A. Nitschke and D. Xu 2016 'Developments in Foreign Exchange and OTC Derivatives Markets', RBA Bulletin, December Quarter. Available at: http://bit.ly/2opXXYW

Gazier, Bernard and Jérôme Gautie 2011 'The "Transitional Labour Markets" Approach: Theory, History and Future Research Agenda', Journal of Economic and Social Policy, 14(1): Article 6.

Genworth Financial 2009 'Mortgage Trends Report', July. Available at: http://bit.ly/2CjNvL9

Gorecki, Stephanie and James Kelly 2012 'Treasury's Wellbeing Framework', Treasury Economic Roundup, Issue 3. Available at: http://bit.ly/2BQkNAM

Geron, T. 2017 'The hidden cash in your assets', Wall Street Journal, 24 April. Available at: http://on.wsj.com/2Fwt4cL

Graber, David 2011 Debt: The First 5000 Years. Brooklyn, NY: Melville House.

References

Greber, Jacob 2017, 'Workers must demand greater share of pie, says RBA
Governor Philip Lowe', *Australian Financial Review*, 19 June. Available at:
http://bit.ly/2tLVVTA

Greenville, J., C. Pobke and N. Rogers 2013 'Trends in the Distribution of Income
in Australia', Productivity Commission Staff Working Paper, Canberra.
Available at: http://bit.ly/2ovPDr1

Hacker, Jacob 2005 'The Privatization of Risk and the Economic Insecurity of
Americans', Paper for the Social Science Research Council's Project on the
Privatization of Risk, October. Available at: http://bit.ly/2GK5x7K

Hacker, Jacob 2008 *The Great Risk Shift: The New Economic Insecurity and the
Decline of the American Dream*, revised and expanded edition. Oxford:
Oxford University Press.

Hacker, Jacob 2009 'A Strong Safety Net Encourages Healthy Risk-Taking', *The
American Prospect*, April 19. Available at: http://bit.ly/2HJvOUO

Hacker, Jacob 2011 'Working Families at Risk: Understanding and Confronting the
New Economic Insecurity' in Plotnick, Robert D. et al. (eds) *Old
Assumptions, New Realities: Ensuring Economic Security for Working Families
in the 21st Century*. Russell Sage Foundation: 31–70.

Haldane, Andrew 2014 'The Age of Asset Management?' Speech at the London
Business School, London, 4 April. Available at: http://bit.ly/1j9i6J6

Hall, Richard 2002 'Labour Hire in Australia: Motivation, Dynamics and
Prospects', ACIRRT Working Paper 76, University of Sydney, April.

Harrington, James 2006 'Labor Market Intermediation, Commodity Chains, and
Knowledge Transfer', University of Washington. Available at: http://bit.ly/
2F6mOL5

Hanewald, Katja and Michael Sherris 2011 'House Price Risk Models for Banking
and Insurance Applications'. UNSW Australian School of Business Research
Paper No. 2011ACTL11. Available at: http://bit.ly/2ENZdzo

Hannagan, Anthony and Jonathan Morduch 2015 'Income Gains and
Month-to-Month Income Volatility: Household Evidence from the US
Financial Diaries', March 16. Available at: http://bit.ly/2BQSWQX

Headey, B. 2007 'HILDA's Household Financial Accounts: Their Value for
Developing Improved Assessment of Economic Well-being and Poverty', July
19–20 2007: Third HILDA Users' Conference, Melbourne Institute of Applied
Economic and Social Research, University of Melbourne, Melbourne.

Headey, B., G. Marks, and M. Wooden 2005, 'The Dynamics of Income Poverty in
Australia: Evidence from the First Three Waves of the *HILDA Survey*',
Australian Journal of Social Issues, 40(4): 541–52.

Higgins H. B. 1907 *Ex parte HV McKay* (Harvester Case). Downloaded from Law Internet Resources, Parliament of Australia, Parliamentary Library. Available at: http://bit.ly/2BQ7u39

HSBC 2013 'The Future of Retirement Life After Work?: Australian Report'. Available at: http://bit.ly/2BPqzCx

Hulse, Carl 2003 'Threats and responses: plans and criticisms; Pentagon prepares a futures market on terror attacks', *New York Times*, 19 July. Available at: http://nyti.ms/2BSPm94

IBIS World 2015 'Funds Management Services in Australia: Market Research Report', August. Available at: http://bit.ly/2oxclht

Illion 2014 'Consumer Financial Stress Index: Stress Forecast to Rise', 22 September. http://bit.ly/2Coezcm

IMF (International Monetary Fund) 2005 'Financial Stability Report April 2005'. New York: International Monetary Fund.

IMF 2008 'World Economic Outlook, April'. Chapter 3: The Changing Housing Cycle and the Implications for Monetary Policy. Available at:

Joye, Christopher 2014 'Bank capital at risk in housing bust', *Australian Financial Review*, 15 November.

JP Morgan Chase Institute 2016 'Paychecks, Paydays, and the Online Platform Economy: Big Data on Income Volatility', February, JPMorgan Chase Institute. Available at: http://bit.ly/1PPDzVE

Kent, Christopher (Assistant Governor, Financial Markets, RBA) 2017 'Some Innovative Mortgage Data'. Speech to Moody's Analytics Australia Conference 2017. August 14. Available at: http://bit.ly/2CIp5qy

Khadem, Nassim 2015, 'David Murray says it's time to tackle superannuation concessions for rich', *Sydney Morning Herald*, 18 February. Available at: http://bit.ly/2F6AR3l

Kirby, M. 2001 'Industrial Relations Law: Call Off the Funeral', *Deakin Law Review*, 6(2): 256–60.

Lacey, R. 1986 *Ford: The Men and the Machine*. Heinemann: London.

Laker, John 2007 *Credit Standards in Housing Lending – Some Further Insights*, The Institute of Chartered Accountants in Australia, Melbourne, June 20. Available at: http://bit.ly/2sUThPC

Lansbury Russell and Greg Bamber 1998 'The End of Institutionalised Industrial Relations in Australia', *Perspectives on Work*, 2(1): 26–30.

Lansbury, Russell 2004 'Work, People and Globalisation: Towards a New Social Contract for Australia – The Kingsley Laffer Memorial Lecture', *Journal of Industrial Relations*, 46(1): 102–15.

Leigh, Andrew 2013 *Battlers and Billionaires: The story of inequality in Australia*. Melbourne: Black Inc.

References

Lewis, Phil. 2017 'We Need to Find New Ways to Measure the Australian Labour Force', *The Conversation*, January 13. Available at: http://bit.ly/2HOp1ti

Lowe Phillip (Assistant Governor, RBA) 2011, 'Changing Patterns in Household Saving and Spending', Address to the Australian Economic Forum 2011, Sydney, 22 September. Available at: http://bit.ly/2F6xCJ4

Lowe, Phillip (Governor, RBA) 2017a Remarks at Reserve Bank Board Dinner, Melbourne, April 4. Available at: http://bit.ly/2nX4U47

Lowe, Phillip 2017b 'Household Debt, Housing Prices and Resilience', Speech to Economic Society of Australia (Qld) Business Lunch, Brisbane, 4 May. Available at: http://bit.ly/2FwtMXt

Macrobusiness 2014 'Is there Demand for Australian Annuities', 19 February. Available at: http://bit.ly/2oxgoud

Maisano, Chris 2013 'The Crisis of American Labor: An Interview with Sam Gindin', *Jacobin*, August 2. Available at: http://bit.ly/2CJcGma

Markey, Ray, Sasha Holley, Louise Thornthwaite and Sharron O'Neill 2014 'The Impact on Injured Workers of Changes to NSW Workers' Compensation: July 2012–November 2014'. Macquarie University Centre for Workplace Futures, December. Available at: http://bit.ly/2FvIgqL

Marks, G. 2007 'Income Poverty, Subjective Poverty and Financial Stress', Social Policy Research Paper no. 29, Australian Government Department of Families, Community Services and Indigenous Affairs, FaCSIA, Canberra.

Martin, Randy 2002 *The Financialization of Daily Life*. Philadelphia: Temple University Press.

McCarroll, Phil 2015, 'Facebook granted a US patent that could deny a mortgage application based on a users' friend list', *Your Investment Property Magazine*, 13 August. Available at: http://bit.ly/2ETajiC

McGaughey, Ewan 2015 'Behavioural Economics and Labour Law', LSE Legal Studies Working Paper No. 20/2014, King's College London Law School Research Paper No. 2015-04. Available at: http://bit.ly/2ERqPDS

Mercer 2014 'Post Retirement Market Trends in Australia', June. Available at: http://bit.ly/2HIZGAO

Millan, Laura 2014, 'Investors should take responsibility for themselves: Medcraft', *Financial Standard*, 25 June.

Minifie, Jim 2016 'Peer-to-Peer Pressure: Policy for the Sharing Economy'. Grattan Institute. Available at: http://bit.ly/2oqSgu6

Mitropoulos, Angela and Dick Bryan 2016 'Social Benefit Bonds: Financial Markets Inside the State', in Gabrielle Meagher and Susan Goodwin (eds) *Markets, Rights and Power in Australian Social Policy*. Sydney: Sydney University Press.

Morduch, Jonathan and Rachel Schneider 2013 'Spikes and Dips: How Income Uncertainty Affects Households', US Financial Diaries, October. Available at: http://bit.ly/1x01ET4

Morduch, Jonathan and Rachel Schneider 2017 *The Financial Diaries: How American Families Cope in a World of Uncertainty*. Princeton, NJ: Princeton University Press.

Morrison, Scott (Minister for Social Services) 2015 'A Good Deal on Welfare'. Address to ACOSS National Conference, Sydney, June 26. Available at: http://bit.ly/2BS9gRd

Mulligan, Mark and Cameron Atfield 2015 'Sydney house price rise "crazy", RBA's Glenn Stevens says', *Sydney Morning Herald*, 10 June. Available at: http://bit.ly/1FQIBv7

Murray, David 2014a *Financial System Inquiry, Interim Report* (D. Murray, Chairman). Available at: http://bit.ly/2F26pHI

Murray, David 2014b *Financial System Inquiry, Final Report* (D. Murray, Chairman). Available at: http://bit.ly/1ul9Qbw

National Commission of Audit 2014 'Towards Responsible Government: Appendix to the Report of the National Commission of Audit', Vol.1. Available at: http://bit.ly/2ERdfjR

Nielson, L. 2010 'Chronology of Superannuation and Retirement Income in Australia', Parliament of Australia, Department of Parliamentary Services, Background Note, 1 June. Available at: http://bit.ly/2oAipWi

North, M. 2016 'How Sensitive Are Owner Occupied Mortgage Holders to Rising Interest Rates', *Digital Finance Analytics*, January 22. Available at: http://bit.ly/2CiSpYV

North, M. 2017 'Mortgage Stress Rises Again', *Digital Finance Analytics*, April 4. Available at: http://bit.ly/2ESgibo

OECD 2014 'Household Saving Rates – Forecasts. Percentage of Disposable Household Income'. May 6. DOI: 10.1787/2074384x-table7. Available at: http://bit.ly/2EQfDaK

OECD 2016 'General Government Debt (indicator)'. DOI: 10.1787/a0528cc2-en. Available at: http://bit.ly/2BOGu4e

Office of the Australian Information Commissioner 2014 Privacy (Credit Reporting) Code 2014 (Version 1.2). Available at: http://bit.ly/2FvniIo

Official Monetary and Financial Institutions Forum (OMFIF) 2015 'Global Public Investor 2015'. Available at: http://bit.ly/2F1yQFH

Ong, Rachel and Gavin Wood, 2014 'Your Home as an "ATM": Home Equity a Risky Welfare Tool', *The Conversation*, 5 February. Available at: http://bit.ly/2sWymMd

References

Pocock, Barbara and Helen Masterman-Smith,2008 *Living Low Paid: The Dark Side of Prosperous Australia*. Sydney: Allen & Unwin.

Pocock, Barbara, Rosslyn Prosser and Ken Bridge 2005 'Only a Casual – How Casual Work Affects Employees, Households and Communities in Australia', *South Australian Policy Online*, University of Adelaide. Available at: http://bit.ly/2F6A5TQ

Popper, Nathaniel 2016, 'After 147 Years, Goldman Sachs hangs a shingle on main street', *New York Times*, 18 June. Available at: http://nyti.ms/2oU9qxH

Price, Fiona and Carl Schwartz 2015 'Recent Developments in Asset Management', *RBA Bulletin*, June Quarter: 69–78. Available at: http://bit.ly/2oyweVl

Productivity Commission 2011, *Caring for Older Australians*, Research Report, Canberra.

Productivity Commission 2013, *An Ageing Australia: Preparing for the Future*, Research Report, Canberra.

Rainmaker Group 2010 'Super Funds and Their Failing Investment Diversification Strategies', *Rainmaker Roundup*, June Quarter. Available at: http://bit.ly/2oye6uJ

Ramesh, Randeep 2010 'Does Getting Tough in the Unemployed Work?' *The Guardian*, June 16. Available at: http://bit.ly/2BSlJEQ

Rappaport, Jordan 2010 'The Effectiveness of Homeownership in Building Household Wealth', *Kansas City Federal Reserve Economic Review*, Fourth quarter: 35–64. Available at: http://bit.ly/2BQyvDA

RBA (Reserve Bank of Australia) 2015 *Financial Stability Review, October 2015*. Available at: http://bit.ly/2ou6M3k

RBA 2017 'Chart Pack – Household Savings; Household Finance', April. Available at: http://bit.ly/2wFMKYT

Read, Matthew, Chris Stewart and Gianni La Cava 2104 'Mortgage-Related Financial Difficulties: Evidence from Australian Micro-level Data', Reserve Bank of Australia Research Discussion Paper, 2014–13, Available at: http://bit.ly/2oxgQIV.

Reagan, Brad 2014, 'A fantasy sports wizard's winning formula', *Wall Street Journal*, 4 June. Available at: http://on.wsj.com/2sRjrmv

Rubery, J., D. Grimshaw and M. Marchington 2010 'Blurring Boundaries and Dis-ordering Hierarchies: Challenges for Employment and Skills in Networked Organisations', UK Commission for Employment and Skills, Issue 6. Available at: http://bit.ly/2pfrQM2

Schmid G. 2006 'Social Risk Management through Transitional Labour Markets', *Socio-Economic Review*, vol. 4, no 1, pp. 1–33.

Schmid G. and B. Gazier (eds.) 2002 *The Dynamics of Full Employment. Social Integration through Transitional Labour Markets*. London: Edward Elgar.

Senate Select Committee 2008 'A Good House is Hard to Find: Housing Affordability in Australia', Parliament of Australia, Senate, Select Committee on Housing Affordability in Australia, Senate Printing Unit, Parliament House, Canberra.

Shaw, Jeff 2004 'Reflections on Industrial Conciliation and Arbitration in Australia', *The Hummer: Journal of the Australasian Society for the Study of Labour History*, 4(3): Summer. Available at: http://bit.ly/2oxQR3U

Simpson, Lisa and Davies, Raewin (2015) 'Interactions between Income System', paper presented to Actuaries Institute of Australia, Injury Schemes Seminar, Adelaide November 8-10, Accessed at: http://bit.ly/2pfsUyZ

Standard & Poor's Ratings Services 2012 'Ratings Direct: An Overview of Australia's Housing Market and Residential Mortgage-Backed Securities', August 27.

Standard & Poor's Ratings Services 2015 'An Overview of Australia's Housing Market and Residential Mortgage-Backed Securities', March 3. Available at: Australian Securitisation Forum Library

Standing, Guy 2011 *The Precariat*. London: Bloomsbury Academic.

Standing, Guy 2012 'The Precariat: Why it Needs Deliberative Democracy', openDemocracy, 27 January. Available at: http://bit.ly/2BOFtsW

Stanwick, J., T. Lu, T. Rittie and M. Circelli 2014 'How People are Transitioning from School to Work', Foundation for Young Australians (FYA), 25 September. Available at: www.fya.org.au

Stevens, Glenn (Governor, RBA) 2008 'The Directors' Cut: Four Important Long-run Themes'. Address to the Australian Institute of Company Directors Luncheon, Sydney, 17 September. Available at: http://bit.ly/2HI57Qp

Stevens, Glenn 2015 'Observations on the Financial System'. Address to the Australian Financial Review Banking and Wealth Summit, Sydney, 28 April. Available at: http://bit.ly/2Ckt80w

Stewart A 2005 'Submission on Independent Contracting and Labour Hire', House of Representatives Standing Committee on Employment, Workplace Relations and Workforce Participation. Available at: http://bit.ly/2FxcWb4

Sunstein, C. 2001 'Human Behavior and the Law of Work', *Virginia Law Review*, 87(2): 205-76.

Tanzer, G. 2015 'The Importance of Culture to Improving Conduct within the Financial Industry'. Speech to Thomson Reuters' Third Australian Regulatory Summit, Sydney, 27 May. Available at: http://bit.ly/2oxBkBnf

Thaler, Richard and Cass Sunstein 2008 *Nudge: Improving Decisions about Health, Wealth, and Happiness*. New Haven: Yale University Press.

The Economist 2013 'Global House Prices: Mixed Messages: America Surges, Much of Europe Sinks', August 31. Available at: http://econ.st/1sr8ATO

References

Tingle, L. 2015 'Scott Morrison tells retirees they must spend their superannuation', *Australian Financial Review*, 24 May.

Titmuss, R. 1956 *The Social Divisions of Welfare: Some Reflections on the Search for Equity*. Liverpool: Liverpool University Press.

Traub, Amy 2013 'Discredited: how employment credit checks keep qualified workers out of a job', *Demos*, http://bit.ly/19hwRIH

Treasury 2004 'A More Flexible and Adaptable Retirement Income System'. Available at: http://bit.ly/2GHCthe

Waite M. and L. Will 2001 'Self-Employed Contractors in Australia: Incidence and Characteristics', Productivity Commission Staff Research Paper. Ausinfo, Canberra.

Warren, Elizabeth and Amelia Tyagi 2003 *The Two-Income Trap: Why Middle-Class Mothers and Fathers Are Going Broke*. New York: Basic Books, 2003.

Welters, R. and W. Mitchell 2009 'Locked-in Casual Employment', University of Newcastle Centre of Full Employment and Equity, Working Paper No. 09–03. Available at: http://bit.ly/2CIpl90

Wesley Mission 2015 'Facing Financial Stress', *The Wesley Report* No. 14, May. Available at: http://bit.ly/1LZ9AZt

Whiteford, Peter 2013 'Income Support, Inequality and Social Risks', in P. Smyth and J. Buchanan (eds), *Inclusive Growth in Australia*. Sydney: Allen & Unwin.

Yates, J. 2007 'Affordability and Access to Home Ownership: Past, Present and Future?', Australian Housing and Urban Research Institute Research, Report No. 10, November. Available at: http://bit.ly/2ETfWBH

Yellen, Janet (Chairperson, Federal Reserve Board of Governors) 2014 'The Importance of Asset Building for Low and Middle Income Households'. Remarks at the 2014 Assets Learning Conference of the Corporation for Enterprise Development, Washington, D.C., September 18. Available at: http://bit.ly/1qhCgRr

Index

www.ingramcontent.com/pod-product-compliance
Lightning Source LLC
Chambersburg PA
CBHW042119190326

41519CB00031B/7555